Introduction

MW01034848

This book presents the major philosophical doctrines of phenomenology in a clear, lively style with an abundance of examples. The book examines such phenomena as perception, pictures, imagination, memory, language, and reference and shows how human thinking arises from experience. It studies personal identity as established through time and discusses the nature of philosophy. In addition to providing a new interpretation of the correspondence theory of truth, the author also explains how phenomenology differs from both modern and postmodern forms of thinking.

Robert Sokolowski is Professor of Philosophy at The Catholic University of America.

Introduction to Phenomenology

ROBERT SOKOLOWSKI

The Catholic University of America

CAMBRIDGE
UNIVERSITY PRESS

CAMBRIDGE
UNIVERSITY PRESS

University Printing House, Cambridge CB2 8BS, United Kingdom

One Liberty Plaza, 20th Floor, New York, NY 10006, USA

477 Williamstown Road, Port Melbourne, VIC 3207, Australia

314-321, 3rd Floor, Plot 3, Splendor Forum, Jasola District Centre, New Delhi-110025, India

79 Anson Road, #06-04/06, Singapore 079906

Cambridge University Press is part of the University of Cambridge.

It furthers the University's mission by disseminating knowledge in the pursuit of education, learning and research at the highest international levels of excellence.

www.cambridge.org
Information on this title: www.cambridge.org/9780521667920

First published 2000

A catalogue record for this publication is available from the British Library

Library of Congress Cataloging in Publication data
Sokolowski, Robert.
Introduction to phenomenology / Robert Sokolowski.
p.   cm.
Includes bibliographical references (p.   ) and index.
ISBN 0-521-66099-8 (hc.) – ISBN 0-521-66792-5 (pbk.)
1. Phenomenology.   I. Title.
B829.5.S576   2000
142´.7-dc21   99-21499
                                                   CIP

ISBN 978-0-521-66099-0 Hardback
ISBN 978-0-521-66792-0 Paperback

To
Owen J. Sadlier, O.S.F.

Contents

Acknowledgments

I am indebted to the late Gian-Carlo Rota for suggesting the topic of this book to me, and for his encouragement and help as the writing progressed. In the Introduction I describe how the concept of the book arose in a conversation between us. The fact that I cannot share the completed work with him is only one of the many sorrows caused by his recent, sudden death.

Many friends and colleagues have commented on earlier drafts of the manuscript, and in several places I have used not only their ideas, but also their formulations. I am grateful to John Brough, Richard Cobb-Stevens, John Drummond, James Hart, Richard Hassing, Piet Hut, John Smolko, Robert Tragesser, and Kevin White. John McCarthy was particularly generous with his remarks. I used an earlier version of this work as the basis for a course at The Catholic University of America, and I am grateful for the response and suggestions of the students who participated in it. Some of Amy Singer's phrases were especially useful. Finally, I am much obliged to Francis Slade for thoughts and formulations that I used throughout the book, especially for his ideas about modernity, which I relied on for the material in the final chapter.

This book is dedicated to Brother Owen J. Sadlier, O.S.F., whose generosity and philosophical judgment have meant so much to those who are fortunate to be his friends.

Introduction

ORIGIN AND PURPOSE OF THE BOOK

The project of writing this book began in a conversation I had with Gian-Carlo Rota in the spring of 1996. He was then lecturing as visiting professor of mathematics and philosophy at The Catholic University of America.

Rota had often drawn attention to a difference between mathematicians and philosophers. Mathematicians, he said, tend to absorb the writings of their predecessors directly into their own work. They do not comment on the writings of earlier mathematicians, even if they have been very much influenced by them. They simply make use of the material that they find in the authors they read. When advances are made in mathematics, later thinkers condense the findings and move on. Few mathematicians study works from past centuries; compared with contemporary mathematics, such older writings seem to them almost like the work of children.

In philosophy, by contrast, classical works often become enshrined as objects of exegesis rather than resources to be exploited. Philosophers, Rota observed, tend not to ask, "Where do we go from here?" Instead, they inform us about the doctrines of major thinkers. They are prone to comment on earlier works rather than paraphrase them. Rota acknowledged the value of commentaries but thought that philosophers ought to do more. Besides offering exposition, they should abridge earlier writings and directly address issues, speaking in their own voice and incorporating into their own work what their predecessors have done. They should extract as well as annotate.

It was against this background that Rota said to me, after one of my classes, as we were having coffee in the cafeteria of the university's Columbus School of Law, "You should write an introduction

1

to phenomenology. Just write it. Don't say what Husserl or Heidegger thought, just tell people what phenomenology is. No fancy title; call it an introduction to phenomenology."

This struck me as very good advice. There are many books and articles that comment on Husserl; why not try to imitate the several introductions that he himself had written? It seemed right to do so, because phenomenology can continue to make an important contribution to current philosophy. Its intellectual capital is far from spent, and its philosophical energy is still largely unexploited.

Phenomenology is the study of human experience and of the ways things present themselves to us in and through such experience. It attempts to restore the sense of philosophy one finds in Plato. It is, moreover, not just an antiquarian revival, but one that confronts the issues raised by modern thought. It goes beyond ancients and moderns and strives to reactivate the philosophical life in our present circumstances. My book is written, therefore, not just to inform readers about a particular philosophical movement, but to offer the possibility of philosophical thinking at a time when such thinking is seriously called into question or largely ignored.

Because this book is an introduction to phenomenology, I use the philosophical vocabulary developed in that tradition. I employ words like "intentionality," "evidence," "constitution," "categorial intuition," the "life world," and "eidetic intuition." However, I do not comment on these terms as though they were alien to my own thinking; I use them. I think they name important phenomena, and I want to make these phenomena available to the readers of this book. I do not, in this work, trace the manner in which these and other terms arose in Husserl's writings and in the work of Heidegger, Merleau-Ponty, and other phenomenologists; I use the words directly because they still have life in them. It is legitimate, for example, to speak about evidence as such, and not only about what Husserl said about evidence. These terms need not be explained only by showing how other people have used them. We do not have to pin them to the wall in order to profit from them.

I will leave a historical survey of phenomenology for the appendix to this book. For the moment, let us simply recall that Edmund Husserl (1859–1938) was the founder of phenomenology, and that his work *Logical Investigations* can justly be considered the initial statement of the movement. The book appeared in two parts, in

1900 and 1901, so phenomenology began with the dawn of the new century. As we now stand at the end of that period of time, we can look back at almost precisely one hundred years of the movement's history. Martin Heidegger (1889–1976), a disciple, colleague, and later rival of Husserl, was the other major figure in German phenomenology. The movement also flourished in France, where it was represented by such authors as Emmanuel Levinas (1906–1995), Jean-Paul Sartre (1905–1980), Maurice Merleau-Ponty (1907–1960), and Paul Ricoeur (b. 1913). There were significant developments in prerevolutionary Russia and in Belgium, Spain, Italy, Poland, England, and the United States. Phenomenology influenced many other philosophical and cultural movements, such as hermeneutics, structuralism, literary formalism, and deconstruction. Through the whole of the twentieth century, it has been the major component in what is called "continental" philosophy, as opposed to the "analytic" tradition that has typified philosophy in England and the United States.

PHENOMENOLOGY AND THE ISSUE OF APPEARANCES

Phenomenology is a significant philosophical movement because it deals so well with the problem of appearances. The issue of appearances has been part of the human question from the beginning of philosophy. The Sophists manipulated appearances through the magic of words, and Plato responded to what they said. Since then, appearances have been multiplied and magnified enormously. We generate them not only by words spoken or written by one person to another, but by microphones, telephones, movies, and television, as well as by computers and the Internet, and by propaganda and advertising. Modes of presentation and representation proliferate, and fascinating issues arise: How is an e-mail message different from a telephone call and a letter? Who is addressing us when we read a Web page? How are speakers, listeners, and conversation modified by the way we communicate now?

One of the dangers we face is that with the technological expansion of images and words, everything seems to fall apart into mere appearances. We might formulate this problem in terms of the three themes of parts and wholes, identity in manifolds, and presence and absence: it seems that we now are flooded by fragments without any wholes, by manifolds bereft of identities, and by multiple absences without any enduring real presence. We have *bricolage* and nothing else, and we think we can even invent ourselves at random by assembling convenient and pleasing but transient identities out of the bits and pieces we find around us. We pick up fragments to shore against our ruin.

In contrast with this postmodern understanding of appearance, phenomenology, in its classical form, insists that parts are only understood against the background of appropriate wholes, that manifolds of appearance harbor identities, and that absences make no sense except as played off against the presences that can be achieved through them. Phenomenology insists that identity and intelligibility are available in things, and that we ourselves are defined as the ones to whom such identities and intelligibilities are given. We can evidence the way things are; when we do so, we discover objects, but we also discover ourselves, precisely as datives of disclosure, as those to whom things appear. Not only can we think the things given to us in experience; we can also understand ourselves as thinking them. Phenomenology is precisely this sort of understanding: *phenomenology is reason's self-discovery in the presence of intelligible objects*. The analyses in this book are presented to the reader as a clarification of what it means for us to let things appear and to be the datives for their appearance. Many philosophers have claimed that we must learn to live without "truth" and "rationality," but this book tries to show that we can and must exercise responsibility and truthfulness if we are to be human.

OUTLINE OF THE BOOK

My introduction to phenomenology generally uses the terminology formulated by Husserl, which has become standard in the movement. In chapter 1, I discuss intentionality, the central issue in phenomenology, and explain why it is an important topic in our current philosophical and cultural situation. Chapter 2 develops a simple example of the kind of analysis phenomenology provides, to give the reader a feeling for its style of thought. Chapter 3 examines three major themes in phenomenology: parts and wholes, identity in manifolds, and presence and absence. These three formal structures pervade phenomenology, and if we are alert to their presence, the point of many issues can more easily be grasped. I would also claim that while the themes of parts and wholes and identity in manifolds (one in many) are found in almost all philosophical schools, the explicit and sustained study of presence and absence is original in phenomenology.

At this point in the book, after we have presented a number of phenomenological analyses, it becomes possible to step back and explain what phenomenology is as a philosophy and to show how its form of thinking differs from that of prephilosophical experience. This initial definition of phenomenology is given in Chapter 4, where "the phenomenological attitude" is distinguished from "the natural attitude."

The next three chapters develop concrete phenomenological investigations in different areas of human experience. Chapter 5 looks at perception and its two variants, memory and imagination. It examines what we could call the "internal" transformation of our perceptions; besides seeing and hearing things, we also recollect, anticipate, and fantasize, and in doing so we live a private, even secret conscious life. Chapter 6 turns to a more public transformation of our perceptions, to words, pictures, and symbols. Here we are conscious of external things that are not merely perceived but interpreted as images or words or other kinds of representations. Finally, Chapter 7 introduces the theme of categorial thinking, in which we do not just perceive things but articulate them, manifesting not just simple objects but arrangements and states of affairs. In categorial thinking we move from the experience of simple objects to the presentation of intelligible objects. This chapter also contains an important treatment of meanings, senses, and propositions. It strives to account for "concepts" and "thoughts" as being more public than they are often taken to be. It tries to show that senses and propositions are not psychological, mental, or conceptual entities. To understand propositions and senses in the right way is a crucial matter in discussing the nature of truth, especially in the philosophical climate generated by modern philosophy. Chapters 5 through 7, then, offer phenomenological descriptions of three domains of experience: the "internal" field of memory and imagination, the "external" field of perceived objects, words, pictures, and symbols, and the "intellectual" field of categorial objects.

Chapter 8 examines the self or the ego as the identity established within all the intentionalities previously described. The self is described as the responsible agent of truth. It is identified within memories and anticipations as well as intersubjective experience, and it carries out the cognitive acts by which higher, intellectual objects such as states of affairs and groups are presented. The self is the one who takes responsibility for the claims that it makes. The issue of the self leads logically, in Chapter 9, to the topic of time and internal time consciousness, which underlies the identity of the self. Temporality is the condition for perceptions, memories, and anticipations and for the self that lives in them. Finally, Chapter 10 examines the world inhabited by the self, the "life world," within which we immediately experience the things around us. This world is the foundation upon which the modern natural sciences are based. The sciences do not provide an alternative to the world in which we live, but arise from and must be integrated within it. This chapter also discusses, very briefly, the theme of intersubjectivity.

Chapter 11 turns to what we could call the phenomenology of reason. It examines not just the various intentionalities that we exercise, but specifically those that lead to the truth of things, those that could be called "evidences." It is especially in this chapter that we see how phenomenology considers the human mind and human reason as ordered toward truth. Chapter 12 discusses eidetic intuition, the kind of intentionality that discloses essential features of things, features that things could not be without. Eidetic evidence reaches not just factual truth, but essential truth. This chapter is a further development of the phenomenology of reason.

The final two chapters of the book return to the question of what phenomenology is. Phenomenology was initially described in Chapter 4, but now a more complete description can be given. Chapter 13 brings out the nature of philosophical thinking by distinguishing phenomenological reflection from what I have called propositional reflection (one of the themes in Chapter 7). Here I show that philosophy, or phenomenology, is not just a clarification of meaning, but something that cuts deeper. The distinctions studied in this chapter bring out more clearly both what philosophy is and what concepts, senses, and propositions are.

Finally, in Chapter 14, I try to describe phenomenology by contrasting it with modernity and postmodernity, and I add a brief remark on how it can be distinguished from Thomistic philosophy.

I define phenomenology by locating it within our present historical situation. Modern philosophy has two major elements, political philosophy and epistemology, and phenomenology explicitly addresses only the latter. However, because it considers human reason as ordered toward evidence and truth, phenomenology can also address in an indirect way modern issues in political theory. If human beings are specified by the ability to be truthful, then politics and citizenship take on a distinctive sense.

In considering reason as teleologically geared toward truth, phenomenology resembles Thomistic philosophy, which represents a premodern understanding of being and the mind, but it differs from Thomism in that it does not approach philosophy from within biblical revelation. Both phenomenology and Thomism are alternatives to the modern project, but in different ways, and contrasting them with one another further clarifies phenomenology as a form of philosophy.

This book introduces the reader to the terminology and the ideas of one of the major twentieth-century developments in philosophy. This development, phenomenology, does not belong only to the past. It can help us as we strive to remind ourselves, at the start of a new century and a new millennium, of things we can never entirely forget. The book began in a conversation between mathematics and philosophy; may it help us cultivate the life of reason expressed in both these human adventures.

1

What Is Intentionality, and Why Is It Important?

The term most closely associated with phenomenology is "intentionality." The core doctrine in phenomenology is the teaching that every act of consciousness we perform, every experience that we have, is intentional: it is essentially "consciousness of" or an "experience of" something or other. All our awareness is directed toward objects. If I see, I see some visual object, such as a tree or a lake; if I imagine, my imagining presents an imaginary object, such as a car that I visualize coming down a road; if I am involved in remembering, I remember a past object; if I am engaged in judging, I intend a state of affairs or a fact. Every act of consciousness, every experience, is correlated with an object. Every intending has its intended object.

We should note that this sense of "intend" or "intention" should not be confused with "intention" as the purpose we have in mind when we act ("He bought some wood with the intention of building a shed"; "She intended to finish law school a year later"). The phenomenological notion of intentionality applies primarily to the theory of knowledge, not to the theory of human action. The phenomenological use of the word is somewhat awkward because it goes against ordinary usage, which tends to use "intention" in the practical sense; the phenomenological use will almost always call up the sense of practical intending as an overtone. However, "intentionality" and its cognates have become technical terms in phenomenology, and there is no way of avoiding them in a discussion of this philosophical tradition. We have to make the adjustment and understand the word to mean primarily mental or cognitive, and not practical, intentions. In phenomenology, "intending" means the conscious relationship we have to an object.

THE EGOCENTRIC PREDICAMENT

The doctrine of intentionality, then, states that every act of consciousness is directed toward an object of some kind. Consciousness is essentially consciousness "of" something or other. Now, when we are presented with this teaching, and when we are told that this doctrine is at the core of phenomenology, we might well react with a feeling of disappointment. What is so important about this idea? Why should phenomenology make such a fuss about intentionality? Isn't it completely obvious to everyone that consciousness is consciousness of something, that experience is experience of an object of some sort? Do such trivialities need to be stated?

They do need to be asserted, because in the philosophy of the past three or four hundred years, human consciousness and experience have come to be understood in a very different way. In the Cartesian, Hobbesian, and Lockean traditions, which dominate our culture, we are told that when we are conscious, we are primarily aware of ourselves or our own ideas. Consciousness is taken to be like a bubble or an enclosed cabinet; the mind comes in a box. Impressions and concepts occur in this enclosed space, in this circle of ideas and experiences, and our awareness is directed toward them, not directly toward the things "outside." We can try to get outside by making inferences: we may reason that our ideas must have been caused by something outside us, and we may construct hypotheses or models of what those things must be like, but we are not in any direct contact with them. We get to things only by reasoning from our mental impressions, not by having them presented to us. Our consciousness, first and foremost, is not "of" anything at all. Rather, we are caught in what has been called an "egocentric predicament"; all we can really be sure of at the start is our own conscious existence and the states of that consciousness.

This understanding of human awareness is reinforced by what we know about the brain and nervous system. It seems unquestionable that everything cognitional must happen "inside the head," and that all we could possibly be in touch with directly are our own brain states. I once heard a famous brain scientist say in a lecture, almost tearfully, that after so many years of studying the brain, he still could not explain how "that avocado-colored organ inside our skulls"

9

could get beyond itself and reach out into the world. I would also venture to say that almost everyone who has gone to college and taken some courses in physiology, neurology, or psychology would have the same difficulty.

These philosophical and scientific understandings of consciousness have become quite widespread in our culture, and the egocentric predicament they force us into causes us great unease. We know instinctively that we are not trapped in our own subjectivity, we are sure that we do go beyond our brains and our internal mental states, but we do not know how to justify this conviction. We do not know how to show that our contact with the "real world" is not an illusion, not a mere subjective projection. For the most part we have no idea how we ever get outside ourselves, and we probably treat this issue simply by ignoring it and hoping that no one will ask us about it. When we try to think about human consciousness, we start with the premise that we are entirely "inside," and we are greatly perplexed as to how we could ever get "outside."

If we are bereft of intentionality, if we do not have a world in common, then we do not enter into a life of reason, evidence, and truth. Each of us turns to his own private world, and in the practical order we do our own thing: the truth does not make any demands on us. Again, we know that this relativism cannot be the final story. We do argue with one another about what ought to be done and about what the facts are, but philosophically and culturally we find it difficult to ratify our naive acceptance of a common world and our ability to discover and communicate what it is. The denial of intentionality has as its correlate the denial of the mind's orientation toward truth.

A colorful expression of the egocentric predicament can be found in Samuel Beckett's novel *Murphy*. About a third of the way through the book, in chapter 6, Beckett interrupts his narrative to undertake "a justification of the expression, 'Murphy's mind.' " He says he will not try to describe "this apparatus as it really was," but only "what it felt and pictured itself to be." The image he presents is the one we have found to be all too common: "Murphy's mind pictured itself as a large hollow sphere, hermetically closed to the universe without." Here the mind, with its "intramental world," there the outside, the "extramental world," each sequestered from the other. However, the mind is not impoverished by being so confined; rather, everything in the outside universe can be represented in the inside, and the representations are, according to Beckett, either "virtual, or actual, or virtual rising into actual, or actual falling into virtual." These parts of the mind are differentiated from one another: "the mind felt its actual part to be above and bright, its virtual beneath and fading into dark."

The mind is not only placed over against the universe or the real world; it is also placed over against the body that is Murphy's other part: "Thus Murphy felt himself split in two, a body and a mind." Somehow or other, the body and the mind interact: "They had intercourse, apparently, otherwise he could not have known that they had anything in common. But he felt his mind to be bodytight and did not understand through what channel the intercourse was effected nor how the two experiences came to overlap." The isolation of the mind from the body entails an isolation of the mind from the world: "He was split, one part of him never left this mental chamber that pictured itself as a sphere full of light fading into dark, because there was no way out." How the body could influence the mind, or the mind the body, remained an utter mystery to Murphy: "The development of what looked like collusion between such utter strangers remained to Murphy as unintelligible as telekinesis or the Leyden Jar, and of as little interest."*

The Cartesian predicament that Beckett describes, with the mind taken as this large, hollow sphere, light-filled but shading off into darkness, closed off from both the body and the world, is the unfortunate situation in which philosophy finds itself in our time. It is the cultural situation, the human self-understanding, within which philosophy must begin. Many of us do not know how to avoid understanding our own minds the way Beckett's Murphy understands his. This epistemological dilemma is the target of the doctrine of intentionality.

THE PUBLICNESS OF MIND

It is not at all otiose, therefore, to bring intentionality to the fore and to make it the center of philosophical reflection. It is not trivial

* From Samuel Beckett, *Murphy* (New York: Grove Weidenfeld, 1957). Reprinted by permission of the publisher.

to say that consciousness is "consciousness of" objects; on the contrary, this statement goes against many common beliefs. One of phenomenology's greatest contributions is to have broken out of the egocentric predicament, to have checkmated the Cartesian doctrine. Phenomenology shows that the mind is a public thing, that it acts and manifests itself out in the open, not just inside its own confines. Everything is outside. The very notions of an "intramental world" and an "extramental world" are incoherent; they are examples of what Ezra Pound called "idea-clots." The mind and the world are correlated with one another. Things do appear to us, things truly are disclosed, and we, on our part, do display, both to ourselves and to others, the way things are. Given the cultural setting in which phenomenology arose and in which we continue to live, a focus on intentionality is not without great philosophical value. By discussing intentionality, phenomenology helps us reclaim a public sense of thinking, reasoning, and perception. It helps us reassume our human condition as agents of truth.

Besides drawing our attention to the intentionality of consciousness, phenomenology also discovers and describes many different structures in intentionality. When the mind is taken in the Cartesian or Lockean way, as an enclosed sphere with its circle of ideas, the term "consciousness" is usually considered to be simply univocal. There are no structural differences within consciousness; there is just awareness, pure and simple. We notice whatever impressions arise in us, and we then arrange them into judgments or propositions that take a stab at declaring what is "out there." But for phenomenology, intentionality is highly differentiated. There are different kinds of intending, correlated with different kinds of objects. For example, we carry out perceptual intentions when we see an ordinary material object, but we must intend pictorially when we see a photograph or a painting. We must change our intentionality; taking something as a picture is different from taking something as a simple object. Pictures are correlated with pictorial intending, perceptual objects are correlated with perceptual intending. Still another kind of intending is at work when we take something to be a word, another when we remember something, and others again when we make judgments or collect things into groups. These and many other kinds of intending need to be described and differentiated one from the other. Furthermore, the forms of intending can be interwoven: to see something as a picture involves, as a foundation, that we also have it as a perceived thing. The pictorial consciousness is layered upon the perceptual, just as the picture we see is layered on a fabric or a piece of paper that could also be looked at simply as a colored thing.

Still other intentionalities can be distinguished, such as the kinds that occur when we think about the past. What sort of intending is exercised when, say, archaeologists find pots and ashes and scraps of clothing and begin to speak about people who lived in a given site seven hundred years ago? How do these objects, these pots and ashes, present human beings to us? How must we "take" them, so that they will serve in that way? What sort of intentions are correlated with finding and interpreting something as a fossil? What sort of intentions are at work when we speak about protons, neutrons, and quarks? They are not the kind that are at work when we see pictures or flags, nor the kind at work when we see something as a plant or an animal; some of the dilemmas associated with particle physics arise because we assume that we intend subatomic entities in the same way that we intend billiard balls. Sorting out and differentiating all these intentionalities, as well as the specific kinds of objects correlated with them, is what is done by the kind of philosophy called phenomenology. Descriptions like these help us to understand human knowing in all its forms, and they also help us understand the many ways in which we can be related to the world in which we live.

The term "phenomenology" is a compound of the Greek words *phainomenon* and *logos*. It signifies the activity of giving an account, giving a *logos*, of various phenomena, of the various ways in which things can appear. By *phenomena* we mean, for example, pictures as opposed to simple objects, remembered events as opposed to anticipated ones, imagined objects as opposed to perceived, mathematical objects such as triangles and sets as opposed to living things, words as opposed to fossils, other people as opposed to nonhuman animals, political reality as opposed to the economic. All such phenomena can be explored when we realize that consciousness is consciousness "of" something, that it is not locked within its own cabinet. In contrast with the cramped confinement of the Cartesian, Hobbesian, and Lockean philosophy of knowledge, phenomenology is liberating. It gets us out of doors and restores the world that was lost by the philosophies that locked us into our egocentric predicament.

Phenomenology recognizes the reality and truth of phenomena, the things that appear. It is not the case, as the Cartesian tradition would have us believe, that "being a picture" or "being a perceived object" or "being a symbol" is only in the mind. They are ways in which things can be. The way things appear is part of the being of things; things appear as they are, and they are as they appear. Things do not just exist; they also manifest themselves as what they are. Animals have a way of appearing that is different from that of plants, because animals are different from plants in their being. Pictures have a way of appearing that is different from that of remembered objects, because their way of being is different. A picture is out there on the canvas or the wood panel; a salute is in the arm being moved, out there between the person saluting and the person saluted. A fact is where the ingredients of the fact are located: the fact that the grass is wet exists in the wet grass, not in my mind when I say the words. My mind in action is the presenting, to myself and to others, of the grass as being wet. When we make judgments we articulate the presentation of parts of the world; we do not just arrange ideas or concepts in our minds.

Someone might object, "What about hallucinations and mistakes? Sometimes things are not as they seem. I may think I see a man, but it turns out that it is only a bush; I may think I see a dagger, but nothing is there. Obviously, the man and the dagger are only in my mind; does not this show that everything is in the mind?" Not at all; the point is simply that things can look like other things, and sometimes we may seem to be perceiving when we really are not. One evening several years ago, in the wintertime, I drove toward my garage and saw some "pieces of glass" on the driveway. I assumed that someone must have smashed a bottle there. I parked my car nearby on the road, intending to come back the next morning to clean the driveway. When I returned the next day, I found only some puddles of water and small pieces of ice; what I had "seen" as glass was in fact only ice. In this experience, my original vision and my later correction were not worked out within the cabinet of my mind; it was not the case that I merely shuffled my impressions and concepts, or that I made up a new hypothesis to explain the ideas that I had. Rather, I was related to the world in different ways, and these relationships were based on the fact that ice can look like glass under some circumstances. Everything, including the "glass" and the ice, is public. Mistakes are something public, and so are concealment and camouflage; all these are kinds of phenomena in which one thing is taken for another. Mistakes, concealment, and camouflage are real in their own way; they are possibilities of being, and they call for their own analysis. Even hallucinations have a kind of reality all their own. What happens when they occur is that we think we are perceiving when we really are imagining, and this disorder can take place only as parasitic on real perceptions and imaginations. In order to be able to hallucinate, we must have entered into the game of intending or targeting things. We could not hallucinate if we were not aware of the difference between perceiving and dreaming.

What phenomenology does through its doctrine of the intentionality of consciousness is to overcome the Cartesian and Lockean bias against the publicness of mind, which is also a bias against the reality of the appearance of things. For phenomenology, there are no "mere" appearances, and nothing is "just" an appearance. Appearances are real; they belong to being. Things do show up. Phenomenology allows us to recognize and to restore the world that seemed to have been lost when we were locked into our own internal world by philosophical confusions. Things that had been declared to be merely psychological are now found to be ontological, part of the being of things. Pictures, words, symbols, perceived objects, states of affairs, other minds, laws, and social conventions are all acknowledged as truly there, as sharing in being and as capable of appearing according to their own proper style.

But phenomenology does more than restore what was lost. That part of its work is somewhat negative and contentious, dependent on an error for its own value. In addition to this refutational work, phenomenology offers the pleasure of philosophy for those who wish to enjoy it. There is much to think about in the way things manifest themselves and in our ability to be truthful, our ability to let things appear. Presentations and absences are exquisitely interwoven, and phenomenology helps us to think about them. It does not just remove skeptical impediments; it also affords the possibility of understanding differences, identities, and forms as philosophers have classically understood them. It is contemplative and theoretic.

It validates the philosophical life as a culminating human achievement. Phenomenology does not only remedy our intellectual distress; it also opens the door to philosophical exploration for those who wish to practice it.

2

Perception of a Cube as a Paradigm of Conscious Experience

We will use a simple example to illustrate the kind of descriptive analysis of consciousness that phenomenology offers us. This example will give us an idea of the type of philosophical explanation that phenomenology provides. It will serve as a model for the more complicated analyses that we will undertake later.

SIDES, ASPECTS, AND PROFILES

Consider the way in which we perceive a material object, such as a cube. I see the cube from one angle, from one perspective. I cannot see the cube from all sides at once. It is essential to the experience of a cube that the perception be partial, with only one part of the object being directly given at any moment. However, it is not the case that I only experience the sides that are visible from my present viewpoint. As I see those sides, I also intend, I cointend, the sides that are hidden. I see more than what strikes the eye. The presently visible sides are surrounded by a halo of potentially visible but actually absent sides. These other sides are given, but given precisely as absent. They too are part of what I experience.

Let us formulate this structure in regard to its objective and its subjective dimensions. Objectively, what is given to me when I see a cube is a blend made up of sides that are present and sides that are absent but cointended. The thing being seen involves a mixture of the present and the absent. Subjectively, my perception, my viewing, is a blend made up of filled and empty intentions. My activity of perceiving, therefore, is also a mixture; parts of it intend what is present, and other parts intend what is absent, the "other sides" of the cube.

Of course, "everyone knows" that perception involves such blends, but not everyone knows their philosophical impact or their philosophical range. All experience involves a blend of presence and absence, and in some cases drawing our attention to this mixture can be philosophically illuminating. When we listen to a sentence being uttered by a speaker, for example, our listening involves a presence of one part of the sentence, flanked by the absence of the parts that have already been pronounced and those that are to come. The sentence itself, as a whole, stands out against the silence, the noise, and the other sentences that precede, follow, or accompany it. The blend of presence and absence in our experience of a sentence is different from that involved in the perception of a cube, but in both cases there is a blend of presence and absence, of filled and empty intendings. Other kinds of objects would have still other kinds of blends, but all of them would be mixtures of presence and absence.

Let us return to the experience of the cube. At a given moment, only certain sides of the cube are presented to me, and the others are absent. But I know that I can either walk around the cube or turn the cube around and the absent sides will come into view, while the present sides go out of view. My perception is dynamic, not static; even if I just look at one side of the cube, the saccadic motion of my eyes introduces a kind of searching mobility that I am not even aware of. As I turn the cube or walk around it, the potentially perceived becomes the actually perceived, and the actually perceived slips into absence; it becomes that which has been seen, that which is again only potentially seen. On the subjective side, the empty intentions become filled and the filled become empty.

Furthermore, other modalities of perception also come into play. I can not only see the cube but also touch it, I can tap it to see what sort of noise it makes, I can taste it (for infants, the mouth is the primary tactile organ), and I can even smell it to see what it is made of. These are all potential presentations that come along with any presentation I have of the cube, potentials that can be activated and brought into direct presence. All of them surround the cube even when it is simply given to my view. It is interesting to note, however, that only vision and touch present the object as a cube; hearing, taste, and smell present the material the cube is made of, not its character of being shaped as a cube.

Let us spell out the visual experience of the cube a bit more precisely. We can distinguish three layers in what is presented to us.

(1) First, there are the *sides* of the cube, six of them. Each side can itself be given under different perspectives. If I hold a side directly before me, it is presented as a square, but if I tilt the cube away from me slightly, the side becomes given at an angle; it looks more like a trapezoid. The farther corners seem closer to one another than do the nearer ones. If I tilt the cube still farther, the side becomes almost like a line, and then, finally, if I tilt it just a bit more, the side vanishes from view. In other words, a side can be given in different ways, just as the cube can be given in different sides. (2) Let us call each of the ways in which the side is given an *aspect*. A side has the aspect of a square when it faces us directly, but it has the aspect of a trapezoid when it is turned at an angle to us. As a cube appears to us in many sides, so each side can appear to us in many aspects, and these aspects, transitively, are also aspects of the cube. But we can go one step farther. (3) I can view a particular aspect at a given moment; I can close my eyes for a minute, then open them again. If I have not moved, I will have the same aspect given to me again. The aspect itself can be given to me as an identity through a manifold of temporally different appearances. Let us call each of these momentary views a *profile* of the aspect; it is, transitively, also a profile of the side and a profile of the cube. A profile is a temporally individuated presentation of an object. The English word "profile" is the translation of the German *Abschattung*, which can signify "profile" or "sketch." Ultimately, therefore, the cube is given to me in a manifold of profiles.

Let us change our example from the perception of a cube to the perception of a building. I look at the front side of the building. I look at that side from a point of view a little to the left of center: at that moment, I see one particular aspect of the front of the building. Suppose I say to you, "This view of the building is very attractive; come and look at it from here." As I move away from the spot and you move into it, you see the same aspect that I just saw, but you will be experiencing profiles that are different from the ones I experienced, because the profiles are the momentary presentations, not the look or the view or the aspect that can be seen by many viewers. An aspect, a side, and of course the building itself are all intersubjective, but a profile is private and subjective. The profile may even depend on my disposition at the time and on the condition of my sensory organs; if I am ill or dizzy, the profile may be wobbly or grayish instead of being steady or blue. The relative and subjective character of profiles does not mean that the aspects or the sides or the things given through them are relative and subjective in the same way.

IDENTITY OF THE OBJECT ITSELF

Perception, therefore, involves layers of synthesis, layers of manifolds of presentation, both actual and potential. Now, however, an important new dimension must be brought into play. When I see the different sides of the cube, when I experience various aspects from various angles and through various profiles, it is essential to my experience that I perceive all these manifolds as belonging to one and the same cube. The sides, aspects, and profiles are presented to me, but in them all, one and the same cube is being presented. The layers of difference that I experience are played off against an identity that is given continuously in and through them.

It would be wrong, however, to say that the cube is just the sum of all its profiles. The identity of the cube belongs to a dimension different from that of the sides, aspects, and profiles. The identity is other to the appearances it offers. The identity never shows up as a side, an aspect, or a profile, but still it is presented to us, precisely as the identity in all of them. We can intend the cube in its sameness, not just in its sides, aspects, and profiles. As I move around the cube, or turn it around in my hand, the continuous flow of profiles is unified by being "of" the single cube. When we say that "the cube" is presented to us, we mean that its identity is given.

At this point, we see a deeper dimension of the intentionality of consciousness than those we examined in Chapter 1. Consciousness is "of" something in the sense that it intends the identity of objects, not just the flow of appearances that are presented to it. The issue of the identity of the object will become important when we examine the transition from perception to intellection, when a perceived object becomes part of a state of affairs or a fact, but it is important even as a constituent of perception. When we perceive an object, we do not just have a flow of profiles, a series of impressions; in and through them all, we have one and the same object given to us, and the identity of the object is intended and is given. All the profiles and all the aspects, all the appearances, are appreciated as being of one and the same thing. Identity belongs to what is given in experience, and the recognition of identity belongs to the intentional structure of experience. Let us also note in passing that this identity itself can be intended in absence as well as in presence, and we can be mistaken about it.

This analysis of sides, aspects, and profiles helps confirm the realism of phenomenology over against the Cartesian and Lockean philosophies of knowledge. According to the latter, all we are immediately aware of are impressions that strike our sensibility; we are enclosed in the circle of our ideas. But once we admit that there are such things as profiles distinguished from aspects, and aspects distinguished from sides, we find that it is quite impossible to account for such structures in terms of simple impressions and ideas within the mind. If everything were simply internal to us, all we would have given to us would be profiles: flashes of color and bits of sound, out of which objects would have to be constructed. We could never distinguish among a profile and an aspect and a side. In contrast, the distinctions between sides, aspects, and profiles make it more obviously clear that the surfaces and looks of things are "out there" for us to perceive; they are not just fabricated out of the impressions that strike our sensibility. The side or aspect that can be seen as the same at different times by the same person, or by several different persons, could not be merely an impression privately affecting each subjectivity. Furthermore, "behind" and "in" the sides, aspects, and profiles, there is also the oneness of the object itself, the identity that is given to us. The identity is public and available to all; it is not just something that we project into the appearances.

We have used the perception of a material object, a cube, as an initial paradigm for the phenomenological analysis of intentionality. Other kinds of objects involve other complex forms of presentation. Before moving on to the analysis of such objects and their corresponding intentionalities, let us consider some formal structures that play an important role in phenomenology.

3

Three Formal Structures in Phenomenology

There are three structural forms that appear constantly in the analyses done in phenomenology. If we are aware of these forms, it will be easier to understand what is going on in a particular passage or the development of a particular theme. The three forms are (a) the structure of *parts and wholes*, (b) the structure of *identity in a manifold*, and (c) the structure of *presence and absence*. The three are interrelated, but they cannot be reduced to one another. The first two of these structures are themes that have been developed by many earlier philosophers; Aristotle has much to say about parts and wholes in the *Metaphysics*, for example, and Plato and the Neoplatonic thinkers, as well as the scholastics, explore the idea of the identity within differences, the one in many.

However, the theme of presence and absence has not been worked out, in an explicit and systematic way, by earlier philosophers. This issue is original in Husserl and in phenomenology. Presences and absences can be blended in remarkable ways, and the exploration of such blends can serve as a valuable theme in philosophy. I believe that phenomenology worked out this new philosophical dimension precisely because it was trying to counteract the epistemological problems of modern thought, the egocentric predicament initiated by Descartes. Phenomenology made a positive advance by responding to a philosophical confusion, much as Plato worked out his understanding of unity and form in response to the challenge of Sophistic skepticism.

We will consider each of the three structural forms as they are developed in phenomenology.

PARTS AND WHOLES

Wholes can be analyzed into two different kinds of parts: pieces and moments. *Pieces* are parts that can subsist and be presented even apart from the whole; they can be detached from their wholes. Pieces can also be called *independent* parts.

Examples of pieces are leaves and acorns, which can be separated from their tree and still present themselves as independent entities. Even a branch of a tree is an independent part, because it can be separated from the tree; when so separated it no longer functions as a living branch and becomes only a piece of wood, but it still can exist and be perceived as an independent thing. Also, the parts of a machine, a member of a troupe of actors, a soldier in a platoon are pieces within their respective wholes. Such things do in fact belong to their larger whole (the machine, the troupe, the platoon), but they can also be themselves and present themselves apart from that whole. When so separated, pieces become wholes in themselves and are no longer parts. Pieces, then, are parts that can become wholes.

Moments are parts that cannot subsist or be presented apart from the whole to which they belong; they cannot be detached. Moments are *nonindependent* parts.

Examples of moments are the color red (or any other color), which cannot occur apart from some surface or spatial expanse, and musical pitch, which cannot exist except as blended with a sound, and also vision, which cannot occur except as dependent upon the eye. Such parts are nonindependent and cannot exist or be presented by themselves. A branch can be cut off from a tree, but the pitch cannot be isolated from a sound and vision cannot float away from the eye. Moments cannot be except as blended with other moments. Moments are the kind of part that cannot become a whole.

Good examples of moments or nonindependent parts can be found in the dimensions that are distinguished in physics. In mechanics, a body in motion possesses the moments of mass, velocity, momentum, and acceleration, and mass and acceleration in turn are associated essentially with force. In electromagnetic theory, an electrical current possesses the dimension of charge per unit of time, which is measured in amperes, and this dimension is associated in turn with electrical potential (volts), resistance (ohms), and power (watts). All these dimensions are interdependent: there cannot be momentum without mass and velocity, or acceleration without mass and force, or current without voltage.

A particular item can be a piece in one respect while being a moment in another. For example, an acorn can be separated from its tree, but as an object of perception it cannot be separated from a background; to be perceived, the acorn has to be seen against a background of some sort or other.

There is a certain necessity in the way moments are blended together into their wholes. Some moments are founded upon others, and a distinction arises between the *founded* and the *founding* parts. Hue is founded upon color, while, conversely, color founds or is the substrate for hue. Vision is founded on the eye, and the eye founds or supports vision. Furthermore, there can be several layers of founding: shade is founded upon hue, which in turn is founded upon color. In this case, shade is only mediately founded upon color (via hue), while hue is immediately founded upon color. Pitch and timbre, however, are both immediately founded upon sound.

Let us add another terminological precision: a whole can be called a *concretum,* something that can exist and present itself and be experienced as a concrete individual. A piece, an independent part, is a part that can itself become a concretum. Moments, however, cannot become concreta. Whenever they exist and are experienced, they drag along their other moments with them; they exist only as blended with their complementary parts.

However, it is possible for us to think and speak about moments by themselves: we can speak about pitch without mentioning sound; we can refer to hue without mentioning color; we can talk about vision without mentioning the eye. When we consider moments simply by themselves, they are *abstracta,* they are being thought of abstractly. The possibility of speaking about such abstract parts, the possibility of speaking abstractly, arises because we can use language; it is language that permits us to deal with a moment apart from its necessary complement of other moments and its whole. However, a danger arises along with this ability: because we can refer to a moment by itself, without mentioning its associated moments, we may begin to think that this moment can exist by itself, that it can become a concretum. We may begin to think about vision, for example, as though it could be by itself, apart from the eye.

The distinction between pieces and moments is very important in philosophical analysis. What often happens in philosophy is that something that is a moment is taken to be a piece, taken to be separable from its wider whole and other parts; then an artificial philosophical "problem" arises about how the original whole can be reconstituted. The true solution to such a problem is not to fashion some new way of building up the whole out of such falsely segmented parts, but simply to show that the part in question was a moment, not a piece, and that it never should have been separated from the whole in the first place. Many philosophical arguments are simply complicated attempts to show that something is a dependent, not an independent part, a moment and not a piece.

This sort of artificial problem arises in regard to the mind and its objects, for example. As we have seen in Chapter 1, people will often take the mind to be a self-enclosed sphere, that is, a piece that can be separated from the worldly context to which it naturally and essentially belongs. Then they will ask how the mind can ever get outside itself and find out what is going on in the world. But the mind cannot be separated out in this way; the mind is a moment to the world and the things in it; the mind is essentially correlated with its objects. The mind is essentially intentional. There is no "problem of knowledge" or "problem of the external world," there is no problem about how we get to "extramental" reality, because the mind should never be separated from reality from the beginning. Mind and being are moments to each other; they are not pieces that can be segmented out of the whole to which they belong. Likewise, the human mind is often separated from the brain and the body as though it were a piece and not a moment founded upon them; the "mind–brain" problem can also be treated as an instance of confusion regarding parts and wholes.

Another example of the logic of parts and wholes can be found in our analysis of the perception of a cube. The profiles, aspects, and sides, as well as the identity of the cube itself, are all moments to one another in the presentation of the object. We could not have the presentation of sides except through aspects, which in turn are only presented through profiles. The cube itself as an identity cannot be presented perceptually except through the manifolds of sides, aspects, and profiles. It would be a case of misplaced concreteness, of looking for the piece rather than the moment, to want to have the cube just by itself, not as founded on its manifolds of presentations.

There is always a danger that we will separate the inseparable, that we will make the abstractum into a concretum, because in our speech we can talk about one moment without mentioning what it is founded upon. We can talk about "the triangle," for example, and after a while we start to think that there exists a triangle apart from embodied triangles. When we allow this to happen, we make a moment into a piece, an abstractum into a concretum, and we begin to ask how on earth we could encounter that piece, how it could present itself to us. We let the abstractness of our speech mislead us into thinking that the thing we talk about could present itself concretely to us. We introduce a separation where we should simply make a distinction.

The contrast between pieces and moments is of great help in our introduction to phenomenology. Many issues that seem very complicated turn out to be simple when formulated in terms of the kinds of parts that function within them. A philosophical analysis usually consists in laying out the various moments that go to make up a given whole. The philosophical analysis of vision, for example, will show how vision is founded upon the eye and also upon bodily mobility (on the saccadic movements of the eye, on the ability of the head to be turned, on the ability of the whole body to go from one place to another, from one viewpoint to another), how both seeing and that which is seen are moments within a whole, and how seeing is conditioned by other sensory modalities, such as touch, hearing, and kinesthesia. A philosophical analysis will help us avoid the temptation to turn moments into pieces, as we might do, for example, when we attempt to separate vision from mobility.

Even the question of the human soul, or the soul of any living thing, can be clarified by an appeal to parts and wholes. The soul is a moment; it bears an essential relation to the body and is founded on the body that it enlivens and determines and in which it is expressed. Human beings are animated bodies, not enmattered spirits. But the soul is often caricatured by being turned into a piece, into a vital force or a thing that could exist and be presented and understood apart from its organic base, even into something that can preexist its body. Of course, the manner in which the soul is a moment to the living body is different from the way hue is a moment to color, but the first step in clarifying the nature of soul is to show that it is not a separable thing that can be understood apart from its involvement with the body.

There is necessity in the way moments, nonindependent parts, are arranged into a whole. Certain moments mediate for others, which join the whole only through the former: in the perception of the cube, aspects mediate between profiles and sides, and sides mediate between aspects and the cube itself (profiles do not present the cube itself, only its aspects and sides and thus mediately the cube). To lay out such arrays of moments provides an understanding of the whole in question. What often happens, however, is that we articulate some of the parts in a whole but neglect others; or we try to segment the moments, taking as pieces the moments we have singled out; or we take one moment as being equivalent to another, that is, we fail to sustain a distinction. We may confuse politics with economics, for instance, within the whole of human relationships, or we may think that economics, which is really only a moment, is the whole. Marx, for example, elevates economics to the whole of social relationships, and Hobbes elevates contractual relations, which are only a part of the social whole, into being the whole. The working out of parts and wholes is central to philosophy and human understanding.

Whenever we think about something, we articulate parts and wholes within it. The parts and wholes make up the content of what we think when we go beyond simple sensibility and rather mute perception. The naming of parts is the essence of thought, and it is important to see the difference between pieces and moments when we try, philosophically, to understand what understanding is.

IDENTITY IN MANIFOLDS

We have already encountered the theme of identity in manifolds when we considered the perception of a cube: the cube as an identity was shown to be distinct from its sides, aspects, and profiles, and yet it was presented through them all. What we can do now is to show how wide-ranging this form of presentation is, and to bring out some of its philosophical implications. The structure operates in the perception of all material objects, as we have seen, but it also operates in any kind of thing that can be presented to us. To begin, let us examine how it functions in the presentation of meaning through language.

When we wish to express something, we can always distinguish between the expression and what is expressed, the exprimend. If I say, "The snow has covered the street," "The street is covered with snow," and "Die Strasse ist verschneit," I have uttered three different expressions, but I can consider all three of them to have expressed one and the same meaning or *exprimend*, one and the same fact or bit of information. The three expressions are like three aspects of one and the same object, except that in this case the object is complicated and its status in being is different from that of a cube. I could amplify the manifold still further by intoning my sentences in different ways: by shouting the sentence once, then whispering it, then saying it in a high-pitched voice, and so on. These would all be various ways of presenting one and the same sentence, and yet all the utterances and all the sentences (and many possible others as well) would present one and the same meaning, and one and the same fact.

The point is that the identical fact can be expressed in a manifold of ways, and the fact is other to any and all of its expressions. Just as the cube belongs to a dimension different from that of the sides, aspects, and profiles, so the meaning or the fact belongs to a dimension different from that of the manifold of expressions and utterances through which it is given. For this reason, it would be misleading to look for a meaning or a fact as some sort of mental sentence, a kind of ghostly analogue of the expressions we publicly utter; to do so would be the usual philosophical mistake of misplaced concreteness, of taking a moment as a piece. The meaning just is the identity that is within and yet behind all of its expressions. We should also notice that the identical meaning is capable of being presented through many other sentences or expressions (in still other languages, in sign languages, through gestures and other symbols) that have not and mostly will not be stated, just as the cube is an identity that could be perceived through profiles we have not yet activated. The horizon of the potential and the absent surrounds the actual presences of things. The thing can always be presented in more ways than we already know; the thing will always hold more appearances in reserve.

As another example of an identity in a manifold, consider an important historical event, such as the Normandy Invasion in the Second World War. This event was experienced in one way by those who participated in it, in another way by those same people when they remembered it, in another way by those who read about it as it was reported in the newspapers, in another way by those who write and those who read books about it later on, in another way by those who join in a memorial celebration on the Normandy beaches, in another way by those who see films taken of the actual event, and in still another way by those who see movies and television shows made about it. The same event was also anticipated by those who were planning to do it and those who, on the other side, were planning to resist it. There are, undoubtedly, still other ways in which one and the same event can be intended and made present, and the identity of the event is sustained through them all.

Let us turn to aesthetic objects. One and the same drama, say, *The Duchess of Malfi*, is presented in all the stagings and all the readings, with all their various interpretations, in which the play is given, and it was also presented to John Webster when he wrote the play. One and the same symphony, such as the Hafner Symphony of Mozart, is given in all its executions. The interpretation given by Bruno Walter is different from that given by Klaus Tennstedt, and indeed the general way of interpreting it in the early twentieth century was different from that common in the late twentieth century, but all the interpretations are of one and the same symphony. It is interesting to note that a recording of a piece of music is different from a live performance because the recording captures just one of the performances, whereas each live performance is different from all the others. If I were to listen twice to the same recording, I would hear the same performance both times, not just the same symphony, and yet my hearing of it would be different each time: some dimensions and not others would come to the fore, my mood might be different, the day itself might be bright or gloomy. When a recording captures just one performance, it is as though a movie captured just one aspect of a cube and only let me see that particular manifestation of the cube itself.

If we turn from the arts that require performance to those that do not, we find further differences in the structure of identity and manifold. A painting is not executed by anything analogous to an orchestra performance; it is presented directly when it is viewed, not when someone performs it. No performer must come between the viewers and the work as the musicians must come between the listeners and the work. However, one and the same painting can be seen at one moment and remembered at another, written analyses of the painting can be given, copies of it can be painted, and prints, "reproductions," of the painting can be made. There is also a difference between how the painting appeared to the artist and how it appears to the viewer, as well as differences between the viewing of a cultivated viewer and a mere curiosity seeker. The painting waits for its viewers in order to be completed as a work of art, but it does so in a way different from how a symphony waits for performances in order to come into actual being. The identities and the manifolds are different in each case.

If we may turn to religious events for further examples, the Exodus was presented to the Jewish people who were involved in it, but the same event is presented to those who read about it in the Scriptures and those who celebrate the Passover. For Christians, the event of the death and resurrection of Christ was experienced by the disciples, and is further presented, in different ways, through the reading of the Scriptures, through the witness of martyrs and confessors, and through the sacraments and especially the Eucharist. Indeed, for Christians the celebration of the Eucharist is not only a presentation of the death and resurrection of Christ, but also a mediated presentation of the Passover and the Exodus. Thus, even the sacred is an identity within a manifold of presentations.

The identity that is given through its manifold of appearances belongs to a dimension different from that of the manifold. The identity is not one member of the manifold: the cube is not one of the aspects or profiles, the proposition is not one of the uttered sentences, the play is not simply one of its performances. The identity transcends its manifold of presentations, it goes beyond them. The identity is not merely the sum of its appearances; to see it as just their sum would flatten out the two dimensions that must be distinguished here. It would make everything just a series of appearances, all in one dimension, instead of recognizing the identity as beyond the dimension of appearances, as something presented through them all, and through other possible appearances as well.

The being of this identity is rather elusive. We think we know rather clearly what an appearance is – an aspect that we see, a sentence that we utter, a performance that we hear – but the identity seems not to be something we can put our hands on or put before our eyes. It seems to elude our grasp. And yet we know that the identity is never reducible to one of its appearances; we know that the identity must be distinguished from this and every presentation that we enjoy of it. If the identity presents itself now in one way, it also holds in reserve other ways of being given and of reappearing as the same thing again, to ourselves and to others; it always both reveals and conceals itself. The thing can always be given again, perhaps in ways we ourselves cannot anticipate. What we try to do in our philosophical analysis is to secure the reality of such identities, to bring out the fact that they are different from their manifolds of presentation, and to show that despite their slippery status they truly are a component of what we experience.

Indeed, perhaps the easiest answer one might give to the question, "What is a phenomenological analysis?" would be to say that it describes the manifold that is proper to a given kind of object. A phenomenology of meaning would spell out the manifold through which meanings are given; a phenomenology of art would describe the various manifolds by which art objects present themselves and are identified; a phenomenology of the imagination would describe the multiplicities of appearance through which imaginary objects are given; a phenomenology of religion would discuss the manifolds of appearance proper to religious things. Each manifold is different, each is proper to its identity, and the identities are different in kind. "Manifold of appearance" and "identity" are analogous terms; the identity of an art object is different from the identity of a political event, and yet both are identities and both have their proper ways of being given. By carefully spelling out the diverse manifolds and identities, phenomenology helps us to preserve the reality and distinctiveness of each. It helps us avoid reductionism by bringing out what is proper to each kind of being, not only in its independent existence, but also in its power of presentation. A moral action, for example, will be more vividly distinguished from compulsive conduct if we are able to formulate the manifold of presentations proper to each.

Most of the examples we have considered of identities in manifolds have been related to a single perceiver or a single knower. When we introduce the presence of other persons, when we include the dimension of intersubjectivity, a much richer array of manifolds comes into play. For example, the manifolds of sides, aspects, and profiles present a bodily object to me, and the manifolds change in response to my own movements in space. But when other perceivers are brought into the picture, the same identity takes on a deeper objectivity, a richer transcendence; I now see it not only as the thing I would see differently if I were to move this way and that, but also as the very same thing that is being seen, right now, from another perspective by someone else. The object is given to other viewers through manifolds that are different from those facing me, and I see the object precisely as being seen by others through viewpoints that I do not share. I realize that it presents facets to others that are not being presented to me, and hence these other facets are cointended by me, precisely as not my own. The identity of the thing is there not only for me but also for others, and therefore it is a deeper and richer identity for me. There is more "there" there; the being and the identity of the thing are heightened by the introduction of intersubjective perspectives. The very dimension of being there for others as well as for me adds to the being and identity of the thing.

The same increase of richness occurs in regard to other identities, such as those of the meaning of a text, artistic and cultural objects, human events, moral situations, and religious identities. One of the possibilities that is opened up, for example, is the power to appreciate that an object, say a text, can be far better understood by another than by me. I may realize that the identity and the manifold given to me are very obscure and confused compared to what is grasped by my colleague, who brings out of the text things I never seem able to discover on my own. Again, I may be quite befuddled by a particular human exchange, while another person immediately grasps and expresses what is going on; as I then perceive this event, I have it given to me as being better perceived and better understood by someone else than by me, and yet I do grasp the event. Even in its obscurity, and precisely as obscure, the event is given to me.

As a final example of the structure of identity in manifolds, let us mention the very awareness we have of our own selves. Our self-identity is something that presents itself through a special set of appearances. While we identify cubes, propositions, facts, symphonies, paintings, moral exchanges, and religious things, we also, always, are establishing our own identities as the ones to whom all these things are given. We are establishing ourselves as datives of manifestation. An important constituent of our personal identity is found in the interplay of memories, imaginations, and perceptions, and in the flow of our awareness of interior time. We will examine these structures in detail later on. Our own identity is obviously not the same as that of any of the objects that are given to us, but it is of the same kind as that of other selves, other persons. However, even in this context, even in intersubjective experience, we stand out as the center of our own consciousness. Even among our own kind, we have a special ineluctable preeminence; we are at our center in a way that we cannot ever escape. We never become anyone else or anything else; we cannot leave ourselves behind.

We will have occasion to apply the structure of identity in manifolds as we examine other themes in phenomenology. Let us for the moment leave this topic and move on to the third of the structures we set out to investigate, that of presence and absence.

PRESENCE AND ABSENCE AND THE IDENTITY BETWEEN THEM

We have already observed that the philosophical theme of presence and absence, or of filled and empty intentions, is quite original with phenomenology. For some reason, the classical philosophers have not focused on the distinction between the present and the absent. I suggest that it was modern, Cartesian skepticism about the reality of the world that provoked phenomenology into examining this issue.

Presence and absence are the objective correlates to *filled* and *empty intentions*. An empty intention is an intention that targets something that is not there, something absent, something not present to the one who intends. A filled intention is one that targets something that is there, in its bodily presence, before the one who intends. Let us look at some examples to bring out these structures.

Suppose we wish to go to a baseball game in Camden Yards in Baltimore. The idea of going arises in a conversation my friends and I are having. We decide that John will get the tickets. He does so. We talk about the game and about who might win. We drive to the game, still talking about it. We walk into the stadium. So far, the game has been absent to us, and yet we have been intending it, but only emptily. We have talked about it in its absence, we have imagined being at the game, we anticipate the game as we walk toward our seats. All these have been empty intendings. Now, as the game starts and we begin to watch it, we exercise filled intentions; the game is gradually presented to us. The empty intentions, what we said and imagined about the game, become filled by the actual presence of the game, which takes some time to unfold. Our watching of the game is our *intuition* of the game. This is all that intuition is in the phenomenological vocabulary. Intuition is not something mystical or magical; it is simply having a thing present to us as opposed to having it intended in its absence. When the event is over, we drive away from the stadium and talk about and remember the game, once again through empty intentions and in the absence of the game, but in a different kind of absence, the kind that is presented to memory, not the kind presented to anticipation. The absences are different. The absences we have given to us after a presence are different from the absences we have before a presence.

As another example, imagine that you visit Washington, DC, and I say that we should go to the National Gallery of Art to see Leonardo da Vinci's *Ginevra de' Benci*. As we go to the gallery I tell you about the painting: all this is done in empty intending, even though your empty intentions are different from mine. You have never seen the painting whereas I have, but nevertheless we both are in the absence of what we are talking about. Then, we walk up to the painting and continue to discuss it, with our intentions now filled. The painting is present to us; we intuit it. When we leave the painting, it is absent again, and we are back to empty intentions.

Still other examples are the following: the "internal experiences" of another person are always irreducibly absent to us; no matter how well you may know me, my actual flow of internal feelings and experiences could never become truly blended with yours in a way that would allow, for example, my memories or fantasies to suddenly start surfacing within your consciousness. On the other hand, a certain kind of sympathy can exist between people who know one another well, and there is a difference between merely talking, say, about someone else's anger in its absence and directly seeing that person enraged. As another example, when I refer to the first two lines said by Hippolyta in *A Midsummer Night's Dream*, I refer to them in their absence, but when I recite the words, "Four days will quickly steep themselves in night;/Four nights will quickly dream away the time," I offer the two lines in their actual presence. When I refer to a certain mathematical proof by name, I signify it emptily in its absence, but when I thoughtfully carry out the proof, I make it present. The play of presence and absence can work for different kinds of things, and in each case the kinds of presences and absences are specific to the thing in question. We noted earlier that philosophical or phenomenological analysis consists in laying out the manifolds that are proper to a particular kind of object; it is also true that phenomenology tries to spell out the blends of presences and absences, of filled and empty intentions, that belong to the object in question.

The concept of intuition is philosophically controversial; it is often taken to be something private, something inexplicable, something almost irrational, a kind of vision that overrides argument and cannot be communicated. But intuition need not be understood in this mysterious way. Phenomenology can give a rather clear and persuasive explanation for the concept: intuition is simply having the object actually present to us, in contrast with having it intended in its absence. The thoughtful experience of a baseball game, the actual seeing of a cube, finding the glasses I was looking for are intuitions, because they bring a thing to presence. Such presentation is played off against the empty intentions directed to the thing in its absence. Paradoxically, it is because phenomenology takes the absence of things so seriously that it can clarify the meaning of intuition; intuition, with the presence it achieves, is made to be much more understandable by being contrasted with empty intentions and their absences.

There is a dimension of presence and absence, of filled and empty intentions, that we have not yet examined. It is the fact that both the empty and the filled intending are directed toward one and the same object. One and the same thing is at one time absent and at another present. In other words, there is an identity "behind" and "in" presence and absence. The presence and the absence are "of" one and the same thing. When we anticipate the baseball game and talk about it, we emptily intend the very same game that we will see. We do not intend an image of that game, or some substitute game that we have in focus now until the real game shows up. We intend the game that is not here, that does not yet exist. If I talk to you about Leonardo's painting, you and I intend one and the same painting, the same one that we will see directly when we walk into the room where it is present. The presence is the presence of the painting, the absence is the absence of the same painting, and the painting is one and the same across presence and

35

absence. The painting is identified across the two. The painting belongs to a dimension different from the presence and the absence, but it could not be except as capable of presenting and absenting itself. The presence and absence belong to the being of the thing identified in them. Things are given in a mixture of presences and absences, just as they are given in a manifold of presentations. We should also notice that it is this identity, this invariant in presence and absence, to which we refer when we use words to name a thing.

In this interplay of presence and absence, special attention must be given, philosophically, to the role of absence, of empty intending. Presence has always been a theme in philosophy, but absence has not been given its due. In fact, absence is usually neglected and evaded: we tend to think that everything we are aware of must be actually present to us; we seem incapable of thinking that we can truly intend what is absent. We shy away from absence even though it is all around us and preoccupies us all the time. Thus, when we want to explain how we can speak about objects that are not present, we tend to say that we are dealing with an image or a concept of the object, which *is* present, and through that image or concept we reach toward the absent thing. But this postulation of a presence to substitute for the absent is highly inadequate. For one thing, how would we ever know that what is given to us is *only* a concept or an image if we did not have some sense of the absence of the real thing, if we did not already intend the thing in its absence? For some reason, philosophers have tended to overlook the radical role of absence in human consciousness, and they have tried to conceal this role by appealing to surreptitious forms of presence, by inserting strange presences, such as concepts or ideas, that will cover up for the absent.

But we do intend the absent, and it is phenomenologically false to deny it. We may need the support of words or mental images to help us intend the absent, but these presences do not impede us from truly intending what is not there before us. The absent is given to us as absent; absence is a phenomenon, and it must be given its due. In fact, there are many human dispositions or emotions that cannot be understood except as responses to a given absence. Hope and despair, for example, presuppose that we can intend some good that is not yet achieved and are either confident or diffident about attaining it. Regret makes sense only because we are aware of the past, and how could homesickness be understood except through a recognition of the absent? When we are looking for something and cannot find it, the absence of the thing is all too present to us. We live constantly in the future and in the past, in the distant and the transcendent, in the unknown and the suspected; we do not live only in the world around us as it is given to the five senses.

The absences that surround the human condition are of different kinds. Some things are absent because they are future, others because they are contemporary but far away, others because they are forgotten, others because they are concealed or secret, and still others because they are beyond our comprehension and yet are given to us as such: we can know that this is something we do not understand. Absences come in many colors and flavors, and it is a great philosophical task to differentiate and describe them. One of Husserl's most original insights was to draw our attention to empty intentions, our ways of intending the absent, and to highlight their importance in the philosophical exploration of being, the mind, and the human condition.

Presences seem to be more familiar to us; it seems easier for us to think about them. We might think they are far less problematic: we think we know what it means for a thing to be given to us in the flesh, so to speak. And yet presences also take on a deeper meaning when they are seen, philosophically, as played off against the absent. When we appreciate the presence of a thing, we appreciate it precisely as not absent: the horizon of its being possibly absent must be there if we are to be aware of the presence. The presence is given as canceling an absence. Sometimes the present object is something we have been looking for. Its absence was vividly given to us while we searched for it through our empty intentions ("Where are my glasses? Where did I leave them?"). Then, when we find the object, its presence comes to light precisely as cushioned by these still-reverberating absences. The object comes to light precisely as what we have been looking for. At other times the object may not have been searched for or awaited but appears suddenly without expectation; it surprises us. Even then, it appears as canceling an absence.

In any case, however, we must emphasize that the identity of the object is given only across the difference of presence and absence. The identity is *not* given only in the presence. Even when the object is absent, we intend the object itself, we intend it in its identity. When it is present, we intend the identity again, this time in its present mode and precisely as not absent.

When we speak philosophically about presence and absence, we focus on the objective side of the correlation between the conscious subject and the object. The object and its identity are given across presence and absence. If we turn to the subjective side, we would say that we exercise empty intentions, that we intend the object emptily, and that these empty intentions can be filled when we succeed in intending the object in actual presence. The empty intention is correlated with the absence of the object, the filled intention is correlated with its presence. However, in addition to the empty and the filled intending, there is also an *act of recognition*, an *act of identification*, that is correlated with the identity of the object itself. This third act transcends the empty and the filled intentions, just as the object's identity transcends its presences and absences.

We have noted the fact that there are many different kinds of absences. It is also true that there are different kinds of presences and presencings, each appropriate to the kind of thing in question. The future comes to presence by letting time go by; something far away is brought to presence by overcoming distance; the other side of the cube is made present by turning the cube around; a difficult mathematical proof is made present by thinking through its steps; the meaning of a foreign text is made present by providing a translation or by learning the language; a danger can be faced only by taking a risk. In each case, the thing in question prescribes the blends of absences and presences that are proper to it.

Sometimes we do not move directly from an empty intention to a fulfillment; sometimes a series of steps is required, or at least is possible, that goes from one *intermediate* fulfillment to another until at last the object itself is reached. I once attended a golf tournament and wanted to see Jack Nicklaus play. I had read about him in the sports pages. I saw his picture in the newspaper. I saw him being interviewed on television. After I got to the tournament, I walked around the golf course, trying to find his threesome. Finally, I saw the leader board (the board identifying the players and giving their scores) with his name on it; on seeing his name there but not yet seeing him, I still intended him signitively or emptily, but now I was closer to fulfillment, because I was no longer seeing his name just in the papers or the sports magazines, but on his leader board, which was something like an indication sign or signal of his presence. Then I saw his caddy, whom I recognized from other pictures (and so I had a further indication of his presence). Finally, I saw Jack Nicklaus himself. At that point I entered into perception and left the empty, signitive intentions, the pictorial intentions, the associative ones, and all the other intermediate kinds. Once I entered into perception, I could not move into any other kind of better fulfillment, but I could continue to have more and more perceptions (and I did, as I followed Nicklaus while he played the next several holes). The further perceptions were, however, not a move into yet another kind of intentionality, but simply more of the same. The fulfillment chain had reached its apogee.

We can distinguish, therefore, two kinds of fulfillment. (1) The one leads through many intermediates, of different kinds, and finally reaches intuition. We might, for example, go from a name of some person to a sketch of his face to a life-sized portrait to a statue to a televised image to the person himself. Each of these stages is qualitatively different from the others, and each fulfills the previous one but still points on to the next. The final one, however, the intuition, does not point on to anything else. It is the terminus, the final evidence. Let us call this sort of chain a *graded* or *cumulative* fulfillment. Again, the final fulfillment, the intuition, has nothing magical or absolute about it; it simply does not point on to any new kind of intending. In this it differs from the intermediate stages, which do point onward. We should also notice that the final intuition of the object collects the sense of all the intermediate stages through which it has been anticipated: it is, precisely, *not* these stages – but it is their completion. Seeing Nicklaus is *not* seeing his name or his picture or his caddy, but it is what all these things were pointing toward.

(2) The other kind of fulfillment chain does not lead up to a climax. It is simply *additive*, providing more and more profiles on the thing in question. As I continued to perceive Nicklaus play, I saw more and more of his person and his golfing skill. There was more as the perception went on, but it was "more" in a different way from the qualitative increase in proximity achieved in a graded fulfillment. Another example of a merely additive fulfillment would be providing more and more definitions of the number 15: as thrice

5, as 16 minus 1, as 12 plus 3, as the square root of 225, and so on. Thus, when we reach an intuition of some particular target, our quest is not over. We may have gone through many of the intermediate presentations that led us up to our intuition, but the target itself now remains to be unfolded. We can discover more of the thing itself, but such exploration is not another new stage in graded fulfillment. It is a deepening of our understanding of what we have brought to intuitive presence.

Let me conclude this treatment of presence and absence by making a point about terminology. At the beginning of this book I spoke about intentionality as the major theme in phenomenology. We have just explored the difference between empty and filled intendings. We might be tempted to think that intentionality is equivalent to empty intentions, to our awareness of the absent. This would not be correct; even when a thing is given to us in its presence, we still intend it. Intentionality as a generic term covers both empty and filled intentions, as well as the recognitional acts that intend the identity of the object.

We should also note that the concept of intentionality has been gradually enriched by the themes developed in this chapter. Intentionality seemed trivial and obvious when it was introduced in Chapter 1, but we now see that it not only counters the egocentric predicament of modern thought, but also accounts for our ability to recognize identities in manifolds of experience, to deal with things that are absent, and to register the identities given across presence and absence.

We have now completed our initial examination of the three structures that run through phenomenology. Whenever we wish to explore a phenomenological issue, we should ask what are the parts and wholes, the identities and the manifolds, and the blends of absences and presences that are at work in the issue in question. Emotional objects have one pattern, aesthetic objects another, and mathematical objects, political objects, economic things, simple material objects, language, memory, and intersubjectivity each have patterns of their own. The three structures will often come to the fore as we proceed with our own analyses in the rest of this book.

Most, but not all, of my remarks so far have been centered on rather simple forms of experience, on things like the perception of a material object such as a cube. It would be logical to move from such perception to more complicated forms of awareness, such as memory and imagination, and to intellection, to the kind of experience we have when we enter into language and syntactic structures, when we begin to register facts and communicate meanings to other people. However, before moving on to these topics, let us interrupt our progress for a moment in order to clarify, in an initial way, what we mean by philosophical analysis. We should consider, at least in outline (for the present), the nature of the analyses we have been carrying out and the point of view from which we have been working. We now have enough samples of philosophical analysis to allow us to convey an initial idea of how philosophy, as understood in phenomenology, differs from prephilosophical experience and speech.

4

An Initial Statement of What Phenomenology Is

In order to understand what phenomenology is, we must make a distinction between two attitudes or perspectives that we can adopt. We must distinguish between the natural attitude and the phenomenological attitude. The *natural attitude* is the focus we have when we are involved in our original, world-directed stance, when we intend things, situations, facts, and any other kinds of objects. The natural attitude is, we might say, the default perspective, the one we start off from, the one we are in originally. We do not move into it from anything more basic. The *phenomenological attitude*, on the other hand, is the focus we have when we reflect upon the natural attitude and all the intentionalities that occur within it. It is within the phenomenological attitude that we carry out philosophical analyses. The phenomenological attitude is also sometimes called the *transcendental attitude*. Let us examine both attitudes or focuses, the natural and the phenomenological. We can understand each precisely in its contrast with the other.

THE NATURAL ATTITUDE

In our ordinary living, we are directly caught up with the various things in the world. As we sit conversing with others at the dinner table, as we walk to work, or as we fill out an application for a passport or for a driver's license, we have material objects presented to us, we identify them through the sides, aspects, and profiles through which they are given, we speak about and articulate them, we have emotional responses to things that are attractive or repellent, we find some things pleasant to look at or hear and others unpleasant and disruptive, and so on. Some things are present to us and other things are absent, we overcome some of the absences and bring things to presence, but we also let other things go out of presence into absences. We identify and recognize one thing after another: the chairs and pictures in our room, the birds singing outside, the car going by down the street, the wind blowing through the trees. Furthermore, in addition to such substantial things, the world also contains mathematical entities such as triangles and squares, closed and open sets, rational and irrational numbers. Such mathematical things require a special kind of intentionality, but they still present themselves as nested within the world, even though they exist in a manner different from trees and trucks. There are also political constitutions, laws, contracts, international agreements, elections, acts of generosity and courage, as well as acts of hatred and cowardice. All such things can be identified within the world in which we live; all such things in their identities are correlated with our intendings.

Moreover, our world does not contain only the things that we have directly experienced. We also intend, emptily, many things that we take to be real even though we have never experienced them. I have never been to China, but from time to time I do intend China, its mountains and rivers, its foreign and domestic policy, its economic condition. The same is true of Brazil, Antarctica, and Greenland. If I were to visit Antarctica I would fulfill many of my empty intentions, some in surprising and others in unsurprising ways. The world we live in expands beyond our immediate experience and beyond our possible experience: we also perceive a domain in the heavens that we could never reach bodily. We might get to the moon or some of the planets, but it is impossible for us to reach to the farthest parts of the universe. We can learn a lot about those places, but much of it will always remain the target of empty intentions rather than fulfillments or perceptions.

So there are many things in the world, all given in different manners of presentation. There is also *the world* itself, which is given in still a different way. The world is not a large "thing," nor is it the sum of the things that have been or can be experienced. The world is not like a sphere floating in space, nor is it a collection of moving objects. The world is more like a context, a setting, a background, or a horizon for all the things there are, all the things that can be intended and given to us; the world is not another thing competing with them. It is the whole for them all, not the sum of them all, and it is given to us as a special kind of identity. We could never have the world given to us as one item among many, nor even as a single item: it is given only as encompassing all the items. It contains everything, but not like any worldly container. The term "world" is a *singulare tantum*; there could only be one of them. There may be many galaxies, there may be many home planets for conscious beings (although there is only one for us), but there is only one world. "The world" is not an astronomical concept; it is a concept related to our immediate experience. The world is the ultimate setting for ourselves and for all the things we experience. The world is the concrete and actual whole for experience.

Another important singularity in our spontaneous experience is the *self*, the *ego*, the *I*. If the world is the widest whole and the most encompassing context, the I is the center around which this widest whole, with all the things in it, is arranged. Paradoxically, the I is a thing in the world, but it is a thing like no other: it is a thing in the world that also cognitively *has* the world, the thing to whom the world as a whole, with all the things in it, manifests itself. The I is the dative of manifestation. It is the entity to whom the world and all the things in it can be given, the one who can receive the world in knowledge. Of course, there are many I's, many egos, many selves, but even among all of them one stands out as the preeminent center, namely me (that is, you, as you read these words and think them through for yourself). These strange facts about the self or the ego are not just tricks of language, not just peculiarities of the first and second person singular; they belong to the kind of being a rational creature is, a creature that can think, that can say "I," and that can have the world even while being a part of the world. The rational soul, as Aristotle says, is somehow all things. The world as a whole and the I as the center are the two singularities between which all other things can be placed. The world and the I are correlated with one another in a way different from the manner in which a particular intentionality is correlated with the thing that it intends. The world and the ego provide an ultimate dual, elliptical context for everything.

All these structural elements belong to the natural attitude in which we find ourselves from the start and always. There is still one more item in the natural attitude that we must examine before we move on to discuss the phenomenological attitude. We must examine the kind of conviction that pervades the natural attitude.

An Initial Definition

The manner in which we accept the things in the world, and the world itself, is one of *belief*. As we experience other people, trees, buildings, cats, stones, and the sun and stars, we experience them as being there, as true, as real. The basic character, the default mode of our acceptance of the world and things in it, is one of belief or, to use the Greek term, *doxa*. Our belief is correlated with the being of things, which first and foremost is simply accepted as such. As time goes on and we become older and more clever, we introduce modalities into our belief; after finding we were mistaken in some instances, we gradually introduce the dimensions of illusion, error, deception, or "mere" appearance. We gradually come to know that things are not always as they seem; a distinction between being and seeming comes into play, but this distinction is exercised only episodically, and it takes great sophistication to bring it about. We may find that this "cat" is only a toy, or that this person's speech was deceptive, or that that "man" was only a shadow, or that the "glass" we seemed to see was really ice; such occasional mistakes, however, do not cause us to become suspicious about everything we experience and everything that is said. The default condition remains one of belief. However, this belief, as fundamental, is now contrasted with a whole array of possible alternatives: suspicion, doubt, rejection, probability, possibility, negation, refutation, all the possible doxic modalities that our intentionality can take on.

Prominent among all our beliefs is the belief we have in the world as a whole. This belief, which we could call not just a *doxa* but the *Ur-doxa* (if we may combine a German and a Greek term), not just a belief but the basic belief, underlies all the specific beliefs we have. *World belief* is not subject to correction or refutation the way any particular belief is. If we are alive at all as conscious beings, world belief is there undergirding any particular conviction we may exercise. We never really learn or acquire our world belief, the way we might achieve our belief in, say, the Empire State Building or the San Juan River in Utah. All such particular beliefs arise concomitantly when we experience or hear about the thing in question, when we come to acknowledge its identity through the manifolds in which it is given to us, whether in presence or in absence. But we could never learn or acquire our world belief. What would be our state prior to learning it? We would have to be in a mute and encapsulated solipsism, a sheer awareness that was not aware *of* anything. Such a state is inconceivable; it would require that the ego think of itself as both the center of things and the sum of things, a hub without a radius. And even if we were to grant its possibility, what on earth (or even outside the earth) could jar us out of such a state? How could the very idea of something "outside" ever arise if it were not there from the beginning?

We cannot start off in the egocentric predicament; our world belief is there from the start, even before we are born, as far back as we go. Even our most rudimentary sense of self could not arise except on the basis of world belief. Similarly, even if we discover that we were wrong about very many things, our world belief remains untouched and the world is still there, no matter how ragged and tattered, unless perhaps we lost our sense of self entirely and fell into a kind of autistic isolation; but even there, some sense of what there is would surely remain, if there is awareness at all. The suffering that must exist in autism is there precisely because the world belief is still at work; if it were not, there would be no awareness at all and no sense of self.

Since we live in the paradoxical condition of both having the world and yet being part of it, we know that when we die the world will still go on, since we are only a part of the world, but in another sense the world that is there for me, behind all the things I know, will be extinguished when I am no longer part of it. Such an extinction is part of the loss we suffer when a close friend dies; it is not just that he is no longer there, but the way the world was for him has also been lost for us. The world has lost a way of being given, one that had been built up over a lifetime.

Both the world and the self invoke the idea of a whole. The paradoxes of set theory, the problem of whether the ultimate set includes itself or not, are less difficult than the problems of the logic of the world and the self: How do these wholes, the world and the self, include or exclude one another, and how are their totalities related to the sum of the things that exist? It may be the case that the paradoxes of set theory are only formalized versions of the problems of how the world contains everything, including the self, and how the self can intend all things, including the world and also itself.

In conclusion, then, in the spontaneous, natural attitude we are directed toward all sorts of things, but we are also directed toward the world as the horizon or context for all the things that can be given, and correlative to the world is the self or the ego, the agent of the natural attitude, the one to whom the world and its things are given, who is both part of the world and yet in intentional possession of it.

THE PHENOMENOLOGICAL ATTITUDE

The reader must have noticed that everything that has been said here about the natural attitude could not have been stated from within the natural attitude. That is, without having drawn attention to it, we have been considering these matters all along from within the phenomenological attitude; we have been doing so in the past several pages and, indeed, practically throughout this entire book, with the exception of the introduction, which had to be written from within the natural attitude. When we considered intentionality in Chapter 1, and perceiving a cube in Chapter 2, we considered these subjects from the phenomenological viewpoint.

There are many different viewpoints and attitudes even within the natural attitude. There is the viewpoint of ordinary life, there is the viewpoint of the mathematician, that of the medical specialist, the physicist, the politician, and so on, and there are even several special kinds of reflective attitudes, as we shall see. But the phenomenological attitude is not like any of these. It is more radical and comprehensive. All the other shifts in viewpoint and focus remain cushioned by our underlying world belief, which always remains in force, and all the shifts define themselves as moving from one viewpoint into another among the many that are open to us. The shift into the phenomenological attitude, however, is an "all or nothing" kind of move that disengages completely from the natural attitude and focuses, in a reflective way, on everything in the natural attitude, including the underlying world belief. In moving into the phenomenological attitude we get "nudged upstairs" in a way that is unique. To move into the phenomenological attitude is not to become a specialist in one form of knowledge or another, but to become a philosopher. From the phenomenological viewpoint we look at and describe, analytically, all the particular intentionalities and their correlates, and world belief as well, with the world as its correlative.

If we are to give a descriptive analysis of any and all of the intentionalities in the natural attitude, we cannot share in any of them. We must take a distance to, reflect upon, and make thematic any and all of them. This means that while we are in the phenomenological attitude, we suspend all the intentionalities that we are examining. We neutralize them. This change of focus most emphatically does not mean, however, that we begin to doubt these intentionalities and the objects they have; we do not change them from, say, doxic assurance to doubt. We do not change our intentionalities, we keep them as they are, but we contemplate them. If we contemplate them, we do not exercise them at that moment. However, we would not be able to contemplate them for what they are if we were to change them from one modality to another; if our move into philosophical reflection meant that we changed, say, our conviction into doubt, or our certainty into suspicion, then we could not contemplate conviction or certainty. Changes from one modality to another take place within the natural attitude. They have to be motivated. We have to have reasons to move from conviction to doubt, from certainty to suspicion; without such reasons, the change in our modality would be irrational and arbitrary.

When we move into the phenomenological attitude, we become something like detached observers of the passing scene or like spectators at a game. We become onlookers. We contemplate the involvements we have with the world and with things in it, and we contemplate the world in its human involvement. We are no longer simply participants in the world; we contemplate what it is to be a participant in the world and in manifestations. But the intentionalities that we contemplate – the convictions, doubts, suspicions, certainties, and perceptions that we examine and describe – are still our intentions. We have not lost them; we only contemplate them. They remain exactly as they were, and their objects remain exactly as they were, with the same correlations between intentions and objects still in force. In a very curious way, we suspend them all just as they are, we "freeze" them in place. And we who become philosophical are also the same selves who exercise natural intentionalities. A kind of enhancement of the self occurs, in which the same self that lived in the natural attitude begins to live explicitly in the phenomenological attitude and begins to carry on the philosophical life.

All human beings, all selves, do this sort of reflective philosophical analysis from time to time, but when most people enter into this kind of life they usually are very confused about what they are doing. They think they are just getting glimpses of some sort of general truths, some sort of laws of nature. They tend to take the move into philosophy as one more adjustment in the natural attitude; they do not see how different it is. The point of our discussion about the phenomenological attitude is to help us to make the shift into philosophy explicitly and clearly, with a fuller appreciation of the difference between the natural and the philosophical attitudes. We make a definite distinction, whereas most people wander unclearly back and forth across the border.

The turn to the phenomenological attitude is called the *phenomenological reduction*, a term that signifies the "leading away" from the natural targets of our concern, "back" to what seems to be a more restricted viewpoint, one that simply targets the intentionalities themselves. Reduction, with the Latin root *re-ducere*, is a leading back, a withholding or a withdrawal. When we enter into this new viewpoint, we *suspend* the intentionalities we now contemplate. This suspension, this neutralization of our doxic modalities, is also called the *epochē*, a term taken from Greek skepticism, where it signifies the restraint the Skeptics said we should have toward our judgments about things; they said we should refrain from judging until the evidence is clear. Although phenomenology takes this term from Greek skepticism, the skeptical overtone of the term is not kept. The *epochē* in phenomenology is simply the neutralizing of natural intentions that must occur when we contemplate those intentions.

Finally, to complete this brief treatment of terminology, let us speak of the term *bracketing*. When we enter into the phenomenological attitude, we suspend our beliefs, and we *bracket* the world and all the things in the world. We put the world and the things in it "into brackets" or "into parentheses." When we so bracket the world or some particular object, we do not turn it into a mere appearance, an illusion, a mere idea, or any other sort of merely subjective impression. Rather, we now consider it precisely as it is intended by an intentionality in the natural attitude. We consider it as correlated with whatever intentionality targets it. If it is a perceived object, we examine it as perceived; if it is a remembered object, we now examine it as remembered; if it is a mathematical entity, we consider it as correlated with a mathematical intention; if it is a merely possible object, or a verified one, we consider it as the object for an intentionality that intends something only possible, or an intentionality that intends something verified. Bracketing retains exactly the modality and the mode of manifestation that the object has for the subject in the natural attitude.

Thus, when we enter into phenomenological reflection, we do not restrict our focus just to the subjective side of consciousness; we do not focus only on the intentionalities. We also focus on the objects that are given to us, but we focus on them as appearing to us in our natural attitude. In the natural attitude we head directly toward the object; we go right through the object's appearances to the object itself. From the philosophically reflective stance, we make the appearances thematic. We look *at* what we normally look *through*. We focus, for example, on the sides, aspects, and profiles through which the cube presents itself as an identity. We focus on the manifold of appearances through which the object is given to us. When we do so, however, we do not turn the identity of the object into one of the "mere" appearances; quite on the contrary, we are better able to distinguish the object from its appearances, we are better able to preserve the reality of the thing itself. We are also better able to provide an appropriate description of the nature of "the world." If we were to try to speak about the world from the natural attitude, we would tend to take it as a large entity or as the sum of all entities. Only from the phenomenological perspective can we get the right terminology to speak about the world as the context for the manifestation of things.

To use a somewhat crude spatial metaphor, when we enter into the phenomenological attitude, we crawl out of the natural attitude, rise above it, theorize it, and distinguish and describe both the subjective and the objective correlates that make it up. From our philosophical perch, we describe the various intentionalities and their various objects, as well as the self and the world. We distinguish between a thing and its appearances, a distinction that has been called by Heidegger the "ontological difference," the difference between a thing and the presencing (or absencing) of the thing. This distinction can be properly made only from the phenomenological perspective. If we try to make the distinction between thing and appearance from within the natural standpoint, either we will tend to substantialize appearances, because in that standpoint we tend to take everything we focus on as a substantial thing, or we will tend to reduce the thing just to its appearances, to being the sum of its appearances. We will be likely either to posit appearances as barriers between us and things, or to make things into mere ideas. We will not get the phenomenological attitude right, and we will not properly understand the natural attitude either.

ARE THERE ARGUMENTS THAT CAN LEAD US INTO THE PHENOMENOLOGICAL ATTITUDE?

Now that we have some sense of the difference between the natural and the phenomenological attitude, we can raise the question of whether there is some way to explain and justify, to other people, the shift between the first and the second. This question amounts to asking whether there is some sort of argument that can persuade someone else to become philosophical, or prove to him that he should do so. The question is not trivial; it asks whether philosophy can introduce itself, explain what it is, and legitimate itself before those who are not philosophers. It also asks whether philosophy can justify itself to itself, whether it can clarify its own origins and thus attempt to be a science without presuppositions.

The issue of the beginning of philosophy is raised in phenomenology under the rubric of the various *ways to reduction*. We are given various "ways" or arguments to help us attain the phenomenological "reduction." As we have seen, the phenomenological reduction is the move from the natural attitude to the phenomenological; it is the restriction of our intentionality from its expansive natural attitude, which targets any and all things in the world, to the apparently more confined phenomenological attitude, which targets our own intentional life, with its correlated objects and world.

We must be careful not to make our task more difficult than it needs to be. We might be tempted to think that the natural attitude is purely natural, purely nonphilosophical, without a shred of philosophy in it, and that the turn to phenomenology is a move into something totally unheard of in the natural focus. If this were the case, it would seem almost impossible for us to convey an idea of what philosophy is to those who have not yet entered it. But in fact, there are anticipations of the philosophical attitude within the natural. There are pseudopods toward philosophy in the natural attitude. Simply as rational beings, we already have a sense of the whole, a sense of self, a sense of intentionality and appearance. However, the trouble is that we try to handle all these things with categories that belong to the natural attitude. We mythologize, psychologize, phenomenalize, or substantialize them; we make the world a thing, appearances become barriers, the self is substantialized, intentions are psychologized. We do not get the terms and distinctions right. The ways to reduction do not try to open up an absolutely new and unanticipated dimension; rather, they try to clarify a distinction that we already possess, between the natural and the philosophical, and they try to explain the transition between the two attitudes. They help us to get the philosophical stance right by showing the change in perspective that occurs when we move into philosophy, and the shift in the meanings of our terms that must follow. We will consider two ways to reduction, the ontological and the Cartesian. These are two approaches that were developed by Husserl.

The *ontological way to reduction* is the less frightening of the two. (The Cartesian seems to plunge us into the most radical doubt and phenomenalism.) The ontological way appeals to the human desire to be truly and fully scientific. It points out that when we scientifically explore a domain of being, we acquire a treasure of knowledge, a system of judgments, about the things in question. Let us say that we have achieved a rather thorough understanding of a field, such as molecular biology or solid state physics. No matter how complete our knowledge of the things in question may be, we still will not have explored the subjective correlatives of the truths that have been achieved. The objective side may be quite completely known, but the subjective accomplishments that are correlated with the objective will have been neglected: the kind of intentions that present the things being studied, the manner of verification proper to the objects, the methods followed, the forms of intersubjective correction and confirmation, and so on.

So long as a science is merely objective, it is lost in positivity. We have truth about things, but we have no truth about our possession of these things. We forget ourselves and lose ourselves even as we are fascinated by the things we know. The scientific truths are left floating and unpossessed. They seem to be nobody's truth. To round out the science, to be fully scientific, we would need to investigate the subjective structural activities at work in the science, and to do so is not simply to continue doing molecular biology or solid state physics. It is to turn from such sciences and to enter into a new, reflective stance, the phenomenological, which does justice to the intentionalities that we exercise but do not make thematic in our prior scientific endeavors. Once we make this turn for molecular biology and solid state physics, we come to see that we cannot do phenomenology just for these two disciplines; we have to expand our effort to cover intentionality as such and even the world as such (as the objective correlate of intentionality), because the intentionalities in any partial science cannot be understood except as completed by wider aspects of intentionality. We could not speak about recognizing the identities in molecular biology without speaking about recognizing identities as such.

By a gradual expansion, therefore, the ontological way to reduction helps us to complete the partial sciences. We move out to wider and wider contexts, until we come to the kind of widest context provided by the phenomenological attitude. The motivation to our expansion is the desire to be fully scientific, to avoid leaving out any dimension that is relevant to the inquiry in question. There may be a kind of partial completeness in a positive science, in molecular biology or solid state physics, but any science that wants to be comprehensive will ultimately have to inquire into the very achieving of the science, into the intentionalities that establish it. So long as these are left out, the science is left dangling and incomplete, lacking its proper context. The ontological way to reduction reminds us of Aristotle's remark in *Metaphysics* IV.1 about the need to go beyond partial sciences to the science of the whole, the science of being as being (and not being simply as material, or quantified, or living, or economic).

It should be clear from these remarks about the ontological way to reduction that phenomenology as a science, as a rigorous, explicit, self-conscious enterprise, is in fact a more concrete science than any of the partial inquiries. We might think that physics or biology is the most concrete of all sciences because it studies the material things right there before us, but so long as such sciences do not look at the activity by which they are achieved, they are really abstract. They leave out an essential part not only of the world but of themselves. The science of phenomenology complements and completes these partial sciences, while retaining them and their validities, so that, paradoxically enough, phenomenology is the most concrete of the sciences. It recovers the wider whole, the greater context. It overcomes the self-forgetfulness of the partial sciences. It considers dimensions the other sciences abstract from, the dimensions of intentionality and appearance. It shows how science itself is a kind of display, and hence it shows the naiveté of objectivism, the belief that being is indifferent to display. The reduction, therefore, really is not a confinement, not a "leading away" from anything. It preserves the natural attitude and everything in it, even as it distances us from it. It amplifies and does not deprive.

We get a very different impression from the *Cartesian way to reduction*. This approach to phenomenology is modeled on Descartes' attempt to initiate philosophy by making a "once in a lifetime" decision to doubt all the judgments he holds as true. Descartes introduces this methodic doubt because he thinks that the judgments he has absorbed from others are contaminated by prejudices. After adopting this universal doubt, he will go on to accept as true only those judgments that he himself can justify, according to the method he has developed.

The problem with Descartes' attempt to begin philosophy is that it changes all our natural doxic modalities into doubted ones. He moves from several natural modalities – certainty, suspicion, verified acceptance, possibility, probability – into another natural modality: doubtfulness. His doubt may only be methodical, but it still is doubt. Descartes tries to lift himself into philosophy, but he succeeds only in sliding over into another one of the natural attitudes, and a radically skeptical one at that. His attempt to put philosophy on the road to being a rigorous science misfires. He veers off to the side, with disastrous consequences for philosophy and science.

The Cartesian way to reduction in phenomenology is an attempt to take up what Descartes was trying to get at and to do it properly. It does not propose that we initiate a universal doubt. Rather, it suggests that we adopt the attitude of *attempting* to doubt our various intentions. This may look like a small difference, but it is crucial. The attempt to doubt is very different from doubt. What happens when we attempt to doubt one of our beliefs is that we adopt a neutral stance toward that conviction; we do not yet doubt it, we only suspend our belief. We stop to see whether we should doubt it. This attempt, this stop, however, is not doubt, but it is something like the neutralization we achieve when we enter into philosophy. This neutral stance then serves as a kind of keyhole through which we can get a sense of what the phenomenological attitude is, the attitude in which we neutralize and contemplate all our intentionalities.

Another important feature of the attempt to doubt is the following. We cannot truly doubt anything unless we have reasons to doubt it. Suppose I know that the door to this room is white, and suppose I see the cat walking into the room. I cannot go on to say that I doubt that the door is white or that the cat is walking across the threshold unless I have reasons to doubt that these apparent things are true: I may suddenly realize that it is the light that makes the door brighter than normal, and that it may be a shade of gray; I may suddenly realize that there is a mirror near the door, and that I may really be seeing only a reflection of the cat walking into another room. As one of the modalities in the natural attitude, doubt needs to be motivated by reasons. I cannot just say I doubt things.

The *attempt* to doubt, however, *is* subject to our free choice. We can attempt to doubt anything, even the most obvious fact before us or the most established opinion. In a similar way, we are free to initiate the neutralization that occurs when we turn to the phenomenological perspective, the suspension or "putting out of action" of our intentionalities, the bracketing of things and the world; these things are in our power and subject to our free choice. We can decide that we want to carry out this kind of life. We do not need to be forced into it by reasons like those that force us into doubt or suspicion. So, whereas doubt is not a good model to use to help us into the phenomenological turn, the attempt to doubt is. The attempt to doubt gives us a good glimpse of what the phenomenological neutralization of our intentions is like. In this manner, the Cartesian way to reduction tries to "kick" us into the philosophical attitude.

Descartes introduced a radical skepticism into the intellectual life that continues to plague the thought that he inspires. Still, it is useful to adopt the Cartesian theme and to modify it in the service of phenomenology, as we have done, because the turn from the natural attitude to the phenomenological is mistakenly seen by many as a relapse into Cartesianism. Even some prominent interpreters of phenomenology cannot get this straight. It is important, therefore, for us to make the distinction between what Descartes does and what phenomenology achieves.

One of the seriously pernicious effects of Descartes' error is that he discredits the intentionalities of the natural attitude. He undermines our natural and valid belief in the reality of the things we experience, the identities we recognize. He introduces the habit of skepticism that makes us tend to believe nothing until it has been proved to us. But this desire for a proof for everything is unreasonable. Proof is only possible on the basis of some truths that are not provable, truths that have their evidence within themselves and do not need proof. We cannot prove everything; we know many things that do not need to be proved. Phenomenology restores the validity of the convictions we have in the natural attitude. It acknowledges that our intentions do, in their various ways, reach the things themselves. It distinguishes and describes how the various intentions are fulfilled and confirmed. It also realizes that we often go beyond the evidence, that we often are vague in what we intend, and that errors are common; but the presence of error does not discredit everything. It only shows that we must be careful. By clarifying the various intentionalities and distinguishing them from one another, phenomenology helps us to be careful.

Finally, we should note the difference between the ontological and the Cartesian ways to reduction. The ontological way proceeds incrementally. It begins with scientific achievements and adds dimensions to them step-by-step, nudging us all the way along, until it arrives at the phenomenological attitude. The Cartesian way tries to do it all in a hurry, in one step. It suspends all the intentionalities at once. It does highlight a little better than the ontological way the new kind of modality, the neutralization, that comes into play in philosophy, but like anything else done in a hurry it can seriously mislead us. It can make us think of phenomenology as skeptical and phenomenalistic, and as depriving us of the real world and the things in it. It even seems to lead to solipsism. The ontological way is slow but sure; the Cartesian way is quick but risky. The best approach is to use both of them, correcting the weaknesses of each by the strengths of the other. In both approaches, however, the key thing is to get a feeling for the difference between the natural attitude and the phenomenological, between our natural involvements and philosophical detachment.

SOME SPECIAL TERMS RELATING TO THE
PHENOMENOLOGICAL ATTITUDE

There are a number of other issues that can help us define the phenomenological attitude more precisely. The treatment of them will be essentially an explanation of several terms in the phenomenological vocabulary.

Our experience and analysis from within the phenomenological viewpoint yields assertions that are, in principle, *apodictic.* Apodictic statements express things that could not be otherwise; they express necessary truths. Moreover, they are *seen* to express such necessary truths. We see that what they say could not be otherwise. There is philosophical necessity in the evidences presented to the phenomenological attitude. Consider, for example, the statement that a material, spatial object like a cube can only be given in a manifold of profiles, aspects, and sides, and that the cube is the identity given in such appearances. Consider also the statement that an identity is given to us in a blend of presences and absences, or the statement that we can only have a temporal present played off against a past and future. These statements are apodictic. We see that a cube could not be given in any other way, and that the present is never specious but always involves the past and future.

Someone might object that such statements are apodictic because they are so obvious, so trivial, almost so gratuitous; but that is exactly the point. Phenomenological statements, like philosophical statements generally, state the obvious and the necessary. They tell us what we already know. They are not new information, but even if they do not tell us anything new, they can still be important and illuminating, because we often are very confused about just such trivialities and necessities. When we think of how most people understand memory (as the viewing of internal pictures), or how poorly many philosophers have described perception (as, for example, the intake of impressions on some sort of internal screen in the brain), then the importance of stating the obvious becomes obvious itself. Phenomenological assertions claim to be apodictic because they are so basic and so unavoidable, so ineluctable. Their apodicticity does not stem from the fact that the people who make them enjoy some special revelation of exotic truths that other people have never heard about.

Furthermore, the fact that phenomenological statements and evidences are apodictic does not mean that we can never improve on them or deepen our understanding of them. A philosophical statement can be apodictic and yet fail in *adequacy*. Adequacy means that all vagueness has been purged from the statement. All the dimensions of the thing have been brought out, all the implications have been drawn. Practically nothing can be so fully presented to us, even in philosophy. The result is that phenomenological statements can be seen to be necessary (we can see that they could not be otherwise), but they can also call for further clarification. It is perfectly possible to know, for example, that the present necessarily involves the past and future but to be unclear about the full meaning of present, past, and future. We can know apodictically that an object is identified in blends of presence and absence, but we can still be vague about the full import of what it is to be present and what it is to be absent.

The phenomenological reduction and the phenomenological attitude are often called *transcendental*. We speak of the transcendental reduction and the transcendental attitude. One even encounters the rather clumsy phrases, "the transcendental-phenomenological reduction" and "the transcendental-phenomenological viewpoint." What does the term "transcendental" mean?

The word means "going beyond," based on its Latin root, *transcendere*, to climb over or go beyond, from *trans* and *scando*. Consciousness, even in the natural attitude, is transcendental because it reaches beyond itself to the identities and things that are given to it. The ego can be called transcendental insofar as it is involved, in cognition, in reaching out to things. The transcendental ego is the ego or the self as the agent of truth. The transcendental reduction is the turn toward the ego as the agent of truth, and the transcendental attitude is the stance we take up when we make this ego and its intentionalities thematic.

When we enter into the phenomenological or transcendental attitude, we have to make appropriate modifications in the words that we use. The new context, since it is so unique, requires adjustments in our natural language. Let us call the new language that results from these changes *transcendentalese*, and let us call the language we speak in the natural attitude *mundanese*. The two attitudes are constituted by the kind of intentionalities proper to each, and the languages spoken in each reflect the differences in perspective. The study of the interplay between the two languages, transcendentalese and mundanese, is a good way of teasing out the differences between philosophy and natural experience.

Some of the words in transcendentalese are drawn from mundanese, words such as "identity," "appearance," "presence and absence," and "ego," but we need to remember that the terms take on a subtle shift in meaning when they are absorbed into the new, philosophical language. The word "science," for example, takes on a sense different from that of physics and biology when it is said that philosophy is a rigorous science. A new kind of exactness is introduced. Phenomenology is a science in a way different from the sciences of the natural attitude, and the whole argument associated with the transcendental reduction is supposed to help us see what the new sense is.

There are also some words that are coined especially for transcendentalese, words that have no basis in the natural attitude or in mundanese. Two of these are *noema* and its correlative, *noesis*. The term "noema" refers to the objective correlates of intentionalities; it refers to whatever is intended by the intentions of our natural attitude: a material object, a picture, a word, a mathematical entity, another person. But more specifically, it refers to such objective correlates precisely as being looked at from the transcendental attitude. It refers to them as having been bracketed by the transcendental-phenomenological reduction. Sometimes the term can be used adjectivally and adverbially: we can be said to provide a noematic analysis, we can study the noematic structure of some thing, we can consider objects noematically. Any phrases in which these words are used are uttered in transcendentalese. They are philosophical phrases. They presume that the neutrality modification proper to philosophy has been introduced. The use of the term "noema" signals that we are in phenomenology, in philosophical discourse, and that the things being talked about are being discussed from a philosophical viewpoint, not from one of the viewpoints within the natural attitude.

These points need to be emphasized because the noema can easily be misunderstood. The noema is often taken to be an entity of some sort, something like a concept or a "sense" distinct from the object of consciousness, something that serves as the vehicle by which consciousness becomes referred to a particular thing. The noema is thought to be that by which intentionality is bestowed on consciousness, as though awareness would be self-enclosed if noemas were not added to it. The noema is also thought to be the entity through which consciousness targets this or that particular object, that by which our consciousness is referred to some specific item in the world outside: the noema is taken as a kind of bombsight for intentionality. This understanding of the noema as a mediating entity is, I believe, incorrect. Later, in Chapter 13, we will see in greater detail why it is problematic and misleading. At present it is sufficient if I introduce the term and give an initial explanation of what it means. The noema is any object of intentionality, any objective correlate, but considered from the phenomenological attitude, considered just as experienced. It is not a copy of any object, not a substitute for any object, not a sense that refers us to the object; it is the object itself, but considered from the philosophical standpoint.

The term "noesis" is less misleading, but it also assumes that we have entered into phenomenology. "Noesis" refers to the intentional acts by which we intend things: perceptions, signifying acts, empty intentions, filled intentions, judgings, rememberings. But it refers to them precisely as looked at from the phenomenological standpoint. It assumes that we have carried out the transcendental reduction. It considers those acts of consciousness after they have been suspended or put out of action by the phenomenological *epochē*. Noeses are less controversial than noemas because we are not tempted by the term to posit another shadow act parallel to the original one, as we are tempted by the term "noema" to posit a shadow "object" or a "sense" parallel to the real object. The reason we are less tempted to posit "a noesis" between ourselves and our psychological acts is that we, living in the Cartesian tradition, have become habituated to accept our introspections as realistic, as putting us in direct touch with our own mental life. This same tradition makes us inclined to deny that we have a direct exposure to things in the world; it makes us demand an intermediary, a representation (the "noema"), to connect us to the things outside.

We might also mention the fact that "noesis" and "noema," both of which were coined in phenomenology, have the same Greek root, the verb *noein*, which means "to think," "to consider," "to perceive." The Greek term *noēsis* means an act of thinking, and the term *noēma* means that which is thought. In Greek the suffix *-ma* added to a verb stem signifies the result or effect of the action expressed in the verb. Thus, *phantasma* signifies the object of fantasizing, *politeuma* means the effect of politicizing (the political entity), *rhēma* signifies the effect of speaking (the word), *horama* means the object of seeing (the view, as in "panorama"), and *migma* means the effect of mixing (the mixture). The term *noēma* then means the thing being thought or the thing we are aware of.

The adaptation of the Greek term to phenomenology is appropriate. The noema is any object of thought, but considered precisely as such, as being thought about or intended, as the correlate of an intentionality. The viewpoint from which we look at it in that way is the phenomenological attitude. The word "noema" is therefore uttered only from within that attitude. What happens, unfortunately, is that people often take "noema" in a psychological, epistemological, or semantic sense. They miss the difference of focus between the transcendental attitude and the natural, and they take the noema naturalistically, epistemologically, or semantically. They posit the noema as an intermediary between the self and things in the world, when it should be seen as the things in the world viewed from a phenomenological perspective. Instead of seeing it as a "moment" (an abstract part) in the manifestation of things, they reify it and make it serve as the link between the mind and things.

The remarks in this section about various terms relating to the phenomenological reduction are not a matter of mere verbal convention. They bring out important aspects of the new attitude that defines phenomenology. Also, the definition of the terms will make it easier to express certain doctrines in phenomenology. Mastery of an appropriate vocabulary is not an incidental matter in a domain of knowledge; the things in question cannot be properly brought to light without the words that name them.

WHY IS THE TRANSCENDENTAL REDUCTION IMPORTANT?

At first glance, we might be tempted to think that phenomenology is essentially an exercise in the theory of knowledge, a study in epistemology, but it is far more than that. It does not just try to deal with "the problem of knowledge," with trying to establish whether or not there is any truth, and with whether or not we can get to the "real world" or the "extramental" world. Phenomenology did arise in the historical period during which epistemology was the major philosophical concern, and some of its vocabulary and argument sound very epistemological, but it succeeded in breaking out of this restrictive context. It surpasses its origins. It comes to terms with modern philosophy and learns from it, but it also overcomes some of its limitations and reestablishes a link with ancient thought. Most of the misunderstandings of phenomenology come from interpretations that are still so caught up in the problems and positions of modern thinking, still so trapped by the Cartesian and Lockean tradition, that they fail to grasp what is new in phenomenology. Phenomenology calls for a major readjustment in the understanding of what philosophy is, and many people cannot make this change, because they cannot free themselves from their background and their cultural context. Phenomenology restores the possibilities of ancient philosophy, even while accounting for new dimensions such as the presence of modern science. Phenomenology provides one of the best examples of how a tradition can be reappropriated and brought to life again in a new context.

The doctrine of the transcendental reduction is especially important because it gives a new definition of how philosophy can be related to prephilosophical life and experience. One of the dangers to philosophy is that it may think that it can replace the prephilosophical life. It is true that philosophy reaches the summit of reason. It encompasses other exercises of reason, such as those found in the particular sciences and in practical life. It studies how all such partial exercises are related to one another and how they fit into a final context. Because philosophy complements prephilosophical reason, it may be tempted to think that it can substitute for such exercises of reason. It may begin to think that it can do better what the more specialized kinds of thinking accomplish. Philosophy may begin to think that it can carry out political life better than the statesmen, better than those who are involved in the perpetual discussion about how our life in community should be led. It may begin to think that it can do a better job than religious persons do in spelling out what the sacred and the ultimate are. It may begin to think that it can replace special sciences such as chemistry or biology or linguistics, because none of them has a sense of the whole. If philosophy tries to substitute for prephilosophical thinking, the result is rationalism, the kind of rationalism introduced into modern philosophy by Machiavelli in regard to political and moral life, and by Descartes in regard to theoretic matters.

The most important contribution phenomenology has made to culture and the intellectual life is to have validated the truth of prephilosophical life, experience, and thinking. It insists that the exercises of reason that are carried out in the natural attitude are valid and true. Truth is achieved before philosophy comes on the scene. The natural intentionalities do reach fulfillment and evidence, and philosophy can never substitute for what they do. Phenomenology is parasitic on the natural attitude and all the achievements thereof. Phenomenology has no access to the things and disclosures of the world except through the natural attitude and its intentionalities. Phenomenology comes only later. It has to be modest; it must recognize the true and valid achievements of the natural attitude, in both its practical and theoretic exercise. It then contemplates these achievements and their correlative subjective activities, but if the achievements were not there, there would be nothing for philosophy to think about. There must be true opinion, there must be prior *doxa*, if there is to be philosophy. Phenomenology may help the natural intentionalities clarify what they are after, but it never replaces them.

When phenomenology "neutralizes" the intentionalities at work in the natural attitude, it does not dilute, destroy, upset, or ridicule them. It merely adopts a contemplative stance toward them, a stance from which it can theorize them. Phenomenology complements the natural attitude; philosophy complements true opinion and science. Phenomenology may also point out the limitations of the truth and evidences achieved in the natural attitude, but the various arts and sciences already are aware of the fact that they are each partial and limited, although they may not be able to formulate their limitations very exactly. And sometimes the particular arts and sciences may want to become imperialistic themselves and dominate over all the others: physics may try to say that it explains the whole and everything in it, or linguistics may try to do so, or psychology, or history. When such partial arts and sciences try to master the whole and the other arts and sciences, they become pseudo philosophies, but philosophy can also falsify itself when it tries to lord it over the prephilosophical forms of knowledge, when it tries to substitute for them.

Phenomenology provides a major cultural restoration by recognizing the validity of the arts and sciences in the natural attitude, and also the validity of common sense, of prudence in the practical order. There is a rationalist tendency in modern thought that wants to make philosophy the perfect substitute for all prephilosophical forms of reason, and phenomenology counteracts this tendency. The modern rationalist trend has, in recent years, broken down into postmodernism, which recoils to the other extreme and denies any center to reason at all. Phenomenology avoids this negative extreme as well, because it never adopted the rationalist position in the first place.

Classical Greek and medieval thought understood that prephilosophical reason achieves truth and evidence, and that philosophical reflection comes afterward and does not disturb what goes before it. Aristotle did not tamper with the political life or with mathematics; he only tried to understand what they were and perhaps to clarify them to themselves. Phenomenology joins this classical understanding, but what it can add to it is the explicit discussion of the change of focus that is required to enter into the philosophical life. The doctrine about the *epochē*, the distinction between the natural and the phenomenological attitude, the idea of neutralizing the intentions in the natural attitude, the role of the world and world belief, are all clarifications of what it means to adopt philosophical detachment and to enter into philosophical thinking. These doctrines associated with the reduction are not mind-bending conundrums that try to make us obsessively introspective, or puzzles about whether we can get out of ourselves into the "extramental" world; they are clarifications of the nature of philosophy. They are useful in showing how philosophical discourse, transcendentalese, differs from the discourse of human practice and the arts and sciences, mundanese, the language of the natural attitude. When properly understood they can illuminate both the prephilosophical and the philosophical life.

Finally, the transcendental reduction should not be seen as an escape from the question of being or the study of being as being; quite the contrary. When we shift from the natural attitude to the phenomenological, we raise the question of being, because we begin to look at things precisely as they are given to us, precisely as they are manifested, precisely as they are determined by "form," which is the principle of disclosure in things. We begin to look at things in their truth and evidencing. This is to look at them in their being. We also begin to look at the self as the dative to whom beings are disclosed: we look at the self as the dative of manifestation. This is to look at it in *its* being, because the core of its being is to inquire into the being of things. "Being" is not just "thing-like"; being involves disclosure or truth, and phenomenology looks at being primarily under its rubric of being truthful. It looks at "human" being as the place in the world where truth occurs. Through all its Cartesian-sounding remarks about the ways to reduction, phenomenology is able to recover the ancient issue of being, which is always new.

5

Perception, Memory, and Imagination

We now have an idea of what phenomenological analysis is and why it is philosophical. We have also gone through an example of such analysis in our examination of the perception of a cube. We have considered the role played in human experience by the structures of parts and wholes, identity in manifolds, and presence and absence. We can now begin to amplify all these themes by developing yet more phenomenological descriptions. What we have done so far have been only preliminary sketches. We will now go back to perception and examine in greater detail how it presents objects to us, and how it is played off against derivative forms of intentionality such as remembering, imagination, and projection into the future.

REMEMBERING

Perception directly presents an object to us, and this object is always given in a mixture of presences and absences. When one side is given, others are absent. Some parts of the object conceal other parts: the front hides the back, the surface hides the inside. If the object is one that we hear, then hearing it at one place excludes the aspects of sound that would be available at another. We can overcome such absences, but only at the cost of losing presences we have, which become absent. Throughout this dynamic blending of presence and absence, throughout this manifold of presentation, one and the same object continues to present itself to us. The identity is given in a dimension different from that of the sides, aspects, and profiles; the identity never shows up as one of the sides, aspects, or profiles.

But the identity can also be given when the object is remembered. Remembering provides another set of appearances, another manifold through which one and the same object is given to us. Memory involves a much more radical kind of absence than does the cointending of absent sides during perception, but it still presents the same object. It presents the same object but with a new noematic layer: as remembered, as past.

We might be tempted to think of memory in the following way: when we remember something, we call up a mental image of the thing and recognize this picture as presenting the same thing we once saw. In this view, remembering would be not all that much different from looking at a photograph of someone and recognizing who the person is and the setting in which the photograph was taken. The only difference would be that the photograph is in the "extramental" world, while the memory image is in the "intramental" world.

This interpretation of remembering is very wrong. It confuses remembering with another kind of intentionality, picturing. It is not surprising that we tend to confuse these two types; it does seem that we have inner images in the mind's eye, and once we learn about the brain it seems inevitable that we are going to postulate some sort of projection of some sort of image on some sort of screen in the brain. But the incoherence of this interpretation becomes obvious when we consider the type of identity that occurs in remembering.

In picturing, we look at one object that depicts another. We look at this piece of colored canvas or that piece of paper, and in it we see something else: a woman, a rustic scene. In remembering, we do not look at one object that depicts another. We simply "see" or visualize the object directly. Remembering is more like perceiving than like picturing something. In memory I do not see something that looks like what I remember; I remember that object itself, at another time. If we are pestered by a memory that will not leave us, we should, strictly speaking, not say, "I can't get that image out of my mind!" Rather, we should exclaim, "I can't stop visualizing that thing!"

Suppose we are willing to say that we do not look at internal pictures when we remember; what else are we supposed to say? How can we express, from the transcendental viewpoint, what happens in remembering? If we do not look at inner pictures, why does it seem that we do, and how can we account for what seems to show up in our mind's eye or our mind's ear? Our reply to such questions can be put this way: what we store up as memories is not images of things we perceived at one time. Rather, we store up the earlier perceptions themselves. We store up the perceptions we once lived through. Then, when we actually remember, we do not call up images; rather, we call up those earlier perceptions. When these perceptions are called up and reenacted, they bring along their objects, their objective correlates. What happens in remembering is that we relive earlier perceptions, and we remember the objects as they were given at that time. We capture that earlier part of our intentional life. We bring it to life again. That is why memories can be so nostalgic. They are not just reminders, they are the activity of reliving. The past comes to life again, along with the things in it, but it comes to life with a special kind of absence, one that we cannot bridge by going anywhere, as we can bridge the absences of the other side of the table by going over to another part of the room and looking at it from there.

A new blend of presences and absences arises through memory, a new manifold of appearance through which one and the same object can be given in its identity. In memory we reactivate not just an object but an object as presenting itself there and then, and yet presenting itself again here and now, but only as past. This is the noematic form that remembered objects take on, a form different from that of perceived objects, which are only here and now, not there and then. We could put the difference between picturing and remembering in the following rather tricky way: when we see a picture, we *see something that seems* to be something else; but in remembering, we *seem to be seeing* something else. This cryptic formulation catches the difference between the two forms of intentionality.

Someone might object, "This sort of thing is nonsense. How could I relive a past perception? How could the very same thing, there and then, be given to me again here and now? This is impossible; there must be a picture of it that I look at." But such reliving of an experience is just what remembering is. It is quite marvelous, but that is how we are wired. We can relive an earlier part of our conscious life, we can reactivate an intentionality. Clearly, there must be some sort of neurological basis for this. The neural activity that is involved in perception is somehow reactivated, the conscious perception is reenacted, and it presents the very same object it had at its original venue. If we are to be faithful to the phenomenon, we have to describe it as it is and not project our wishes onto it. We do stretch into the past through memory; we bring back an elapsed world and a situation in it. We can live in the past as well as in the present. In fact, unless we had the general sense of the past that comes to us through memory, how could we interpret a "mental picture" as an image of something we saw in the past? How would the sense of pastness ever arise for us? The very dimension or horizon of the past is given to us through remembering, as we have described it phenomenologically.

In memory the object that was once perceived is given as past, as remembered. Moreover, it is given as it was then perceived; if I saw an automobile accident, I remember it from the same angle, with the same sides, aspects, and profiles, from which I saw it. One and the same accident is given to me again, and if I have to testify about the accident, I may have to rerun the event a few times to try to bring the details back to mind. ("Try to remember: Did the pedestrian step into the street before or after the traffic light changed?") When I do rerun the event, I do not inspect an inner picture; I try to exercise again the perception I had then and bring back the thing I saw, and I do this the way it is done when we remember things. Of course, errors do creep in; often I project things into the remembered event that I want to see or that I think I should be seeing. I oscillate between memory and imagination. Memories are notoriously elusive; they are not tamper proof, but such are the limitations of memory. Because memories are often wrong does not mean that they do not exist or that they are always wrong. Only because there are memories can they be sometimes deceptive. Furthermore, their way of being right and their way of being wrong are different from the ways of being right and wrong in perception. A new manifold, a new possibility of identity, is introduced by memory, and new possibilities of error arise as well. It is the task of phenomenology to bring out the structures in question and to distinguish them from those at work in perception and in other kinds of intentionality.

So far in this treatment of remembering we have been focusing on the noematic side, on the object remembered. We have mentioned the noetic side when we said that remembering is not the perception of an image but a revival of a perception. But we must move a bit farther to the subjective and talk about the self who is the agent of remembering. New dimensions of the object arise through memory, but new dimensions of the self arise as well.

When I remember something past, I also displace myself into the past. A distinction arises between me here and now, sitting in a chair in a room and perceiving the walls, windows, and sounds around me, and me then, watching an accident occur on the corner of Wisconsin Avenue and Macomb Street yesterday, or me involved in a painful farewell last week. The revival of my earlier perception involves a revival of myself as perceiving at that time. Just as the past object is brought to light again, so my past self as an agent of that experience is brought to light again. Through memory a distinction is introduced between the remembering self and the remembered self.

We might be tempted to say that my "real self" is the one here and now, the one doing the remembering. The reactivated self is only an image of some sort. But this would be inaccurate. It would be more appropriate to say that my self is the identity constituted between myself now remembering and myself then remembered. My self, the self, is established precisely in the interplay that occurs between perception and memory. This displacement of myself into the past introduces a whole new dimension into my mental or inner life. I am not confined to the here and now; I can not only refer to the past (and to the future, as we shall see), but I can also live in it through memory.

Sometimes this living in the past can be troublesome. If we have done things we are deeply ashamed of, or if we were caught up in traumatic incidents, we may be unable to rid ourselves of the experiences in question. They help constitute my self, and I cannot cut loose from them; no matter how far away we travel, we take them with us. We are glued to them. The mountaineer Peter Hillary, speaking of brushes with death he experienced in the Himalayas, says, "Surviving is sometimes the most painful role to play in this life. You . . . re-enact in your mind those closing scenes again and again and again" ("Everest is Mighty, We Are Fragile," *New York Times*, Saturday, May 25, 1996, p. A19). A man involved in the killing of prisoners says, "I have spent many nights sleeping in the plazas of Buenos Aires with a bottle of wine, trying to forget. I have ruined my life. I have to have the radio or television on at all times or something to distract me. Sometimes I am afraid to be alone with my thoughts'' ("Argentine Tells of Dumping 'Dirty War' Captives," *New York Times*, Monday, March 13, 1995, p. A1). A man who had been in an automobile accident is quoted as saying, "For months, I relived the crash in slow motion." We are something like spectators when we reenact things in memory, but we are not just spectators, and we are not like viewers of a separate scene. We are engaged in what happened then. We are the same ones who were involved in the action; the memory brings us back as acting and experiencing there and then. Without memory and the displacement it brings we would not be fully actualized as selves and as human beings, for good and for ill. Identity syntheses occur on both the noetic and the noematic side of memory.

IMAGINATION AND ANTICIPATION

Memory and imagination are structurally very similar, and one easily slips into the other. The same sort of displacement of the ego or the self that we find in memory also occurs in imagination. In both forms of intentionality, I here and now can mentally live in another place and time: in memory the there and then is specific and past, but in imagination it is in a kind of nowhere and "nowhen," but even in imagination it is different from the here and now I actually inhabit. I am displaced into an imaginary world, even as I live in the real one. Furthermore, an object in imagination, an imaginary object, might well be taken from my real perceptions or from my memories, but it is now projected into situations and transactions that did not occur.

The major difference between memory and imagination lies in the doxic modality proper to each. Memory operates with belief. The memories I call up, or that intrude on me, are of what really happened and what I did experience and do. It is not the case that I first have the memories and then add belief to them; rather, they originally come with belief (of how it was), just as my perceptions come with belief (of how it is). We have to make an effort to delete the belief in memory, or to change it into another modality, such as doubt or denial.

Imagination, on the other hand, is pervaded by a kind of suspension of belief, a turn into the mode of "as if." This modal change is a kind of neutralizing, but one different from the kind that comes into play in the transcendental reduction. In imagination I displace myself into an imaginary world, but the real world around me remains as the believed-in, default context within which I imagine, from which I am displaced. All the things I imagine are pervaded with a sense of unreality; imagined events do not strap me with the true regret or terror that horrible events from my past can inflict on me. It may be the case that an overactive imagination can skew my memories and make me think that some things happened that did not, but such a breach of the boundary between memory and imagination is possible only if imagination and memory are indeed two different kinds of intentionalities.

However, even when I imagine, the identity synthesis that is proper to all intentionality remains in force. An imaginary object stays one and the same through many imaginings of it. There is a manifold with an identity at its core even in imagination. We can take things we have actually perceived and enroll them into imaginary scenarios, and the things remain the same; or we can fabricate purely imaginary things and put them into an imaginary routine, and they too remain the same throughout. Obviously, imaginary objects do not have the thick solidity of perceived objects, since we can fantasize them into all sorts of improbable situations, but we are not totally free even in our imaginings; the things we imagine put some restrictions on what we can fantasize about them. If the thing is to remain itself, certain things cannot be imagined about it; if they were to be proposed, the thing would become something else. I can imagine a cat flying through the air (although I cannot remember a cat doing this), but I cannot truly imagine a cat being read as a poem, or a cat smiling and talking to me. A cat is not the kind of thing that can be read out loud, and a cat that smiled and spoke would not be just a cat any longer. It makes no sense to blend the "ideas" or even the images in that way.

Imagination therefore works in a doxic modality different from that of perception and memory; it is unreal, only "as if." However, there is a form of imagination that has to get realistic, that has to move back into the mode of belief. It is the kind of imagination we engage in when we are planning something, when we imagine ourselves in some future condition that we can bring about through the choices that we make. This is an anticipatory form of imagination, and it brings us back to earth, so to speak, from the flights of pure fantasy. Suppose that we wish to buy a house. We look at several homes, we narrow the possible options down to two or three, and then we deliberate about which to buy. Part of our deliberation involves imagining ourselves living in each of the houses, using the rooms, walking outside, and the like. Such projections come back to a doxic mode analogous to that of memory; we come back to a mode of belief, correlated with a sense of reality in what we imagine. If we are serious about buying the house, we do not imagine ourselves floating over it like a balloon or crawling through the walls like a termite. That sort of imaginary projection is all right for dreams and fantasy, but it is not helpful in buying a house. (It is interesting to note how television advertising takes advantage of the difference between fantasy and serious projection. It displays all sorts of attractive but totally unreal situations – a car surrounded by beautiful people, a truck flying over the Grand Canyon, a romantic encounter facilitated by toothpaste – with the intention of getting the viewer to realistically imagine himself into a future in which he buys the product.)

The advance experience of ourselves in a new situation is a displacement of the self, but it is the reverse of memory. Instead of reviving an earlier experience, we anticipate a future one. Since the future has not yet been determined, we can realistically anticipate ourselves in several possible futures and not only one: we imagine how we will have been if the choice has been made, and we can at this point still imagine ourselves in several different circumstances. We project ourselves into the future perfect in different ways. In the enterprise of buying a house, we project ourselves as living in three or four different homes; we try them on for size. We might do so while actually visiting the houses or else afterward, when we daydream about what it would be like.

We may take such projections of the self for granted and assume that anyone can easily perform them, but in some situations it takes considerable ego strength to be able to carry them out effectively. For some people at some times the strain of realistically imagining themselves into new circumstances is too great; they collapse emotionally and get all confused, and their self does not have the flexibility plus the identity to project into circumstances they have not yet lived through. They may panic at the thought of moving to a new place or changing a job or leaving a certain person. Part of the terror of death lies in the fact that our imagination turns blank in the face of it.

One might object that deliberation about future action is more intellectual than this. When we deliberate, we set down our goals, we draw up lists of advantages and disadvantages, and we figure out the means by which we can attain what we want. We weigh the pros and cons and make our decision. Such rational calculation is indeed part of deliberation, but the whole sense of its being deliberation about the future is given to us first of all by our imaginative projection. The list of pros and cons only applies if we realize that this information has to do with the way we will be in the future, and it is our imaginative projections that open that dimension to us. We sample in advance our future selves. We imagine certain wished-for satisfactions. We may in some cases find that our anticipations were quite wrong; things may not turn out as we imagined they would; but such errors are possible only because we are dealing with the future in the first place. That new dimension, of a future that has a range of possibilities that can be determined into actuality by the choices we make, is opened up to us not by rational lists, but by imaginative projections. Only because we can imagine can we live in the future. And the imaginative projections also enter into the motivations that nudge us into this choice or that; we feel more "comfortable," as the saying goes, with one particular future perfect than with others, and so we are inclined to make the choices that lead to that one. The intellectual lists are played off against the imaginative anticipation.

DISPLACEMENT OF THE SELF

The formal structure of displacement, in which I here and now can imagine myself or remember myself or anticipate myself into a situation somewhere and sometime else, thus allows us to live in the future and the past, as well as in the no-man's-land of free imagination. These displaced forms of consciousness are derivative upon perception, which gives the raw material and content for them. It is not the case, moreover, that we first of all live simply in perception, then at some moments decide to plunge into displacements; rather, the perceiving and the displaced selves are always being played off against one another. Even perception cannot be what it is without being contrasted with imagination, memory, and anticipation. All these forms differentiate themselves from an initial undifferentiated condition of consciousness. It also takes some sophistication to introduce the differences in doxic modality associated with each form. To know that some experiences are truly past, to know that some are just fantasy, is not achieved by everyone. Many people think that dreams and daydreams are true perceptions of unusual kinds of things.

Whenever we live in the kind of inner displacement just described, we live, so to speak, in two parallel tracks. We live in the immediacy of our surrounding world, which is perceptually given to us, but we also live in the world of the displaced self, the remembered or imagined or anticipated world. Sometimes we can drift more and more into one or other of these: we might get so wrapped up with what is immediately around us that we lose all imaginative detachment from it, or we may drift more and more into reverie and daydreaming, becoming practically, but never entirely, disconnected from the world around us. Furthermore, the imaginative intentions we have stored up within us serve to blend with and modify the perceptions we have. We see faces in a certain way, we see buildings and landscapes in a certain way, because what we have seen before comes back to life when we see something new and puts a slant on what is given to us. Displacement allows this to happen.

Both the self and the object, both the subjective and objective poles of experience, take on a much greater reservoir of manifolds of appearance when memory, imagination, and anticipation are differentiated from perception. All these structures and amplifications operate in the natural attitude, but they can be recognized and described from the transcendental, phenomenological attitude.

It might be helpful, at the close of this chapter, to show how the natural and the phenomenological attitudes, which were distinguished in Chapter 4, each approaches memory in a different way. To the natural attitude, the past is dead and gone; it is definitely not there any longer. The natural attitude is swallowed up by the present. In this attitude we resist attributing any presence to the past, and therefore when we try to explain memory we are inclined to posit something (an image, an idea of memory) as a present substitute for the past. We look around for a thing to stand in for the event that we remember. Thus, trying to handle the phenomenon of memory from within the natural attitude leads to a philosophical distortion of our experience of the past. From the transcendental perspective, however, with its more refined and differentiated understanding of presence and absence, we are able to recognize the special kind of presence that the absent past has for us. We see that there is no need to posit a picture as a kind of surrogate for the past object, and that, indeed, it is impossible to do so. Such memory images, as we now can see, are incoherences.

We might also observe that the dimension of the past in memory sheds light on the experience of the present we have in perception. Because we are aware that things can be past, we can advert to their presence when they are given to us: they now are given as not yet having elapsed into temporal absence. It is not only they that are present to us; their presence itself becomes present to us. We become able to distinguish between a thing and the presence of a thing. Once again, however, if we try to handle this presence from within the natural attitude, we will turn it into another thing (a sensory datum, an image in the brain), because the natural attitude tends to substantialize whatever it is concerned with. The presence (as well as the absence) of things is so subtle and fragile, so close to nothing, that only the phenomenological attitude, with its sense of the delicacy of presencing, can find the proper terms and grammar to express it. The natural attitude, rather ham-handed in these matters, always looks for a thingly stand-in to mediate between us as datives and the things that are present and absent to us.

6

Words, Pictures, and Symbols

We have considered perception and its variants, but all the variants we have examined belong to our "internal" life: memory, imagination, and anticipation. This internal reenactment of our experiences is not the only domain in which changes in intentionality occur. Perception puts us in touch with things in the world, and variations can take place in how we directly interpret the objects that the world offers us.

Sometimes we just accept the object that is given to us (a tree, a cat). We are then engaged in simple perception. But sometimes we modify the way we take the thing being presented: we have some sounds or marks given to us, but we take them not just as sounds or marks, but as words; we have a panel of wood given to us, and we take it as a picture; we have a small pile of stones given to us, and we take it as a trail marker. In these cases we add to and hence modify the perception that remains as the base for such intentionalities. We introduce new intentionalities founded upon perceptions. We continue to perceive the marks, the wood, and the stones, but besides just perceiving them we intend them in a new way. These higher intentionalities, of course, are quite different from those at work in memory, imagination, and anticipation, which are internal reenactments of perception, not intentions built upon it.

The new kinds of intentionality we will study in this chapter will allow us still more manifolds through which we can identify the objects that we encounter, and still more manifolds within which we establish our own identity as human persons.

THE PRESENCE OF WORDS

Suppose we are looking at a sheet of paper that has decorations inscribed on it: interwoven curlicues cover its surface. We perceive and admire the intricacy and elegance of the lines. Then, suddenly, some of the lines configure themselves into words, "The Burritt Hotel." The words leap out of the patterns. We inspect the paper more closely and find a whole sentence hidden in the decorative lines: "The Burritt Hotel has the best prices." The ornamented paper is really a cryptic advertisement for the local hotel.

What interests us as philosophers is not the bargain prices at the Burritt Hotel, but the change in intentionality that takes place when the words suddenly stand out. Before the change, we simply perceived something that was there before us. The perception was a continuous process that involved changes of focus and movements of attention from one part of the paper to another. But when the words stand out, we no longer intend just what is before us. A new kind of intending comes into play, one that makes these perceived marks into words and at the same time makes us intend not just the marks that are present, but the Burritt Hotel, which is absent. The new kind of intending is called a *signitive* intention, because it bestows meaning on the marks. It is obviously an empty intention. It is a founded intentionality, a nonindependent part of a larger whole, because it rests upon the perceptual base that presents the marks that become the words.

Such signitive intending is extremely important philosophically. We must define it more exactly by making a few comparisons.

Signitive intending is not the same as imagining. We might be tempted to say that when the words stand out for us, we suddenly have a visual image of the Burritt Hotel, and that this image is what serves as the meaning of the words. This explanation would be false; internal images are not the meaning of words. We might well have such a visual image, but then again we might not, and we could still have the same meaning. The image that comes to mind when we hear a word might be only accidentally related to the word: the name "The Burritt Hotel" might call up in my mind the image of John Smith, the owner of the hotel. The "arrow" of the signitive intention goes right through the perceived word toward the real Burritt Hotel, not to an image. The Burritt Hotel might be fifty miles away from us; it might even have been demolished to make room for a highway, and yet we do intend it through the words that appear to us. The Burritt Hotel may be absent, but we still are directed toward it through the words. We are capable of such empty intending; we are formed that way, and this ability to intend the absent is a major element in establishing the human condition.

For some reason, we seem to resist the idea that we truly intend the absent. We want to posit something present as the meaning of the words: an image, a concept, a sense impression, the word itself. So long as we try to reduce empty intending to other forms of intentionality, so long as we deny that we can intend the absent, so long as we try to find presences as substitutes for the absent, we will be blocked from a proper understanding of what we are and what the structure of consciousness is. We cannot even understand perception unless we know what its contrary, the signitive intention, is. We must get a more precise sense of the absent and its role in human awareness.

Furthermore, signitive intending is also different from the kind of empty intentions that accompany perception. When I see the front of the building, I cointend the absent sides, the back, and the inside, but this sort of emptiness is different from the kind at work in the use of words. The empty intentions pervading perception are continuous and ever changing. They are like a cushion or a halo that slides around whatever is centrally given. They give way gradually to presence. The verbal signitive intention, on the other hand, is discrete and not continuous. It means its target all at once and as a whole. It specifies its target more exactly and more explicitly than do the empty intentions in perception. Signitive intentions are not smooth and gradual, but choppy, more identifiable as one: by virtue of the words, "The Burritt Hotel," I mean the Burritt Hotel just by itself, nothing more. Signitive intentions therefore establish discrete meanings that can be placed into syntax and built up into statements. Signitive intentions are the entrance into reason, while the empty intentions pervading perception remain in sensibility. Once it dawns on us that certain sounds or marks are names, and once we realize that all things can be named, we have entered into a world different from that of animal perception, calling, and signaling; we have entered into linguistic reasoning.

Let us think back to the shift from perceiving marks on paper to intending the absent Burritt Hotel through words that stand out of the lines. We experience this change, and most of us have had some such experience at one time or another; however, the experience we have of it is not necessarily emotional or palpable. We do not feel the change in our chest or in the pit of our stomach or behind our eyes. The shift is simply a change of intentionality. It is a purely rational change from one kind of intending to another. How do we become aware of such intentions? Do we "see" them by introspection? Are they mental things that we somehow look at or feel? No; and yet we do know when one or the other is operative within us, we do know whether we are perceiving or signifying. We know the difference between these two activities, and we also know the difference between them and other intentions, such as picturing or remembering. I do not necessarily feel anything when I suddenly take a surface as a picture, but the new way of taking the surface is different from the old, in which I simply perceived it.

These differences in intentionality become the focus of our direct attention when we adopt the transcendental attitude. They are differences that we recognize even before we enter into philosophy; before we make the transcendental turn, we already know that seeing a pattern is not the same as seeing a word, and we know that seeing a surface is different from seeing a picture. Philosophy takes these differences as already given, and it systematically investigates them. It turns explicitly toward them.

Critics of phenomenology often say that it relies on introspection and on the intuition of subjective, mental things. But the things phenomenology looks at are those that have already been recognized by anyone who thinks and speaks, things like perceptions, signitive intentions, and pictorial intentions. Phenomenology examines these intentions, these noetic activities, and it also examines their objective correlates, their noemas, the kinds of objects that are established or targeted by them: the perceptual object, the picture, the word, the verbal meaning, the verbal referent.

We have used as our introductory paradigm the example of what happens when we suddenly discover a name within a pattern of lines. This type of discovery, which happens to us from time to time and which we can easily understand, is useful as an example, but it is not typical of how we use words. In fact, as human beings we always live in a verbal manner; words are not just sporadic or occasional events. We are always already in a linguistic mode. We are always recognizing words around us in the chatter and speech of others, in signs ("Exit," "Do Not Enter"), and in our internal imaginary life. Words always abound, and the signitive intentions that establish them as words abound as well. Even our perceptions are modified by the words that are called to mind when they occur; when we see, for the first time, a site we have heard and read about, such as a battlefield or the home of a famous person, all sorts of names and vague assertions arise within us, like a flock of blackbirds suddenly rising from a tree after a shot has been fired. The perceptual intuition fulfills many empty signitive intentions and stimulates many more.

The presence of signifying intentions makes it possible for us to perceive things in a specifically human way. The signifying intention is ordered to the thing in its absence, but this intention can also find fulfillment in a perception, in an intuition. We have already noted the interplay of empty and filled intentions, of absence and presence, in establishing human rationality. Amid all the kinds of empty and filled intentions, those associated with signifying acts are among the most properly human kinds of intentionality. Because we can name and articulate something in its absence, we can also go to the thing itself and see whether we can name and articulate it in its presence, in its own evidence, in the same way that we have heard it spoken about in its absence. We ask whether the signitive articulations can be transformed into perceptual articulations. We can receive messages from others about how things are and then go to the things themselves and find out on our own whether they are the way they were said to be. It is especially in the interplay between linguistic absence and presence that a heightened form of the identity of things can be achieved. We can name and articulate in words with far greater exactness than we can merely imagine or anticipate.

There is one more point to be made before we close this treatment of signifying intentions. We have noted that when we suddenly see the words, "The Burritt Hotel," in the pattern on the page, we intend no longer just the decorated paper but the Burritt Hotel itself, in its absence. The signitive intention is directed toward the hotel. Secondly, the same intention establishes some of the marks as a word. And thirdly, the same intention establishes a meaning as part of the word. The introduction of the signitive intention thus introduces three elements: a reference, a word, and a meaning or sense. The first two, the reference and the word, seem noncontroversial, but what about the third? How does the meaning fit in all this? The meaning is not just the marks that have become a word, nor is it simply the hotel. The meaning seems to be a strange intermediate entity between the word and the object, an entity that seems to spring into being in response to the signifying act. It seems to be a mentalistic being of some sort, an "intension," as it has been called. Where is this meaning, and what kind of thing is it? Is it in the mind or in the word? Does it exist at all? The status of the verbal meaning is a philosophical perplexity. We note this problem now, but we will not explore it here; we leave it for more extensive treatment in Chapter 7.

If words can sometimes surprise us and leap off a page, so can pictures. Suppose we are looking at the same decorated sheet of paper I spoke of earlier; suddenly, besides the words, "The Burritt Hotel," the face of Harry Truman appears in the network of lines. Perhaps the owners of the Burritt Hotel would like to suggest that President Truman stayed there once. We now have not just a word but also a picture asserting itself before us, and correspondingly we have entered not into a signifying intention but into a pictorial or imaging intentionality. Perception remains as a base for both intendings, but the two, the signifying and picturing, are different from each other. Taking something as a word is different from taking it as a picture. Once again, the picturing intentionality is not rare or surprising, but very common in our conscious life; pictures surround us. I see the photograph here, the landscape there, the portrait of Francis Bacon on the wall above my bookcase.

There are differences between signitive and pictorial intentions. In signification the "arrow" of intentionality goes through the word to an absent object. It is outward bound. It goes away from me and my situation here to something somewhere else. In picturing, however, the direction of the arrow is reversed. The object intended is brought toward me, into my own proximity; the presence of the object is embodied before me on a panel of wood or a piece of paper. Signitive intentions point away to the thing, pictorial intentions draw the thing near. The direction of the intending is different. In the picture I intend Francis Bacon here and now, not there and then. Francis Bacon as he was there and then is made present here and now.

Another difference between signitive and pictorial intending is that the signitive intends the object at one stroke, all at once, as a whole (I signify just the Burritt Hotel pure and simple when I utter its name, I do not mean it under any special angle), while the pictorial presents the object under a certain perspective, in a certain light, with a certain pose, at a certain moment, with certain features highlighted. Picturing is more concrete, signifying is more abstract.

Furthermore, pictorial intending is more like a perception than is signitive intending. Pictorial intending is very much like seeing or hearing the thing: we do not really see or hear it, of course, because we are given only a picture and not the thing itself, but the way the picture is given has analogies with the way the thing itself would be given. Like perception, pictorial intending is continuous, we can focus on one or another part of the image, the image can be clear or faded, its parts can be more or less vividly articulated. There are differences, however, between picturing and ordinary perceiving: there is, for example, no "other side of the cube" for objects that are depicted; there is only the other side of the wooden panel on which the picture exists. The only sides, aspects, and profiles of the pictured object are those that are depicted.

Signifying and picturing are two kinds of intentionalities, but they can interact. We can use words to talk about a picture, and when we do so we can talk about either the bodily material or the content of the image. Picturing involves a perception of a substrate or a vehicle (the wood panel, the colored paper) and an intending of the depicted object (Francis Bacon, Wyvenhoe Park). We can direct our verbal intentions either to the substrate or to the theme: we can describe Bacon in the picture as coy, as disdainful, as elderly, and we can describe the house in Wyvenhoe Park as hidden by the trees, and the cattle as grazing in the meadow. But we can also say that the paint is cracked, and that these blue patches contrast nicely with those white ones. Some of the pleasure of looking at paintings comes from shifting between a focus on the theme and a focus on the substrate: we might step up very close to the painting, or we might narrow the scope of our vision, in order to concentrate on the material substrate, to appreciate the brushstrokes and colors in these particular spots; then we move back for a view of the wider whole, retaining all the while our recent grasp of the materiality of the thing. The interplay between substrate and form enhances the presence of the work of art, and such an interplay is possible because of the various signitive intentions we train on the thing we are looking at.

The interaction of signitive and pictorial intending occurs also when we identify what the picture is about. If we were to hold up a picture of the Brooklyn Bridge and ask, "What is this?" people would normally answer, "The Brooklyn Bridge," but strictly speaking this is only one of the possible answers. One might just as well have said, "A picture" or "A piece of paper." One would generally identify it as the Brooklyn Bridge because one assumes that one should enter into the pictorial intentionality that seems to be presupposed by the question. The clever ambiguity of the presence of the picture shows us how many intentionalities are always at work in our ordinary experience.

Let us observe, finally, that picturing is based on more than similarity. A picture may resemble what it depicts, but it is not made to be a picture by virtue of the resemblance; one twin sister resembles another, but she is not a picture of the other. Being a picture is not just being like something else, it is being the presentation of what is depicted. If I see a picture of Harry Truman, I see *Truman* depicted, in his individuality; I do not just see something that looks like him.

INDICATIONS, SYMBOLS, OR SIGNALS

If I am hiking along a trail and see a pile of stones about eighteen inches high, I take it as a sign that I am still on the trail. I will look ahead and try to see another pile or a mark on a tree, to confirm the continuation of the trail. The pile of stones is not a word, nor is it a picture; it is another kind of sign. In phenomenology, such signs have been called *indications*, but we could also call them symbols or signals. They bring forth another kind of intentionality, the symbolic or the indicational.

Indication signs are like words in that they generally point us to an absent object (a lock of hair reminds us of someone, a flag with four stars represents an army general), but they are unlike words in that they do not specify very clearly how we are to intend the object. They only call the indicated object to mind. In contrast, words generally articulate the object for us; they name the object and then say something about it. When we name something we usually make it ready for predication, and even a single word usually presents the object under a certain aspect (the words "dog" and "cur" both designate the same animal, but with a different sense). A symbol, however, just refers us to the object and stops there. It just signals the object and brings it to mind without qualification.

An important difference between indication signs and words is that the former do not enter into syntax while the latter are essentially syntactic. Symbols do not enter into grammar. It is true that one indication might well lead on to another (the pile of stones makes us look for the next trail marker, the starting shot calls for the flag signaling the end of the race), but this is concatenation and not syntax. There are not different ways in which the series of symbols could be composed; they are merely placed in sequence, as at the start and the end of a race. The syntax in language allows great flexibility; we can intend a thing in many different ways because we can articulate it through the grammar of our language, but symbols do not leave us free to shape the presence of the thing in that way. They merely bring the thing to mind.

ENRICHMENT OF MANIFOLDS, ENHANCEMENT OF IDENTITY

In Chapter 3 we considered identities that are given to us in manifolds of appearance. The single cube is given to us through an array of sides, aspects, and profiles. Now that we have examined the modifications that perception can take on, we see that the manifolds of sides, aspects, and profiles are only a few of the manifolds through which things are presented to us. All the intentionalities we have considered in this chapter and in Chapter 5 expand the manifolds of appearances. Let us summarize the forms we have examined. In our internal life, experience can be modified in the following ways:

1. Perception
2. Remembering
3. Imagination
4. Anticipation

One and the same cube can be not only perceived through many perspectives, but also imagined, remembered, and anticipated, and it is one and the same cube in all these experiences.

However, such "internal" modifications of perception belong rather to the level of sensibility. As important as they are in establishing the human condition, they are also found, in simple forms, in the higher animals: dogs dream, and cats have some sense of awaiting a mouse. The other range of intentions we have studied in this chapter are built upon perception and are more properly rational and human intentions:

1. Perception
2. Signification
3. Picturing
4. Indication

In each group, all the variants are interdependent. We could not have memory without imagination and anticipation; we could not have the power to picture without also having the power to carry out signifying intentions and the power to establish and recognize indication signs. Our perceptual intercourse with the world branches off into variations in our internal life, in which we displace ourselves into remembered, imagined, and anticipated situations and into variations in our way of taking the things in the world: signifying particular things and states of affairs, picturing things that are not present to us, and symbolizing what cannot be pictured or brought into words.

One and the same object or event can be now symbolized, now pictured, now verbally intended, and now perceived; it can also be imagined, remembered, and anticipated. Through all these permutations it remains the same thing. We do not see many different appearances that we just relate to one and the same thing, but rather one and the same thing is itself given in new and varied ways. In this flow of presentations, the same thing is recognized over and over again. Its own identity is increased and intensified. We could even say its being is enhanced through the enrichment of its manifolds of presentation, since the being of a thing is not unrelated to its truth, and certainly the thing enjoys more truth as its displays are enlarged. There is more to *A Midsummer Night's Dream* after centuries of interpretation and staging than there was before. There is more to an animal and to a human being after they have manifested themselves through the events of life than there was before. The actuality involved in truth perfects not only the perceiver, but the entity that is displayed as well.

The various intentionalities we have investigated are achieved while we are in the natural attitude. We perceive, imagine, remember, and anticipate, and we also signify, picture, and symbolize, while maintaining the world belief and world-directed focus that characterize the natural attitude. All the identities we have considered here are given to us while we remain in the natural attitude: the trail markers, Francis Bacon and his portrait, Wyvenhoe Park and the painting that depicts it, the Burritt Hotel and its name, are all recognized through the layers of appearance that occur to us in the natural attitude. However, the reflective descriptions of all these activities, manifolds, and identities are carried out in the transcendental, philosophical attitude. We as philosophers take a distance to all these intentionalities and their objects; we contemplate, distinguish, and describe them, from a point of view different from that in which we achieve them. We suspend our natural intentionalities, we bracket the identities correlated with them, and we unravel the complexities that make up our condition as rational human beings who have a world and experience things in it. We provide a noetic and a noematic analysis and thus shed light on what it is to be in the world as datives of manifestation, and we clarify what it is for beings to be and to be manifest.

7

Categorial Intentions and Objects

The kinds of intentionality we explored in Chapters 5 and 6 were rather colorful and concrete. We examined imagination, picturing, memory, and other familiar elements in our experience. In this chapter we will move to a kind of intentionality that is more austere and more purely rational. We will examine what phenomenology calls *categorial* intentionality. This is the kind of intending that articulates states of affairs and propositions, the kind that functions when we predicate, relate, collect, and introduce logical operations into what we experience. We will examine the difference, for example, between simply intending an object and making a judgment about that object.

We recall that the word "categorial" is related to the Greek term *katēgoreō*, which originally meant the act of denouncing or accusing someone, of stating publicly that some feature belongs to him, that he is a murderer or a thief. In philosophy, the term came to mean the act of saying something about something. The phenomenological term "categorial" draws on this etymology. It refers to the kind of intending that articulates an object, the kind that introduces syntax into what we experience. A house is a simple object, but the fact that the house is white is a categorial object. The meaning of the term "Fido" or "dog" is a simple meaning, but the sense of "Fido is hungry" or "Dogs are domesticated" is categorial. When we move to the categorial domain, we move from simple, "one-rayed" intentions to complex, "many-rayed" intentions. How do we move from the simple to the categorial? How do we infuse the things we experience with syntax? How do we move from perception to intellection?

The issue we are about to study is a development of the signitive intentions that were introduced in Chapter 6. Signitive intentions, those associated with words, practically always put us into syntax and categorial form. We almost never just say a single word, and when we do, the word usually serves more as an exclamation or expletive ("Harry!" "Trouble!" "Hurry!") than as a fully operative linguistic unit. We exercise our humanity most fully, we act as rational animals most intensely, when we use words, and our achievement of truth and thinking is implicated in our use of language; the discussion of categorial intentionality is therefore of great importance in phenomenology, in our study of what it is to be human and what it is to be a dative of manifestation. Furthermore, it is especially in its treatment of categorial intending that phenomenology provides resources to escape the egocentric predicament of modern philosophy. Some of phenomenology's most original and valuable contributions to philosophy are found in its doctrines about categorial intentions.

THE GENESIS OF JUDGMENTS FROM EXPERIENCE

Before we examine the importance of categorial intentions, let us try to obtain a more complete idea of what they are. How do categorial intentions arise from the experience of simple objects? To spell out the process, we must distinguish three stages.

Suppose we are perceiving an object; suppose we are looking at a car:

(1) At first, we just look at it in a rather passive way. Our gaze moves from one part to another, we go through the manifolds of sides, aspects, and profiles, we go through the color, the smoothness, the shine of the surface, its feel of hardness or softness. All this is a continuous perception, all carried out on one level. No particular thinking is engaged as we continue to perceive. Furthermore, as we go through the various manifolds of presentation, one and the same car is continuously given to us as the identity in the manifold.

(2) Now, suppose that some abrasions on the surface of the car catch our attention. We zero in on them. We highlight this part of the car; not just this spatial part, but this feature, this abrasiveness, in the spatial part. This focus is not just more of the dawdling perception that preceded; this highlighting is qualitatively different from what had been going on continuously before. However, it is not yet the establishment of a categorial object. So far, we are at an in-between point: we continue to experience the appearances of the

car, and we continue to recognize one and the same car in all the appearances, but we have now spotlighted one of the appearances and brought it to center stage; it stands out from all the rest. A part comes into the foreground against the general background of the whole.

(3) One more step is needed to establish a categorial object. We interrupt the continuous flow of perception; we go back to the whole (the car), and we now take it precisely as being the whole, and simultaneously we take the part we had highlighted (the abrasion) as being a part in that whole. We now register the whole as containing the part. A relation between whole and part is articulated and registered. At this point we can declare, "This car is damaged." This achievement is a *categorial intuition*, because the categorial object, the thing in its articulation, is made actually present to us. We do not just have *the car* present to us; rather, *the car's being damaged* is made present.

What happens in this third stage is that the whole (the car) is presented specifically as the whole, and the part (damaged) is presented specifically as a part. The whole and its part are explicitly distinguished. A relation between them is distinctly registered. An articulation is achieved. A state of affairs clicks into place. We have moved from sensibility to intellection, from mere experiencing to an initial understanding. We have moved from the single-rayed intentionality of perception to the many-rayed intentionality of judgment. We have entered into categorial thinking.

In the first and second stages, the whole and the parts were experienced or lived through, but they were not made thematic. Strictly speaking, they were not yet articulated. Even in the second stage, when the part was brought to the fore, it was highlighted, but it was not yet acknowledged explicitly as a part. The part was brought to the fore, but its being a part was not brought to the fore. In this second stage the part is being prepped, so to speak, to become acknowledged as an attribute, but it has not been so identified as yet. In the third stage the whole and the parts are explicitly articulated.

We should note, however, that the third stage could not be reached without the preparation afforded in the second, without the first blush of structure, the concentration on a feature, that goes beyond simple continuous perception. The first stage is not differentiated enough to yield a categorial structure directly. The special focus that occurs in the second stage is needed. We have to begin to experience a part within the whole (the abrasion) before we can articulate it as such ("The car is damaged!").

A lot of philosophical material is contained in what we have just described. We have described the shift in intentionality that occurs when we go from simple perception to categorial intending, to thinking. The intentional achievement we have described is the thoughtful basis for human language and speech. Language does not float by itself on top of our sensibility; the reason we can use language is that we are capable of the kind of intending that constitutes categorial objects. The syntax that defines language is grounded on the articulation of wholes and parts that takes place in categorial intending. Syntax in language simply expresses the relations of part and whole that are brought out in categorial consciousness. The reason we can communicate, the reason we can tell someone, "That car over there is damaged," is because we have the power to go from perception to categorial thinking. It is not the case that we can think because we have language; rather, we have language because we can think, because we have the ability to achieve categorial intentions. The power of rational consciousness underlies the capacity for language. It is true that the language we inherit pressures our categorial activities in this direction or that, into these or those categorial forms, but the very ability to have language is based on the kind of intentionalities that we enjoy in the categorial domain.

It will take us some time to unpack the implications of this transition from experience to judgment. First of all, we should note that the move into the categorial domain is obviously discontinuous with the experiencing that preceded it. The move into the categorial is not just more perception; it is not just a further unrolling of the manifolds that are given in perception. In the third stage noted earlier, when we go back to the whole and register it precisely as the whole containing the part in question, we interrupt the continuity of perception. We start again on a new level; we go back over what we had been experiencing and initiate a new level of identity. This new beginning installs a new kind of consciousness and a new kind of object, the state of affairs, as the objective correlate of that consciousness.

Second, the state of affairs that is registered, the car's being damaged, is a "one," a unity in a way that is different from the identity that was given in perception. It is a heightened unity. It is more discrete and identifiable. The continuous perception just went on and on as more and more profiles were given, in a process that could have continued indefinitely. Now, however, we have a single state of affairs ("The car is damaged") that can be picked up and carried around, so to speak; it can be detached from the immediacy of perception and from our present situation. It can be conveyed to someone else in a communication. (In contrast, we cannot really hand our perceptions or our memories over to someone else.) It can be logically related to other states of affairs that we register. The theme of identity, which was so important even in perception, where an identity is given through manifolds, acquires a new sense and a new level of intensity. We now have identity in categorial consciousness, the kind of identity that is presented, preserved, and transported through speech.

Third, the identity of the categorial object is presented all at once. In perception we have a process in which profiles follow one another sequentially, but in categorial registration the whole and the part are given simultaneously. It is not the case that we first have the whole all by itself ("the car") and then, as a separate achievement, the part or the predicate ("damaged"), and then a relation drawn between the two ("is"). Rather, even as we register the car as the whole, we must already have the part in mind. The whole-with-part comes all at once, synchronously. When we have an articulated whole given to us, we do not have the whole first and then the articulation. The whole as such is presented only as articulated. This simultaneity of the categorial object is a further aspect of its discreteness, which must be contrasted with the continuous character of perceptual experience.

In phenomenological terminology, the establishment of categorial objects is called their *constitution*. The term "constitution" should not be taken to mean anything like a creation or an imposition of subjective forms on reality. In phenomenology, to "constitute" a categorial object means to bring it to light, to articulate it, to bring it forth, to actualize its truth. We cannot manifest a thing any way we please; we cannot make an object mean anything we wish. We can bring a thing to light only if the thing offers itself in a certain light. The thing has to show up with certain aspects that we can spotlight if we are to be able to declare that it has certain features. If we did not experience something like the abrasions in the car, we would not be able to constitute the car as damaged. Of course, we might be misled by false appearances, in which the car merely seems to be scraped, and we might erroneously declare that it is damaged when it is not; but then we remedy this situation simply by further and closer experience of the car, or by listening to what other people have to say about it, or by figuring out what must really be the case; we will then come to see that we were wrong. We have to submit to the way things disclose themselves. To submit in this way is not to place limitations on our freedom, but to achieve the perfection of our intelligence, which is geared by its nature to disclosing the way things are. To submit in this way is to bring about the triumph of objectivity, which is what our minds are supposed to do. To "constitute" a state of affairs is to exercise our understanding and to let a thing manifest itself to us.

Some further remarks on terminology: the development of categorial objects from experience is called *genetic* constitution, because of the stages through which the higher objectivities come to be from the lower. The categorial objects and intentions are obviously *founded* on the simple objects and intentions. They are *nonindependent* parts. Human intellectual activity is based on the sensible. Finally, *predicative* intentionality, in which we predicate a feature of an object and declare that "*S* is *p*," is the preeminent form of categorial activity; the term *prepredicative*, in contrast, is used to designate the kind of experience and intentionality that precedes the categorial. One of the major topics in phenomenology is that of prepredicative experience, the sort of experiencing that precedes but also leads up to categorial achievements.

NEW LEVELS OF IDENTITY, NEW MANIFOLDS

We have remained with predication in our analysis of categorial intentionality, but there are many other kinds of articulation that can take place once we move into this higher-level form of consciousness. Besides saying, "The car is damaged," we can articulate other internal features of the car: "The car is large," "It is old," "It is a Ford." We can articulate its external relations: "It is in the parking lot," "It is next to the Honda," "It is smaller than my truck." We can include it in a collection: "There are five cars," "Three of the cars seem to be damaged." We can introduce independent and subordinate clauses, conjunctions, prepositions, relative pronouns and relative clauses, adverbs, adjectives, and many other grammatical features, all of which express various ways of allowing things to be articulated. The range of the categorial is very wide, as extensive as the grammar of human language.

This whole domain of categorial articulation, in all its variety and nuances, rests, together with picturing and symbolizing, upon the "lower" intentionalities of perception, imagination, remembering, and anticipation. The categorial linguistic intentionality humanizes our perception, imagination, remembering, and anticipation; it raises them to a more rational level than they achieve in the animal kingdom. Categorial intending introduces new manifolds that supplement and penetrate the manifolds found in prepredicative experience.

Categorial intentionality is itself a new kind of identification, a new kind of identity synthesis, that also supplements and penetrates those achieved in prepredicative experience. When we categorially intend the cube, we have not just the identity of a cube that is perceived through a manifold of sides, aspects, and profiles, and through the manifolds of memory, imagination, and anticipation; we also have the identity achieved through the statements we can make about it, the statements we can hear others make about it from their points of view, and the fulfillments we can achieve when we listen to what others say and then try to confirm their opinions by going and looking and directly articulating for ourselves. A whole new range of manifestation and truth is opened up in the categorial domain. Even our imaginings, memories, and anticipations take on a categorial complexity: we can anticipate not only "water" but "the cool water from the mountain spring." In human consciousness, perception, imagination, remembering, and anticipation all show the effects of being ordered toward their completion in rational thinking. The way we exercise these forms of intending is shaped by their involvement in categorial intentionality.

What happens in categorial intentions is that the things we perceive become elevated into the space of reasons, the domain of logic, argument, and rational thinking. Categorial experience is the transit point leading from perception to intelligence, where language and syntax come into play. Through categorial articulation, the things we perceive become registered and admitted into the field of reasoning and conversation. Simple perception is more of a physiological and psychological process, while categorial registration is the first move into logic.

When I spoke, in Chapter 3, about the object as an identity within a manifold of presentation, I insisted that the identity itself never shows up as one of the sides, aspects, and profiles through which it is given. Its identity belongs to another dimension. It is this identity, however, that we refer to when we name the object and bring it into categorial articulation. Thus, the cube that is perceptually given in and through a manifold of sides, aspects, and profiles is the identity that we refer to when we utter the words "the cube" and begin to predicate features of it. The identity of the cube is the bridge between perception and thought.

CATEGORIAL OBJECTS

Through our categorial intentions, we establish categorial objects. We constitute states of affairs, such as the fact that the car is damaged. These categorial objects truly are objects; they are not just arrangements of concepts or ideas. They are not "intramental" objects; they are intellected crystallizations that take place in the things we encounter. In categorial activity we articulate the way things are presented to us; we bring to light relationships that exist in things in the world. We have this world-directed focus, moreover, whether we intend things that are present to us or things that are absent. We must emphasize the fact that categorial objects are ways in which things appear; they are not subjective, psychological "things in the mind."

To bring out the objectivity of categorial objects, let us examine a few other examples. We have already talked about the state of affairs expressed by the statement, "This car is damaged." As another example, suppose I am engaged in a discussion with two other people. The discussion progresses, but then something fishy begins to surface; something smells strange in what they are saying and the way they are saying it. This intermediate stage is like the stage, in our previous example, when the abrasions on the car begin to attract our attention. Then, suddenly, I register the situation: "They are trying to put something over on me!" The state of affairs clicks into place, a categorial intuition is achieved, the wholes and parts are articulated, syntax is installed into what I experience.

Again, suppose I am walking along a trail, looking at the rocks along the side. Suddenly I realize that the thing over there is not a rock but a fossil. The rather passive level of perception, the continuous identification of one and the same object through many profiles, gives way to a registration of the state of affairs, "That is not just a rock; it's a fossil in the ground!"

The examples we have examined – the damaged car, the deceptive behavior, the fossil and not the rock – are articulations of things that are before us. They are not mental entities, they are not just meanings in the mind; they are modifications in the way things are being presented to us. These modifications, these changes in the mode of presentation, are "in the world," but obviously they are not in the world in the manner in which a tree or a table is in the world. Rather, they are higher-level objects. They are "out there" as more complex modes of presentation, more intricate ways of being manifested. The states of affairs expressed by the words that we use ("The car is damaged," "They are deceiving me") are truly parts of the world. They are how certain segments of the world – this car, this behavior – can be articulated.

The states of affairs in these examples are there directly before us. We intuit them. Most of the time that we speak, however, the states of affairs that we express are absent from us. We talk about what is not present: yesterday's football game, how our congressman is voting, what happened at the Battle of Sharpsburg. The human possession of language gives us enormous reach; we can talk about things long ago and very far away, even about galaxies that are incredibly distant from us and periods of time billions of years ago. Most of our talk does not reach quite that far; most of it is much more local ("What did she do after you slammed the door?" "Was the dentist careful?"), but it still reaches largely into what is absent.

An extremely important point is the fact that when we speak about the absent, we still are articulating a part of the world. We are not turning to our ideas or concepts as substitute presences for the things that are absent. We are so constituted that we can intend things in their absence as well as in their presence. The intentionality of consciousness is such that it reaches outward all the time, even when it targets things that are not before it. If I give a speech about the Battle of Antietam, I and my audience intend that battle even though it happened over one hundred thirty years ago; if you and I, here in Washington, DC, talk about the Empire State Building, it is the building we are talking about, not some meanings or images that might come to mind during our conversation.

Our discourse about the absent is, however, punctuated by episodes in which we speak about what is present. Sometimes we might just have something to say about the objects that are nearby, objects that we can perceive. At other times, our speech about absent things might demand that we go and find out whether what we say is true or not. We might be questioned about what we say, and at least in some cases we can resolve the question by going to see what is the case, that is, by going somewhere and categorially registering the situation in its presence ("See; I told you that an owl was nesting in this barn"). When we cannot do this, we may resort to the witness of others, to documents, to relics, and to other forms of indirect confirmation, but many of these in turn will have been based on direct categorial registrations that were carried out by someone else.

Thus, although our speech is mostly directed toward things that are absent, it can turn to things that are present to confirm or disconfirm what we say about the absent. An identity synthesis takes place between the state of affairs that we intended in its absence and the same state of affairs we now intend in its confirming presence. We identify the situation given now as the same as the one we intended when we only spoke about it.

THE ELIMINATION OF MEANINGS AS MENTAL OR CONCEPTUAL THINGS

In discussing the transition from categorial actions dealing with the absent to those dealing with the present, we have introduced the issue of truth. We noted that in our worldly experience we try to see whether the statements made in the absence of the objects are true or not. But something seems to be missing in our analysis so far.

Where does "the meaning" of our words exist? Where are the judgments we perform? Traditionally, the meaning of our words, the judgments or the propositions that we make, the ideas that we possess, have all been taken as some sort of mental or conceptual things, something closer to us, some sort of things that are never absent. Because such things were thought always to be directly present to our minds, they seemed able to serve as a bridge between us and what we intend, especially when we intend something that was absent. These things could explain how we could be directed toward that which was not near us. This understanding of meanings and propositions can be found in some medieval thinkers, in Descartes, the British Empiricists, and Kant, in contemporary cognitive science, and in many philosophers of language.

Furthermore, the issue of truth seems to require some sort of meaning or concept or judgment between us and the thing: when we claim we have told the truth, we imply – do we not? – that what we said, the meanings we had, correspond to what is out there. If there are no meanings and propositions apart from the things we know, how can we ever say that our judgments conform to things as they are? What is there that could conform to the facts? How can we explain what truth is if we do not posit meanings and judgments as some sort of mental things? Common sense seems to demand that we posit meanings as some sort of entities in the mind.

And yet, although we seem forced to posit meanings and judgments as mental or conceptual things, such things turn out to be philosophically embarrassing and perplexing. We never directly experience them. They are postulated as something we cannot do without, but no one has ever seen one of them. They are theoretical constructs rather than familiar entities. They are postulated, not given, and they are postulated because we think we cannot explain knowledge and truth without them. How do they exist? What sort of entities are they? Are they in the mind or in some sort of third realm between the mind and the world? How do they do their work of referring us to objects? How many of them do we have? Do they come into actual existence and then go out of it, moving from virtual to actual and back to virtual again, as we call them up? They seem to be duplicates of the things and states of affairs outside us; why do we need to posit them? But how can we avoid doing so? Propositions and meanings as mental or representational entities seem to be a pis aller, a cul de sac, an aporia. We are boxed into them by philosophical confusions.

I believe that one of the most sophisticated and most valuable contributions of phenomenology to philosophy lies in its treatment of judgments and meanings. Phenomenology is able to show that we need not posit judgments and senses as mental entities or as intermediaries between the mind and things. We need not introduce them as the philosophically perplexing, strange beings that have the magical power of relating our consciousness to the world outside. Phenomenology provides a new interpretation of the status of judgments, propositions, and concepts, one that is simple, elegant, and true to life. It does so in the following manner.

Suppose you tell me that the flatware you are showing me is sterling silver. At first I simply go along with what you say and see it as silver. Following your lead, I register the state of affairs, "This flatware is silver." Then I begin to have doubts. The whole thing does not add up; how could you have so much silverware? Besides, it does not look or feel like sterling; it is too light; it is too tinny.

What happens at this point is that I have changed my attitude toward the state of affairs that I had just constituted. Originally, I simply intended the flatware's being silver; I intended it naively and straightforwardly. Now, I begin to hesitate. I enter into a new, reflective attitude. I still intend the flatware as silver, but now I add the qualifier, "As proposed by you." I no longer simply believe; I suspend belief, but I still intend the same thing-and-feature. I have changed the state of affairs, "This flatware is silver," into the mere judgment or meaning, "This flatware is silver." It is no longer a simple state of affairs for me; it is now, for me, a state of affairs *as being presented by you;* this qualifier makes it into just your judgment, not the simple fact.

The change from being a state of affairs to being a judgment occurs in response to a new attitude I have adopted. Let us call my new attitude the "propositional attitude," and let us call the reflection that establishes it the "propositional (or judgmental) reflection." It can also be called *apophantic* reflection, because it establishes and turns toward the judgment, which is called *apophansis* in Greek. The judgment, the proposition, the meaning, the sense arise in response to this new attitude. The judgment, proposition, or concept is not there ahead of time as a kind of mediating entity before it is reflected upon. It is not there beforehand doing its epistemological work of relating us to the real world. It is not there already, waiting for us to turn to it or to infer its presence. Rather, it is a dimension of presentation, a change in the mode of presentation, that arises when we enter into the propositional attitude by means of a propositional reflection. It arises when we change our focus. The proposition is not a subsistent entity; it is part of the world being articulated, but being taken as just someone's presentation: in this case, it is being taken as your presentation. It is your judgment.

The benefit of this new explanation of how propositions and meanings come to be is that it avoids the need to posit propositions and meanings as mysterious mental or conceptual entities. It preserves the world directedness of all intentionality; even when we refer to a judgment, we are referring to the world, but to the world precisely as it has been proposed by someone.

This phenomenological analysis of judgment also allows us to clarify the correspondence theory of truth. Usually, the biggest problem discussed in the correspondence theory of truth is how to explain the "match" between the proposition and the state of affairs. But in fact, a deeper problem is the question of what propositions are in the first place; how do they come to be? What mode of existence do they have? Before we say how they can correspond to things, we have to say what they are like.

Instead of postulating judgments, propositions, and senses as mediating entities, phenomenology sees them as correlated to a propositional attitude and propositional reflection. They arise in response to our taking a state of affairs as being merely proposed by someone. In this analysis, not only is a state of affairs "in the world"; even a proposition is "in the world," but in the world only as being projected by someone. It is how the world is being projected as being, through what someone is saying.

We have reached the following point in our phenomenological analysis: we have moved from naively intending the state of affairs to reflectively taking the same state of affairs "as stated or proposed by you." The flatware "is" silver, but only as stated or presented by you; I am no longer intending it purely and simply as such. What happens next? At this point we have a state of affairs as intended by you. We do not yet have the truth of the question resolved.

What happens next is that I go back to the flatware and inspect it more closely, look at its bill of sale, look for inscriptions on it, perhaps ask other people's opinion, and so on. Then, after sufficient inspection of my own, I might conclude, "Yes, it is silver after all." If this is the outcome of my inquiry, then I find that your judgment does correspond to the way things are. I no longer take the state of affairs as just being proposed by you. I go back to a straightforward intending of the "being silver" of the flatware, but my return is not like the original naive intention. I now have the state of affairs as confirmed, as having gone through the acid test of propositional reflection and confirmation. The state of affairs is the same one I originally intended, and the same I took as just proposed by you; but now it takes on a new layer of sense, a new noematic dimension: it is now a confirmed fact and not just a naively intended state of affairs.

This explanation of the correspondence between judgment and fact can be called a "disquotational" theory of truth, because it involves the step of first merely "quoting" the state of affairs (during the critical analysis, when I take the state of affairs as merely proposed by you) and then removing the quotation marks, annulling the propositional reflection, leaving the propositional attitude, and going back to the straightforward acceptance. However, it is a disquotational theory that deals with more than the merely linguistic phenomenon of introducing and removing the quotation marks; the theory provides more than a linguistic explanation, because it describes the shifts in intentionality that underlie the quotation and disquotation. We begin with the state of affairs simply, then move to the state of affairs as proposed, then move to the state of affairs as confirmed.

Of course, my investigation might well result in the conclusion that the flatware is not silver after all; then, the "state of affairs as proposed" continues permanently. I do not disquote, I do not annul the propositional reflection; the flatware never was silver, it was only proposed as such by you. Therefore, that particular "state of affairs" was and is only your proposition, only your judgment, only your meaning, never the way the things are. The state of affairs becomes permanently disqualified from being truly the case; it will always remain just your opinion, and a false one at that. It is interesting to note, incidentally, that an opinion or a judgment is usually attached to someone whose proposition it is, while a fact is not the possession of anyone in particular; it is there for everyone.

This phenomenological theory of truth, instead of moving between mental or semantic entities and real entities, operates entirely in the domain of presentation. It distinguishes varieties in the kinds of presentation (the simple, the categorial, the propositional, the confirmatory) and speaks about the identities that are achieved within the new manifolds that these varieties introduce. The perceptual object, given through profiles, is now further identified through categorial articulation and heightened still further as an object through the moves of critical reflection and confirming identification.

The dimension of linguistic categorial verification also introduces great richness and variety, because it involves an intersubjective dimension. We have not only the other side of the cube that someone else can see while I see this side; we also have, say, the statements made by people centuries ago, confirmed or disconfirmed by people now, or statements made by people very different from us, living in different times and places, and yet understood and to some degree verified or falsified by our own thoughtful experience. We also have the statements made by us that will be confirmed or disconfirmed by others in other places and times. Speech allows intersubjective exchanges that range far more widely than do the exchanges based on simple common perceptions.

The steps in intentionality that we have considered – of naive, categorial intending, of critical, propositional reflection, and of the return to confirmation or disconfirmation – are all carried out in the natural attitude. The phenomenological theory of truth and meaning analyzes these steps and their elements from the vantage point of the transcendental, phenomenological attitude. From this perch, it reflects on the true and false intentionalities that are carried out in our prephilosophical engagements and clarifies what goes on in them.

FURTHER REMARKS ON CATEGORIAL ACTS AND OBJECTS

Obviously, we are more active when we enter into categorial intentions than when we simply perceive, imagine, remember, and anticipate things. There is something like a new "product" in categorial intentionality, the categorial object, whether that object be taken as a state of affairs or a judgment (which is a state of affairs taken as proposed). The new product, the categorial object, can be detached from its immediate context and related somewhere else through the use of language. By speaking to you, I can "give" you the same categorial object that I see and articulate now. You can articulate that selfsame object even in its absence. This sort of distancing is much more radical than that which occurs in the displacements of remembering or imagining, in which I can also present things to myself in their absence. Remembering and imagining give us an original sense of the absent, but they do not allow the sort of communication of the absent, and the kind of control we can have over it, that occur in speech.

Categorial intentionality elevates us into a properly human form of truth, the truth that involves speech and reasoning. But if it allows this form of truth, it also allows a properly human abuse of truth; it makes possible errors and falsehoods on a scale that dwarfs the misperceptions, failed memories, and misimaginings of the lower intentions. If I can "give" you a state of affairs that you have not experienced, I can also "give" you a false version of it in my speech, or I can "give" you a state of affairs that never happened at all. Also, I can even contradict, that is, speak against, my own self. I can have one conviction and then have another that annuls the first. I may hold as true the state of affairs that this person is good to be with, and also hold as true the state of affairs that this person is hateful to be with. I can believe that "S is p" and also hold, at least by implication, that "S is not p." Often, such contradictions are caused by emotional involvements, in which we desire two things that cannot be possessed together and we do not wish to face up to the fact that we cannot have both; they can also be caused by confusion, inattention, and inability to master the intellectual material of the thing at hand. We will examine this intellectual root of contradiction when we come to the topic of vagueness.

Entry into the categorial domain also permits the introduction of logic. Logic does not belong to the lower level of perception and its variants, but it does come into play on the categorial level. Once we have constituted categorial objects, we can formalize those objects and pay attention to the consistency or inconsistency of the forms that result. Instead of dealing with the categorial object, "The car is damaged," we can deal with the pure form, "S is p," in which the content of the object is rendered indifferent and the syntax is kept in place. Instead of "car" we deal with "any object whatever," and instead of "damaged" we deal with "any attribute whatever." Then, we can examine the relations among various forms and see, for example, that the form "*S* is not *p*" is not consistent with the form "*Sp* is *q*." If we were to assert the latter and then go on to assert the former ("This red house is expensive; this house is not red"), we would be contradicting ourselves. Logical consistency is a necessary condition for the truth of statements; if statements contradict themselves by virtue of their logical form, then a priori they cannot be verified by our experience of the things themselves.

A distinction is introduced in phenomenology between two kinds of formal systems, those belonging to objects and states of affairs and the "ontological" side of things, and those belonging to judgments or propositions and the region of sense or meaning. The science of the formal structures of objects and states of affairs is called *formal ontology*, while the science of the formal structures of senses and propositions is called *formal apophantics*.

Let me make one more comment about the doctrine that takes concepts, judgments, meanings, or senses as mental or conceptual entities, the doctrine that I have attempted to refute. To think that such entities are needed to explain knowledge betrays a failure to recognize the intentionality of consciousness. It is to take consciousness as simple, sheer awareness, conscious only of itself, and to assume that intentionality must be added to it by the insertion of some kind of representation: a concept, a word, a proposition, a mental image, a symbol, a sense, or a "noema." In this view, it is not consciousness that is essentially intentional, but the representation. It is the insert that makes consciousness intentional and specifies what the consciousness intends and how it intends it: the insert establishes an intention, a reference, and a sense. The representation relates us to the objects "outside" and gives them a certain meaning. But how could such an additive bestow intentionality on our awareness? How could we know that what is given to us is a word or image or a concept, and that it represents something "beyond" itself? How would the very dimension of an "outside" arise for us if it were not there in the beginning? If consciousness does not start out being intentional, it could never figure out how to become so.

THE PHENOMENON OF VAGUENESS

We have been considering categorial intentions and their correlative objects, as well as truth, meaning, judgments, states of affairs, verification, and logic. Phenomenology also treats another topic that plays a strategic role in this network of phenomena, one that is only infrequently and marginally treated by most philosophers. It is the phenomenon of *vagueness*. Vagueness is important not only in regard to the more scientific issues of logic, meaning, and verification, but also in regard to the ordinary use of language and the establishment of a responsible speaker.

When we say or read something, it is usually assumed that we think through what we say or read. This is often not the case. Words are frequently used without thought. We might be superficially reading something, or we might hear someone talk but fail to pay attention to what he says, we might even say things ourselves without being properly aware of the meaning of what we say, or we might be reciting something by rote. Sometimes the material we are talking about is beyond us; we really do not understand what we are saying. Much of what people say about politics, for example, is like this. Much of what they say is vague: slogans are repeated, favorite ideas are trotted out, statements made by others are stated verbally but without comprehension. Most public opinion polls measure vague thinking. The human power of speech, the noble power that gives us our dignity as human beings, also makes it possible for us to seem to be thinking when we really are not. This is a specifically human way of failing to be what we should be, and it is very important in human affairs.

What occurs in thoughtless speech is that the categorial activity that should accompany the speech is not adequately achieved. There is some categorial activity, but it is not up to the issues being discussed and asserted. There is a succession of ideas but not a thought. If I speak vaguely, someone who listens to me, and who is more thoughtful than I am, will usually find, as time goes on, that what I am saying makes no sense. It is garbled. He will ask me to clarify what I mean, to make sense out of the hodgepodge I am presenting. If he tries to argue with me he will be continuously frustrated; arguing with someone who speaks vaguely is like trying to use hand grenades to disperse a fog. A listener who is no more thoughtful than I am, however, will not perceive that I am speaking vaguely. In his own vagueness, he will, if he likes the position I seem to take, feel that I am successfully articulating our common belief: "Un fou trouve toujours un plus fou qui l'admire." If the listener does not sympathize with what I seem to be saying, he will be upset with me and express what seems to be another viewpoint. But in all this, neither his mind nor mine is truly active; we are expressing something like emotional attitudes rather than distinct opinions. There is no real argument, only a collision of half-formed thoughts.

Vagueness should be distinguished from two other failures in regard to truth and categorial objects: ignorance and error. In ignorance we simply do not try to articulate the categorial objects in question; we just are silent about the issue. We do not pretend to think about it, and we do not seem to be thinking. When we are in error, we formulate an opinion about something, and we do so explicitly, but it turns out to be incorrect. Our opinion would not stand up if we went to the things we are talking about and tried to experience and register them as we state them to be. Our propositions would be disconfirmed. In such error, we do achieve distinct thinking, and we do articulate a categorial object, but the thinking and the object are false. We must have overcome vagueness and reached distinctness if we are to be incorrect.

Vagueness comes between ignorance and error. It is inchoate thinking. It is an attempt to think that does not quite get there, but it uses the words that generally indicate thinking, and hence it dissimulates, however unintentionally. The words are paraded and give the impression of thought, but there is insufficient thought behind them.

In some cases, it is possible for the speaker who begins with vagueness to think through the things he is saying and to articulate the states of affairs and judgments that he wishes to declare. In this case, the speaker has moved from vagueness to *distinctness*. He successfully achieves the categorial objects he was striving to constitute. He now thinks distinctly. He now presents the state of affairs or the judgment he was earlier trying to present.

When the speaker goes from vagueness to distinctness, he may find that the judgment he finally achieves is indeed the same one he had been vaguely stating; the judgment is the same in the two modes of presentation, the vague and the distinct. But he may also find that the distinct judgment is not the same as the vague one; rather, he may find that the vague judgment harbored contradictions within itself, and now that distinctness has been achieved, the contradictions come to the fore; they had been hidden, precisely because of the vagueness. Thus, the possibility of logical contradiction or consistency demands that we have brought the judgment to distinctness, that we have distinctly articulated it. Until a judgment is brought to distinctness, we cannot really say whether it is true or false, or even consistent or inconsistent with itself and other judgments, because we do not yet really know what the judgment is. It does not yet exist as a distinct meaning, one that could be true or false, consistent or inconsistent. We have to know what someone is saying before we can determine whether what he says is true or false.

Vagueness can harbor inconsistency, but it can also harbor *incoherence*. Inconsistency means that one part of what we say contradicts another part in regard to formal logical structure: we say both "*S* is *p*" and "*S* is not *p*." Incoherence, on the other hand, means that the content, as opposed to the form, of our judgments is not properly assembled. It means that we are using content words that make no sense when they are put together: we might, for example, say that, literally, the nation is a big family, or that a political constitution guarantees a job for everyone, or that the brain knows who is coming through the door (it is the person, not the brain, that knows things). Contradiction deals with the form of judgments, incoherence deals with their content, and both can occur in the fog of vagueness. Words mean things, but it is possible to put the words together in such a way that the whole does not mean one thing. Some parts of the whole "speak against" other parts, or some parts are not blended properly with other parts (features that belong to families are blended with nations, features of the whole person are blended with one of the person's organic parts).

Everyone is vague at some time, and there is nothing regrettable about that. We have to start with vagueness when we enter into a new domain of thinking. Ideas that come to mind are almost always vague at first and ask to be brought to distinctness, when the inconsistencies and incoherences in the idea will be filtered out. The student beginning mathematics is usually quite vague about the categorial objects he is articulating. If he is a good student, he will move on to distinctness. Some people can get to distinctness more easily and more quickly than others. Some people can never get out of vagueness in certain domains, while other people can hardly ever get out of vagueness in any domain. They just do not think clearly and distinctly, and yet they use language, which might make it seem to others that they are thinking properly. A chatterbox is a living example of vagueness. Public opinion is awash with vagueness, demanding contradictory things from public figures. What "they" say, what "on dit," what "man sagt," is notoriously vague, but it is still the starting point for authentic thinking. Our thoughts, the categorial objects we constitute, do not come finished and polished from the start.

Finally, our treatment of vagueness has dealt with its appearance in speech and thought, but vagueness also occurs in action. Someone who chronically speaks without thinking is likely to act in the same manner, lurching from one half-baked move to another and making a royal mess of things. In this case, it is deliberation and choice that are pervaded by the inconsistency and incoherence that vagueness brings. The spectacle of such conduct, whether in personal, institutional, or political affairs, arouses either pity or grief in the observer, depending on how he is affected by the action in question.

CATEGORIAL OBJECTS AND HUMAN INTELLIGENCE

Instead of closing this chapter with the theme of vagueness, which is a deficiency in human thinking, let us end on a more positive note and consider some of the excellences of the domain of categorial objects.

Human language differs from animal sounds because it contains syntax. Human language contains sound, but its sound is structured by phonemic patterns and by grammatical particles, inflections, and placements. It is the grammatical ordering of language that makes the linguistic sign system amenable to human control, that makes it a system of such exquisite complexity and refinement, and that lets it become the vehicle for the exercise of truth. Syntax elevates animal sounds into human discourse. In phenomenology, the syntactic elements of language have been called the *syncategorematic* parts of language, because they "come along with" the expressions that merely name objects and features, the *categorematic* parts of speech.

The syntactic parts of language obviously serve to link words. They are the grammar of a language. This linguistic work, however, is not all that they do. They also function in intentionality: the syntax of language is related to the way things can present themselves to us, to the way we can intend and articulate them. Syntactic parts of language serve to express the combinatorics of presentation, the way things can be presented to us in various part–whole relationships. Phenomenology does not just consider the linguistic role of grammar, as structural linguistics does; it also relates syntax to the activity of being truthful, to evidencing.

The nonsyntactic elements of language (terms such as "tree" and "green") simply name things and features, but the syntactic elements express the manner in which the things and features are displayed. The syntactic parts of expressions have objective correlates. In the statement, "The tree is green," the terms "tree" and "green" obviously name things and features that can be given to perception, but the copula "is" also has objective reference, because the statement does not just present the tree and the green color: it presents the tree's being green, or the state of affairs that the tree is green. The "being featured" of the tree corresponds to the copula "is." The copula "is" does not just link the words "tree" and "green," but also allows the tree's being green to be intended by us, even in its absence. To take another example, if we were to conjoin two terms, such as "pepper and salt," the grammatical particle "and" would correspond to the "being together" of the two items: the two are not just individually presented, but presented as being together, as taken as one.

Thus, the way things can be articulated for us, the way they can be intended in either presence or absence, the way they "fall apart" and "fall into wholes" for us, is made possible by the syntax of language, and the grammatical genius of each language provides a style of presentation that is distinctive to that language. Phenomenology relates syntax to the modes of presentation.

When we register a categorial object, we move from the continuity of perception to the more abrupt, discontinuous presence of intellected objects, with wholes and parts being explicitly recognized. We present higher-level, categorial objects, and such objects come in discrete packets. There are many of them, expressed in the many statements we make, and they are all interrelated. The objects given to intellection form a network. We document each categorial object when we express it; we put ourselves on record, we state precisely this or that. We say one thing, then another, then yet another, but as we move on to other statements the ones we made earlier remain in force, and what we say subsequently has to be consistent with what we said before. The connections among all these categorial objects are logical and not just associative. We can ask whether this categorial object or sense is consistent with that one; we can call upon the speaker to avoid contradiction (that is, to avoid saying something "against" what he said before). We can also call upon the speaker to explain what he has articulated, to give reasons and clarifications for it. The categorial domain is the space of reasons, and phenomenology explores the intricate intentionalities that constitute it.

When we succeed in lifting the objects we experience into the precision of categorial objects, we do not fragment them into pieces disconnected from one another. Rather, we make available a more profound continuity among things. Instead of a perceptual flow we are given interrelated states of affairs and, behind them, the sense of a world or a cosmos. The categorial domain brings a new, articulated sense of the whole; it is not the case that only the precategorial is holistic. Precision and distinctness in thinking do not atomize things, but yield a much keener appreciation of the whole picture, allowing us to apprehend the forest precisely because we apprehend trees.

Syntactic parts of speech express categorial forms, and in doing so they help express the way the world presents itself to us, but they also serve another function. They also serve to *indicate* or to signal that the speaker is carrying out the acts of thinking that constitute the categorial objects. They signal that the speaker is speaking and voicing an opinion, and not just groaning or burping. When we listen to someone speak, we hear more than sounds; we also hear the grammatical ordering of sounds. By virtue of this encoding we have the world and the things in it expressed to us, and we also have given to us the presence of a speaker who takes responsibility for their being expressed in this way. Language and syntax are used to reveal a world and the things in it, but they also, in a different way, reveal the speaker who is using the language and syntax at the moment. They reveal a transcendental ego, a responsible agent of intentionality and evidence.

In this chapter we have considered categorial intentionality, the form of intending that supervenes on the more basic forms of perception and its variants. Categorial intending is the domain of reason or logos. It establishes categorial objects, objects that are pervaded by syntax, with parts and wholes explicitly registered. Categorial objects are found on the ontological side of things (states of affairs, things, attributes) and also on the apophantic side (judgments, propositions, senses, subjects, predicates). Verification moves between these two sides, between the ontological and the apophantic. States of affairs and judgments have to be brought to distinctness before they can be confirmed or disconfirmed, and even before they can be understood (indeed, to bring them to distinctness is precisely to understand them). They are brought to distinctness out of the matrix of vagueness, which is a sort of basement and source for categoriality.

Our attention has been directed to categorial objects, but, as we have noted, the domain of the categorial also involves the emergence of a responsible speaker. It requires a self elevated beyond the self constituted in perception, memory, and imagination. Categorial objects involve categorial activity, which requires in turn an agent of truth who carries it out. It is to this self, the transcendental ego, that we now turn.

8

Phenomenology of the Self

The things we experience present themselves as identities within manifolds of appearance. Our own self, our "ego," also establishes and presents itself to us as an identity in a manifold of appearances, but the manifold in which we are presented to ourselves is different from those in which things are presented. We never show up to ourselves in the world as just one more thing; we stand out, each of us, as central, as the agents of our intentional life, as the one who has the world and the things in it given to him. Our power of disclosure, our being the dative of manifestation for things that appear, introduces us into the life of reason and the human way of being.

There is a marvelous ambiguity to the ego: on the one hand, it is an ordinary part of the world, one of the many things that inhabit it. It occupies space, endures through time, has physical and psychic features, and interacts causally with other things in the world: if it falls, it falls like any other body; if it is pushed, it topples over like any other thing; if it is treated with chemicals, it reacts like any living organism; if light rays hit its visual organs, it reacts electronically, chemically, and psychologically. "I" am a material, organic, and psychological thing. If we were to take the self simply as one of the things in the world, we would be treating it as what can be called the *empirical ego.*

On the other hand, this very same self can also be played off against the world: it is the center of disclosure to whom the world and everything in it manifest themselves. It is the agent of truth, the one responsible for judgments and verifications, the perceptual and cognitive "owner" of the world. When considered in this manner, it is no longer simply a part of the world; it is what is called the *transcendental ego.*

The empirical and the transcendental egos are not two entities; they are one and the same being, but considered in two ways. Moreover, it is not just our manner of considering the ego that introduces the distinction between the empirical and the transcendental; it is not just our adoption of an empirical or a transcendental stance that establishes the duality in the self. Rather, the ego exists in this double manner. We can consider it in this dual way only because it enjoys the kind of being that allows it to be so considered. We could not attribute a transcendental ego to a tree or a cat.

The ambiguity of the ego consists in the fact that something that is a part of the world can stand over against the world, and even "possess" or be correlated with the world. The ego seems to be both a part and yet not a part of the world. This is not to say that the ego could be detached from the world, that it could be found or even imagined to exist without a world. Even as transcendental, the ego's intentional character requires that it have things and a world correlated with itself. The ego and the world are moments to one another. However, when the ego is considered as having a world, it is no longer just a part of it. It is correlated with the world as the dative to whom the world is "given."

There is a strong tendency to reduce the transcendental ego to the empirical. When we deal with human cognition, we tend to want to treat it as merely one more item in the causal exchanges that go on in the world, on a par with things simply engaged in mechanical, chemical, and biological causation. Thus, the generation of knowledge in the mind is often taken to be just like the generation of chemical changes in the body. We think we can give an exhaustive explanation of what knowledge is by giving an account of what happens, say, in the brain and nervous system when we come to know things. Many writers in cognitive science, for example, try to reduce knowledge and other rational achievements to merely physical brain states. To try to handle knowledge in this way could be called *biologism* or biological reductionism.

Another kind of reductionism, a more sophisticated kind, is the psychological; it is called *psychologism.* From its beginning in the early twentieth century, phenomenology attacked the psychologistic interpretation of truth, reason, and the ego; psychologism was the foil against which phenomenology originally defined itself. Nevertheless, paradoxically enough, many people mistakenly regard phenomenology itself as a form of psychologism.

What is meant by "psychologism"? Psychologism is the claim that things like logic, truth, verification, evidence, and reasoning are simply empirical activities of our psyche. In psychologism, reason and truth are naturalized. Laws of truth and logic are taken to be high-level empirical laws that describe how our minds function; they are not seen as constituents of the very meaning of truth and reason. For example, in psychologism, the principle of noncontradiction would be taken simply as a statement of how our minds work; it would state how we happen to arrange our ideas; it would not be seen as governing how things have to reveal themselves. It would tell us about the habits, whether innate or acquired, of our mind, not about how things have to be and how they have to disclose themselves. Also, the fact that human languages require syntax would be presented as simply a historical fact about human beings and their psychological development. Psychologism, along with biologism, treats meaning and truth as a matter of empirical fact, not as a dimension that underlies and hence transcends the empirical, not as a dimension that belongs to the being of things.

Psychologism is the most common and the most insidious form of reductionism. Biologism follows closely behind it. Once we reduce laws of meaning, truth, and logic to psychological laws, we will be inclined to reduce them one step farther to the biological structures that underlie our psychology. Thus, in biologism the fact that human language essentially involves syntax would be taken as caused simply by the way the brain is wired and the way it has evolved. It would not be based on the fact that things must be articulated when they are disclosed. The entire explanation for syntax would be brain based, with no regard paid to the way things exist and present themselves.

A phenomenological approach, on the other hand, would obviously agree that the wiring of the brain is one of the causes for syntax in language, as well as for perception, categorial intentions, and knowledge and science, but it would then claim that one must also provide an explanation of another kind based on the things that appear. Besides looking to the wiring in the brain, we must also look to the fact that things can be distinguished into wholes and parts, that they can be perceived and pictured, that essentials and accidentals can be distinguished in them when they present themselves to us. This second kind of explanation is different, obviously, from the kind of explanation that studies the wiring in the brain and our psychic dispositions; it may be hard to get clear on what kind of explanation this second kind is, but it cannot be dispensed with.

Phenomenology has waged a heroic struggle against psychologism from the beginning. It tries to show that the activity of achieving meaning, truth, and logical reasoning is not just a feature of our psychological or biological makeup, but that it enters into a new domain, a domain of rationality, a domain that goes beyond the psychological. It is not easy to make this distinction. The ego is indeed both empirical and transcendental, and one can limit one's consideration to the empirical side of things. Meaning and truth also have their empirical dimensions, but they are more than just empirical things. To treat them as simply psychological is to leave out something important. However, it is not easy to show what that extra something is.

WHAT IS THE TRANSCENDENTAL EGO?

We need now to consider the nature of the rational domain and how it differs from the biological and the psychological, how the transcendental domain differs from the empirical. We can do so by examining human knowledge and human virtue, both of which occur in the transcendental domain. The essential point to be made is that when we exercise our rationality, when we act as agents of truth and meaning, we become involved in activities that cannot be adequately treated from a merely empirical point of view.

Consider the natural sciences. Psychologism would claim that reasoning, argument, knowledge, and science are merely a matter of our psychological makeup. The sciences of physics, biology, and mathematics, for example, are said to be ways in which our organism adapts to its environment; they are not seen as telling us the truth about anything. The very idea of truth becomes problematic in psychologism; the judgments or propositions we make are ultimately just organic or psychic responses, not really all that different from the beating of the heart, the digestion in the stomach, or a mood of elation or depression. Even in the sciences, according to psychologism, we do not disclose what is; we just react.

In contrast, phenomenology would insist that even though we are biological and psychological creatures, even though our perceptions and judgments require a brain and nervous system and subjective reactions, when we get into the activity of judging, verifying, and reasoning, we formulate meanings and achieve presentations that can be distinguished from our biological and psychological way of being. They can be communicated to others, who may have subjective feelings that are very different from ours; they can be recorded, they can be used as premises in arguments, and they can be confirmed or disconfirmed. They have a kind of subsistence. They can be shown to be true or false in themselves, quite apart from our subjectivity. It is the meanings themselves that are consistent or contradictory; it is the judgments themselves that are true or false. Meanings and judgments belong to what can be called the "space" of reasons, and we enter into that space when we carry out categorial activities. Thus, besides being biological, psychological, and subjective beings, we also enter as agents into the space of reasons, we enter into the domain of the rational, and when we do so we "go beyond," we transcend our subjectivity; we act as transcendental egos.

Consider also the virtue of justice. As a child develops into a mature person, he becomes a rational being. He reaches a stage in which he can understand an argument and act according to its conclusions. He can work with ideas and not just with inclinations and feelings. In the early stages of life, the child is largely a bundle of tendencies and impulses, with only an inchoate rationality. As time goes by, the child begins to appreciate that he has to see himself as only one among many, that he cannot simply prefer his own satisfactions all the time. He has to see that others are there, and that he has to give them their due. In this way, a sense of justice arises in the child. Early stages of this sense are present even among small children, who are quick to judge that this or that action "is not fair."

Two things are needed for the development of the virtue of justice. The person in question must, through guidance and repeated activity, become morally virtuous, but in addition, and as a deeper condition of possibility, the person must also have become a rational agent. He must have entered the space of reasons and become able to exercise categorial activities. The emergence of a sense of justice requires the presence of reason in the young person. It is through the power of reason that we can take an objective view of a situation and judge what is truly due to each person involved in it, ourselves included. The virtue of justice is the exercise of reason par excellence in practical matters. Other virtues also involve the development of reason, but justice does so to a greater degree, because it requires the ability to determine equalities, to say what is appropriately "the same" for myself and others.

Our entire moral and emotional life as human beings is made possible by the fact that we exercise rationality. A mature person is one who can listen to arguments about practical things, evaluate them, and act accordingly. Some people cannot do this. They dissolve into emotion or impulse; one cannot argue with them. When this occurs, whether it be a permanent or an intermittent state, the transcendental egos of such persons are diluted by vagueness. The categorial thinking that should enter into their conduct cannot prevail.

In both theoretical and practical matters, therefore, our transcendental ego is that part of us that is the agent of reason and truth. The transcendental ego is each of us taken as an agent of truth, as one who can responsibly declare what is the case. Besides being biological and psychological organisms, we are rational beings who belong to what Kant called the "kingdom of ends"; when we recognize ourselves as such, we treat ourselves as transcendental egos. Phenomenology attempts to describe what structural forms go into being a transcendental ego. Phenomenology is the exploration of the transcendental ego in all its intentional forms, along with the noematic correlates that are found as the targets of these intentionalities. Since our rationality is what makes us human, phenomenology is the exploration of ourselves in our humanity.

Philosophers have often had a too limited understanding of what makes us rational. They have taken our rationality as primarily the power to abstract universal concepts from particular experiences, the power to carry on syllogistic reasoning, and the power to have insight into self-evident truths. However, our rationality consists in far more than these abilities; it involves also the intentionalities by which we identify things in both their presence and their absence, the intentionalities by which we introduce syntax and part–whole compositions in what we experience, the specifically human ways of remembering, imagining, and anticipating, and the forms of evidence and verification that we can carry out. It also involves the intentionalities by which we are established as responsible moral agents. All these and many more forms of intentionality are as essential to us as rational agents as are the power to abstract universals and the power to reason syllogistically. All the structures described in this book are constituents of what it means to be a transcendental ego, a responsible agent of truth and verification. Phenomenology provides a much more ample description of what we are as datives of manifestation.

Indeed, one of the constituents of rationality is the ability to say "I," the power to use a certain sign design in a particular language to refer to ourselves specifically as using the language and making a truth claim at the moment we use the word. If I say something like, "I believe that the door is open," my use of the term "I" does three things: first, it simply refers to me, it picks me out as the one being spoken about; second, it signifies me as the one speaking the English sentence; but third, it signifies me as the agent of truth for the particular declaration that follows. I signal myself as the one responsible for the categorial articulation, and the truth claim in it, expressed by the sentence. Only a transcendental ego can say "I" in this way. It can use a language to say that it is asserting something in that language.

To help us understand the distinction between the empirical and the transcendental ego, let us develop an analogy between the ego and a chessman. Let us consider a chessman both outside and inside the game of chess. In one sense, a chess piece is a merely empirical thing. If I were to throw a rook on the table, I would be treating it as a simple thing in the world, an "empirical rook." Even if I were to move it from one square on the chessboard to another, I might still be treating it as an ordinary object: I might be taking it just as a colored piece of wood that is being moved ten inches away from me. However, if I were to take the piece as involved in the game of chess, as, say, setting up a checkmate, I would be treating it as a "transcendental rook," not merely as an empirical one. I would be treating it, and it would be acting, as a player in the game of chess. Analogously, my bodily organism is active as a transcendental ego when it plays according to the rules of reason and is engaged in the game of truth. The analogy would fit better, of course, if the rook somehow moved itself in the game of chess (instead of being moved by me), and if it could declare itself as moving. The transcendental ego can do all these things: it not only acts on its own initiative in the game of truth (which is the game of life), but also expresses itself as doing so.

Animals have consciousness, but they do not have transcendental egos. They may approach something like language and truth, but they do not enter fully into the space of reasons. If my dog does something "wrong" (he snaps at me or soils the carpet), I might do something to him there and then, but it would make no sense to come to him a month later and try to refer to that "action" or to an "opinion" he voiced earlier. But it does make sense for you to complain about what I said last year or what I did last month, because I spoke and acted within the space of reasons; I made a move in the game of truth, and what I said or did is documented and subsists as such a move even beyond the situation in which it occurred. I can act as a transcendental ego, but a nonhuman animal cannot.

PUBLICNESS OF THE TRANSCENDENTAL EGO

The life of reason is a public thing. It is not enclosed in the solitude or privacy of a "sphere of consciousness." It is expressed in manifest conduct and achievements, in human beings who are walking around, talking to one another, examining scientific instruments, focusing a laser beam on a target, digging a trench at an archaeological site, writing a letter to a friend, trying to persuade someone to vote for a certain proposal. It is present in words, pictures, and flags. The life of reason is as public as a field goal in a football game or a technical knockout in a boxing match. An archaeological dig or a political argument cannot be explained without involving terms like "tools," "words," "statements," "reasons," and "truth," and such terms refer to public behavior and not to private, internal episodes. It is the rational animal, not the solitary awareness, not the large, hollow sphere of consciousness, that enters into rational life.

The public life of reason is lived by the transcendental ego, who is also a public entity. When we talk about the transcendental ego, we may be tempted to imagine it as a wispy sort of thing lodged within us, a speck located somewhere in the middle of our cortex, living a secret life. Such an interpretation would be incorrect, and to counter it I would like to provide a more concrete picture of what the transcendental ego is.

As I write these pages, it is the month of November, and people are recalling the armistice, the end of the First World War, which occurred on the eleventh hour of the eleventh day of the eleventh month of the year 1918. Stories about the war are being presented on television. In one of them, photographs were shown of three young British men who went to the war and did not return. Consider one of these pictures, an image of a twenty-one-year-old man. He was once alive, he was photographed in uniform, and he was killed in the war. A sense of sadness surrounds the picture, the kind we project onto images of those we know have died in combat, during that war or others; the eyes in the picture seem ready to be closed.

What was lost when that young man died? Not just a biological life, but the life of reason that would have taken place in him and in his surroundings had he filled out his three-score-and-ten. This life of reason would have been not only the true and false utterances he might have made during those years, but also the deliberations, choices, and human exchanges that he would have carried out. What he would have done as a responsible agent of truth vanished with the extinction of his organic life. The way the world would have seemed to those eyes and ears never came to pass. His death was not just the reshuffling of chemical elements, or the termination of a living organism, but the conclusion of a human life, a life in which reason illuminates the things around it and permits moral interventions. The self that identified itself behind the face in the picture, the one that had assembled memories and anticipations and experienced itself in them, ceased to be a dative for the way things appear in the whole we call the world. What was loved by those who loved him was not just a pleasant companion, not just a complicated version of an animal, but someone who could enter into a kind of life that a mere animal could not: someone responsible for the truth of what he said and did, someone who could love in return because he could appreciate another as worthy of being loved.

The ego in that young man, his transcendental ego, was not an entity distinct from him; it was that man as a player in the game of truth, one who could claim and confirm, quote and infer, deceive and unmask, deliberate and decide. The ego is not a separate thing, but the man as capable of living a rational kind of life. It is the entity that can say "I" and take responsibility for what is said. Furthermore, the transcendental ego is not just the agent of science; it is not just "intellect" making inferences and constructing hypotheses; it is not merely a calculating engine. Besides being the agent of science, the transcendental ego is also the agent of truth in human conduct, where actions are free and responsible because they are the outcome of intelligent assessments. The "I" that can say, "I think this or that," is the same one that can say, "I intend to do this or that," and the same one that others can call on for an explanation for what "you" did. The ability to say "I" and to intervene in the world through a responsible act depends on the organic life that underlies thinking, the organic life in which the life of thinking is embodied, but it is not just that organic life: it enters into the space of reasons and the kingdom of ends.

And if the picture of someone who died before his time may, by the very absence of a future, give us an impression of what the responsible ego is, the picture of someone not yet born, someone who is almost all future, with even a name still to come, may serve the same purpose. We have seen pictures of the early stages of life, during fetal development, when the eyes look like spots and the mouth is speechless and immersed in amniotic fluid. The mouth that opens and closes silently at that time is the same one that will be used to say "I" later on, and the early sense of self that is being established in the synesthesia of touch and hearing and bodily motion is the same that will have memories and project actions in the years after the baby is born. The transcendental ego, the dative of manifestation, is already there, establishing the basis for its future categorial activity and moral interventions. The early self is already something of a player in the game of truth.

Thus, both the mind and the transcendental ego are public, and the life they live is public. An act of the agent of truth, such as a judgment, is in principle a public act. It can be compared to a salute, which can only occur between two or more people. A judgment is a move in the game of truth, and it involves, in principle, an agent, receivers, and onlookers. It does not occur merely inside us. Even a perception is more like a salute than like a stomach ache; it too is an initial move in the game of truth, disposing us to make a claim, to discredit what someone else has said, or to take some other step in the human conversation. The acts of the transcendental ego are as public as the body that is involved in making them. They are actual or potential interventions, not just private thoughts.

To bring out the publicness of the transcendental ego, it is helpful to remember that there is also a "transcendental you." That is, the transcendental ego can be recognized not only by himself but also by others, and when he is so recognized he is called a "you." However, for some reason, the Latin *tu*, as a counterpart to *ego*, does not sound appropriate here.

THE EGO IN THE PHENOMENOLOGICAL ATTITUDE

We note that all the activities of the transcendental ego we have been considering are done in the natural attitude. They are exercises in the achievement of truth, responsible operations of reason. The ego that is the agent for all these activities is the ego that has a world and continues to sustain his underlying world belief. When we enter into the phenomenological attitude, we disengage from the natural attitude and contemplate and describe the transcendental ego and all its achievements, all its intentionalities, and we also contemplate the special manifolds through which it is constituted as the transcendental ego. We describe how the ego establishes and presents itself, to itself and to others, as an agent of manifestation.

This move into phenomenological reflection "stretches" the ego even farther than do its activities in the natural attitude. When we enter into phenomenological reflection, we become agents of truth in a new, philosophical way. We make truth claims from a new perspective, one radically different from all the perspectives that function within the natural attitude. We can say "I" from a new angle, with a new sense. And yet, the philosophical self who views the natural ego is not another entity, not somebody else; it is the same "me," but now stretched into a new form of reflection.

It is *not* the case, furthermore, that the transcendental ego comes into play only within the phenomenological attitude. It is not the case that only the philosophically reflective ego is the transcendental ego. The transcendental ego is already active in the natural attitude. Any achievement of truth, any exercise of rationality, is the work of the transcendental ego. Any categorial intentions that raise the issue of truth are the work of the transcendental ego. The transcendental ego achieves truth in the natural attitude, but this naive achievement of truth calls for a completion in philosophy, which theorizes truth. The truth achieved in the natural attitude is incomplete because it does not contemplate itself. Philosophy, carried out in the phenomenological attitude, brings to a new level the manifestations achieved in the prephilosophical life. In the natural attitude we have a world, we exercise rationality, we identify across presence and absence, we confirm and disconfirm, and we also lie, deceive, and fall into error; but in the phenomenological attitude we clarify what it is to do all these things.

It would be helpful to outline three stages in the identification of the ego.

(1) In the first stage, an identity is achieved for the agent of the intentional acts of perception and its variants: an identity of the ego occurs between, say, the ego living in a situation here and now and the ego displaced in remembering, imagining, and anticipating. For example, the remembering and the remembered ego, as we have seen in Chapter 5, are one and the same.

(2) In the second stage, a heightened identity is achieved for the agent of categorial activity. The person who syntactically articulates what he perceives or remembers does more than just perceive and remember; he brings about categorial objects, with all the dimensions of responsibility and verification that they imply. The ego that actualizes itself at this stage is able to refer to itself when it explicitly takes a position about some matter of truth or manifestation and says things like, "I know that p" or "I suspect that p." The ego that emerges here is obviously the same one that emerged in memory, imagining, and anticipation, but it now emerges with greater responsibility and epistemic vigor. It now takes positions and has opinions that it can vouch for. Obviously, it could not have come to be an ego on this level had it not first consolidated its identity on the first level, and psychological disruptions on the lower level can impede activities on the higher. Emotional disturbances can undermine rational thinking.

(3) In the third stage, a further identity is achieved when the ego does not just develop more and more opinions or scientific truths, but reflects on what it is to have opinions and to pursue and verify

scientific claims. Now the ego "hovers over" all the intentionalities in the first and second stages and analyzes them. It also takes possession of its own self in a new way; it acquires a responsibility as an agent of truth that is different from the responsibilities it had in the second stage.

We will examine the special character of phenomenological truth, and the responsibility associated with it, in Chapter 13. At present, it is sufficient to have noted how the sense of the ego or the self develops in these various stages.

THE EGO AND CORPOREALITY

Even as transcendental, as an agent of truth, the ego exists corporeally. The way the ego experiences its own body is different from the way it experiences other things in the world, and yet the body is also a thing in the world and is presented as such. We experience our own bodies from the inside and from the outside. Furthermore, we hold sway over our own bodies in a manner radically different from the control we have over other things in the world. What are some of the features of the ego's corporeality?

The peculiarities of how we experience our own bodies are shown especially in the sense of touch. (1) When I touch one part of my body with another (I touch my left elbow with my right hand), the part being touched is being treated like any other object I might touch in the world. The touching hand is where my transcendental ego, in its perception and categorial articulation, is active at the moment, and its attention is directed toward another part of myself, the elbow ("My elbow seems to be getting swollen"). (2) Even at this stage, however, the touched part, the elbow, feels the pressure of the hand, so I am also perceiving, somewhat passively, from that direction as well, as I sense how it feels to have the elbow rubbed. (3) But then, the touched part can become the actively touching one: even as my hand touches the elbow, I can "reverse direction" and begin to notice how the hand feels to the elbow. However implausibly, the elbow can become the actively perceiving organ. I then touch the hand through the elbow and begin to move the elbow as the touching part. Thus, the touched and touching roles can be reversed; the transcendental ego can work in either direction.

Only in my own body, and only in regard to the sense of touch, which is the most basic of all the senses, is this reversal possible. An embrace of another person may be an analogue of this, and it may also be an attempt to approximate the unity we have with ourselves (we may be said metaphorically to become one body with those we embrace), but it could never really become the same. Shakespeare reminds us of this ambiguity of touch when in *Troilus and Cressida* (IV.5) he has Cressida ask, "In kissing, do you render or receive?"

The curious reversibility found in the sense of touch shows that even as transcendental egos, even as agents of truth, we are partitioned out into a body. Furthermore, there are other ways of experiencing the body, all related to the sense of touch, that help establish our corporeality: the sense we have of our position in space, the experience of the disposition of our limbs, our sense of balance and the resistance we feel to the pull of gravity, and the pressure we feel from the chair or the floor. Our felt corporeality sets up a place within which the transcendental ego exercises all its intentionalities, from perception and its variants to categorial articulations to phenomenological reflection. All our seeing, hearing, and tasting take place within the space of the body, and our memories are stored there as well. All the intentional activities, whether perceptual or categorial, occur within the space marked out by the top of the head and the soles of the feet, our front and back, and our right and left sides and arms.

The spatiality of the body is not only tactile, but also mobile. We hold sway over the parts of our body and can move them directly; if we wish to move other things, we can do so only by first moving parts of ourselves (we lift something only by lifting our hands and arms, but we do not have to move anything else in order to raise our hands and arms). The parts of the body can move in relation to one another, and the body itself moves through the space of the world. But we do not move only to introduce motion into other objects; even our perceptions, and hence our thinking, involve motions of some sort or other; we move around to see the other side of the cube, to get to a better spot to hear the violin, to get a better whiff of what is cooking; we move our fingers over the sandpaper to see which grade it is, and we roll the food over our tongue to appreciate its taste. Our vision requires motion: even a single eye can adjust its focus to the near and the far; two eyes together, with their slight convergences, give perspective and stereoscopic views; the head can be moved from side to side; and the motion of the whole body allows the eyes to range over all sides of the object being seen. In fact, points in objective space are established for us only when we are able to move around in space; if we were immobile, we could visually experience some surfaces as occluding others, but we could not get the sense of a fixed point around which things can circle.

Thus, there are many parts and wholes, many moments, in human sensibility, and they serve as a basis for the articulation of parts and wholes that occurs in categorial action. The several senses achieve identities through synesthesia, the recognition of a single object given through the various senses distributed throughout our own bodies. These varieties of sensible parts, both noetic and noematic, serve as manifolds through which objects become identified from more and more perspectives: the tree is seen, heard (in the wind), touched, smelled; we walk around it and climb it; we trim its branches and break off pieces of dead bark; and in all this, one and the same tree is registered in its identity and its many features.

This registration of the tree, moreover, is accomplished by the transcendental ego that perceives and articulates the tree, and while identifying trees and other things in the world, the ego also continuously identifies its own body over time as the privileged object "in" which it is living its life, the object that provides the ineluctable corporeal "here" that the ego can never flee. The way the body is "here" for me is different from the way any worldly place can be "here," even the most familiar and the most loved of all domiciles. Furthermore, as the ego identifies the things in the world and its own body, it also continuously identifies itself. It is the same ego that remembers itself climbing that tree twenty-five years ago, that anticipates seeing the same tree in snow next winter, and that imagines what the tree would look like if certain other trees were to be planted next to it.

One of the most interesting facets of our corporeality is the way our memories are stored in our body. Our identity as a transcendental ego is established through the displacements and identifications made in remembering: I here and now am the same one that I remember as being there and then in the memory that comes to mind. But the remembered parts of my life are not always active; they mostly remain latent and stored in my neural system, in the body that differentiates itself from my surroundings. Everything I have lived through is somehow there, and parts of it come to light now and then. While it remains stored it is purely chemical and organic, but when it is activated it becomes part of my transcendental life again. The ambiguity between the transcendental and the empirical ego is particularly prominent in regard to the latency of memories.

One of the tasks of phenomenology is to work out in detail, from the transcendental attitude, how our various senses and mobilities work to establish our own corporeality. I have sketched only a few of the descriptions that could be made. It should be mentioned that the structures of disclosure that present our bodies to ourselves are part of the same cognitive life that reaches to things like categorial thinking, exact science, formal logic, and mathematics. The one dative of manifestation is at work on all these levels of intentionality.

THE NONPUNCTUAL SELF

One of the complaints sometimes made concerning phenomenology is that it seems to substantialize the self, that it makes the ego into a kind of fixed point that escapes its own history, an "ego pole" that is self-contained, unambiguous, and unaffected by what it suffers and does. The self, it is said, is much more elusive, flexible, and engaged than this. But phenomenology does not punctualize the self: it recognizes the special identity of the self by describing the manifolds that are proper to it. The self recognized in phenomenology is not a point that stands behind or outside its perceptions, memories, imaginations, choices, and cognitive acts; rather, it is constituted as an identity through such achievements. It is actualized through delays and differences. It is, for example, one and the same as remembering and remembered. It comes "between" and not "behind" its present perceptions and its displacements. Also, the self is scattered through the lived body and is active in all its parts, not stationed behind it. It is identifiable in its unconscious and even its bodily life. The ego that is getting old in body and psyche identifies itself as the same that was once a child and once young (one's own baby pictures have something uncanny about them). The self is constituted in a distinct way even by seeing its own bodily reflections in a mirror, when it gets a view of itself as it is seen by others.

The same self that perceives, imagines, and remembers, and that is latent in the memories stored in its body, is also the one that says "I" and executes categorial actions. This self, this ego, also articulates situations (through its deliberation) and hence lays out possibilities of practical and moral conduct. It imaginatively displaces itself into the future perfect, estimating how it will be if it performs this or that action. In more theoretic matters, the self holds opinions about the way things are, and it maintains those opinions over against the views of other selves who may think otherwise. It listens to argument and may concede that it has been wrong, and when it does so it differentiates itself as it is now from itself as holding its earlier belief.

One of the most impressive manifolds through which the self is established is found in the phenomenon of quotation, when the ego uses its own voice to express the mind of someone else, to constitute categorial objects not as its own but as belonging to another: I here and now, with the world appearing to me as it does, can manifest through my own words a part of the world as it has appeared to someone else. A kind of duplication of the mind occurs, and along with it a duplication of the one who says "I." The self that comes to light in all these differences and activities is not a punctual thing, not an always completed identity, but one that is there only within a rich manifold of appearances and conduct. There is an identity of the self, but it is achieved precisely through decentering.

Still, the self does get punctuated at certain moments: if I am among a group of people who hold positions strongly different from mine, I stand out as "the one" who insists that this or that is indeed the case. I need ego strength to hold fast. If a serious situation builds up around me and it becomes evident that no one will act if I do not, then I am punctuated by the practical demand. All the lines converge on me, on me and on none other. I am highlighted in this way precisely because I am the prominent agent of the categorial activity, the agent of evidence and the owner of a claim of truth, whether in the theoretic or the practical order. I am such an agent not because I am a physical or psychological entity, but because I am someone who can say "I." Even these strong identifications of the self, however, are not absolute: even while my self is in the spotlight, I am still the same one who can remember and anticipate other situations, the one who holds sway within the body that is for the moment at the center of things, the one whose emotions may well up and overcome the decision I am trying to make.

The manifolds that are proper to the self are not realized in rocks, trees, or nonhuman animals. They are specific to the dative of manifestation, whose self is both flexible and yet continuously the same throughout its conscious lifetime. Phenomenology acknowledges the complexity and the mystery of the agent whose voice not only speaks about the way things are, but registers itself, when it says "I," precisely as speaking about them.

9

Temporality

Phenomenology has developed a highly articulated theory of time and temporal experience. The temporality that it describes plays an important role in the establishment of personal identity. Furthermore, it is in the domain of temporality that phenomenology approaches what could be called the first principles of the things that it examines. Time pervades all the things, both noematic and noetic, that are discussed in phenomenology, and the description of the phenomenological "origin" of time gets to a kind of philosophical center.

LEVELS OF TEMPORALITY

Three levels of temporal structure can be distinguished.

1. The first is *world time*, the time of clocks and calendars. It can also be called *transcendent* or *objective time*. This is the time that belongs to worldly processes and events. When we say that a dinner lasted two hours, or that Mary returned two days before Doris, or that the overture precedes the opera, we arrange such things and events in world time. Such time can be compared to the spatiality of the world, the geometric extension that things possess and the local relatedness that they have with one another. Like such space, objective time is public and verifiable; we can use a clock to measure exactly how long a process takes, and we will all agree on the measurement. The time being measured is located in the world, in the common space we all inhabit.

2. The second level is *internal time*. It can also be called *immanent* or *subjective time*. This kind of time belongs to the duration and sequence of mental acts and experiences, the events of conscious life. Intentional acts and experiences follow one another, and we can also call back certain prior experiences through memory. If I

remember seeing the play last night, I now reenact the perceptions I had then. The way my intentions and feelings are temporally ordered, both in regard to one another and in regard to my present experiences, takes place in internal time. Such immanent temporality can be compared to the bodily spatiality that we experience "from the inside." There are sequences in internal time, since one activity or experience can be before, after, or concurrent with another, but such sequences and durations are not measured by world time, no more than the felt internal "distance" between my elbow and my wrist, or between my chest and my stomach, can be measured by a yardstick. I do experience one conscious event as following or preceding another, but I could not "time" the sequence the way I time someone running a race. Internal time is not public, but private.

3. One might think that the two levels of time we have distinguished would exhaust the possible forms of time. One might think that it is enough to distinguish between objective time and subjective time. However, a third level must be added to these two, that of the *consciousness of internal time*. This is a step beyond the second level. The second level is inner temporality, but this third level is the *awareness of* or the *consciousness of* such internal temporality. In other words, the second level alone is not enough to account for its own self-awareness; we must introduce a third level to account for what we experience on the second. This third level enjoys a special kind of "flow," one different from those in transcendent and internal time. This third level, however, does not require the introduction of yet another level beyond itself.

The third level thus achieves a kind of closure and completeness. No further levels need to be posited beyond it. In phenomenology, this third level, with the special flow that occurs in it, is an absolute. It is the domain in which the first beginning of things as phenomena is reached. It does not point beyond itself to anything more basic. It is the ultimate context, the final horizon, the bottom line. It provides the setting for all the other more particular things and events that are analyzed in phenomenology, and it does not in turn presuppose any more ultimate context. It founds everything else but is not founded upon anything. The domain of internal time consciousness is, in phenomenology, the origin of the deepest distinctions and identities, those that are presupposed by all the others that occur in our experience. It is also, obviously, a domain about which it is very difficult to speak, because it requires a transformation of the vocabulary that is geared first and foremost to worldly objects. However, if we make use of the forms of parts and wholes, identity and manifolds, and presence and absence, we may be able to express more clearly the issues that arise in this domain.

Before approaching the vexing issues of internal time consciousness, however, let us say a word about the interaction between transcendent and immanent time, between the first and second levels of temporality that we distinguished at the beginning of this chapter. We might think that objective time is the most basic, because worldly duration would go on even if we, with our subjectivity, ceased to exist. As a phenomenon, however, objective time is dependent on immanent time: level 1 is dependent on level 2. Worldly things can be measured by clocks and calendars, and can be experienced as enduring, only because we experience a succession of mental activities in our subjective life. If we did not anticipate and remember, we could not organize the processes that occur in the world into temporal patterns. When we try to give a phenomenological analysis of world time, we must mention the structures of immanent time as a condition for such time. The display of objective time occurs to us only because we possess subjective, immanent time. The noematic structure of world time thus depends on the noetic structures of internal time. As we look down on intentionality from our perch in the phenomenological attitude, therefore, we see world time as correlated with internal time. Transcendent time is founded, as a phenomenon, on immanent time.

Of course, as living organisms we are caught up in objective time. You became sunburned after staying three hours in the sun; I could not think clearly after staying all afternoon in a stuffy room; she is late for an appointment. Like all objects, we are subject to the causal effects that operate in the world. But we are not just things in the world; we also are datives of manifestation or transcendental egos, and as such we stand over against the world and have it appearing to us, and the temporal flow of our conscious experiences is a condition for the appearing of the world and the things in it. The paradoxical relationship of the self as both a part of the world and the one who has a world comes to the fore again in regard to temporality: the internal flow of consciousness is nested within the processes going on in the world, but it also stands over against the world and provides the noetic structures that allow the world to appear. We find ourselves living in both objective and subjective time. The dative of manifestation, the transcendental ego, is not a single and static point; it involves a process that goes on in time, but in its own internal temporality, not in the objective temporality of clock and calendar.

Now, if internal time is a condition for the appearance of objective time, the third level of temporality, the consciousness of internal time, is in its turn a condition for the appearance of internal time.

THE PROBLEM OF INTERNAL TIME CONSCIOUSNESS

Let us explore the issue of internal time consciousness. The internal temporality that is played off against world time is, as we have said, not the final kind of time; it is not the final context. We are not left with just the objective stream of time and the subjective stream correlated with it. Rather, the stream of immanent time calls for something more basic upon which it is founded. This more basic something is the domain of internal time consciousness. The three levels can be schematized as shown in Figure 1.

Internal time consciousness is, so to speak, "more immanent" than immanent time. It constitutes the temporality of the activities that occur in our conscious life, such as the perceptions, imaginations, rememberings, and sensible experiences that we have: it allows such inner objects to appear as temporally extended and ordered. However, these intentions themselves are just the presentation of the things that they target: they are the perceptions, imag-

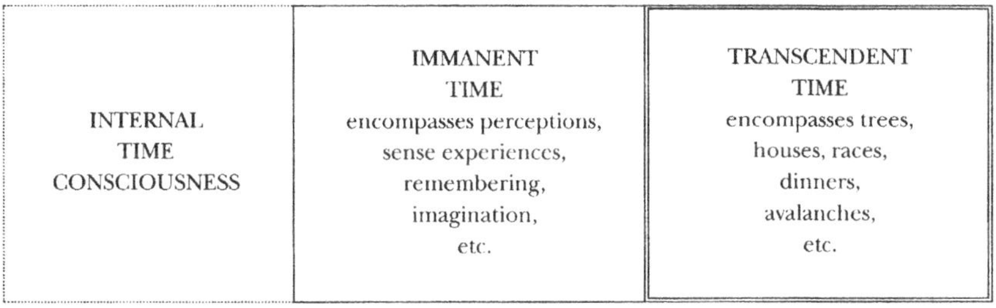

INTERNAL TIME CONSCIOUSNESS	IMMANENT TIME encompasses perceptions, sense experiences, remembering, imagination, etc.	TRANSCENDENT TIME encompasses trees, houses, races, dinners, avalanches, etc.

Figure 1

inings, and categorial intendings of the objects and processes in the world. Consequently, the effect of internal time consciousness extends to such transcendent objects and to their transcendent time as well. Internal time consciousness constitutes not only the internal temporality of our conscious life, but the objective temporality of worldly events. Internal time consciousness is the core for the temporality of all other forms of intentional constitution.

All these claims may seem rather bombastic. They may well seem somewhat improbable and contrived. They seem to imply that internal time consciousness is like a Neoplatonic source of being from which both subjective experience and the things in the world emanate. Internal time consciousness seems to be given a kind of metaphysical priority over everything else. Is it not rather speculative and extravagant to endow it with such powers? How can such a hidden section of the world, something so tiny and so internal that it is even more immanent than our intentional acts, have such a powerful effect on the being of things? Phenomenology seems to go off into artificial constructions when it enters into this domain; it does not seem to be faithfully describing what appears to us.

The phenomenological description of internal time consciousness is indeed an unusual doctrine. Some of its terminology seems to be excessively internal; it seems to say that at the core of our being we are locked into a kind of solitary confinement that is even more private than the subjectivity reached through the transcendental reduction. The rhetoric and vocabulary of this issue of temporality do seem disturbing at first. However, before we dismiss the doctrine, we should examine what it has to say about our experience of time. There may be more here than meets the casual glance.

THE STRUCTURE OF THE LIVING PRESENT

When we try to explain how we experience temporal objects, we are usually tempted to say that we have a series of "nows" presented to us, one after the other. We tend to say that temporal experience is very much like a film being run, with one exposure (one presence) quickly following another. One state of the object impacts us after another. But our experience of temporal duration could not be like this; if it were, we would never get the sense of a duration, of a continual temporal process, because all we would have at any given moment would be the frame in the film that is given at that moment. Furthermore, not only the film being shown, but our experience of the sequence would be discrete and staccato as well; we ourselves would be jumping from one experience to the next, and we would never have a sense that we are seeing something that goes beyond the frame that is being given at the instant. We would also not have a sense of our experience or even of ourselves as enduring through time. The sense of a continuous flow would never arise for us. Thus, neither the object nor our experience nor we ourselves would have any temporal continuity. We and what we experience would be nothing but momentary flashes, momentary presences, momentary exposures.

We might try to introduce continuity and sequence into our description of our experience by saying the following: it is true that we have only one frame given at any moment, but while we have that one given, we remember some of the frames that preceded; we relate them as earlier frames to the one being given now. We would remember at least the few frames that just preceded the present one. Replicas of earlier frames arise for us. It would be through such memory, which accompanies our perception, that a sense of continuity would arise.

This explanation, however, does not cut deeply enough. If we say we *remember* an earlier frame, we presuppose the fact that we already have a sense of the past; but how could such a sense of the past ever have dawned on us? If we just have one frame and then another frame and then another, all we have ever experienced would be present frames, and even if we called back an earlier frame, it would be given to us as yet another present one. All we would have would be sheer presence. No sense of pastness could ever have been disclosed to us, even in the replicas of earlier frames. The very dimension of being past would never have differentiated itself from the present.

We should also add that besides having to posit remembrances of the past frames, we would also have to posit anticipations of the coming frames, because our experience extends into the future as well as the past. Our perception would have to be accompanied by acts of immediate memory and acts of proximate anticipation. But once again, how would we ever appreciate the anticipations as directing us toward the future if the sense of the future had not been given from the beginning? How would we know that the anticipated frames are future and not just more of the present? Neither the future nor the past would be different from the present.

It is necessary, therefore, to say that in our immediate experience we do not just have frames of presence given to us; right in our most elementary experience, we have a sense of past and future directly given. To use the phrase of William James, our experience of the present is not a knife edge but a saddleback. Whatever is given to us in perception is given as trailing off and also as coming into presence. If our experience of the present were not like this, we never would acquire a sense of past or of the future. To try to insert such senses into our experience "later on," after our initial experience, would be too late. A primary sense of past and future has to be given right from the start.

Furthermore, claiming that we have such a rudimentary sense of past and future is not just a postulation that we are led to by argument; it is not a hypothesis or an inference. Rather, it fits the way we experience things: whatever we experience, whether things and processes in the world or subjective acts and feelings, we experience as "goings-on," as passing as they exist. Only because they trail off now can we remember them later and recognize them as past, and only because they come into view now can we anticipate them at a greater distance. When we reflect on our experience, we find it to be an exposure into the immediate past and future. The initial absences of pastness and futurity are present in all our experience.

There are several technical terms that have been introduced in phenomenology to help describe the immediate experience of time. The term *the living present* signifies the full immediate experience of temporality that we have at any instant. The living present is the temporal whole at any instant. This living present, as the whole, is composed of three moments: *primal impression, retention,* and *protention.* These three abstract parts, these three moments, are inseparable. We could never have a retention just by itself, nor could we have a primal impression or a protention just by itself. The living present is a whole made up of these three parts as moments. The structure of the living present can be diagrammed as shown in Figure 2.

Retention, as the word suggests, points to the past. It "retains" something. What does it retain? It retains the living present that has

Figure 2

just elapsed. This point is both subtle and important. The retention does not immediately retain an earlier phase or frame of the temporal object that is being experienced, such as the melody or the feeling of anger. It retains the elapsed living present, the elapsed experience of temporality.

Now, this elapsed living present was itself made up of a primal impression, protention, and retention. Thus, in retaining the elapsed living present, the current one also retains the retention that had elapsed within it. This retention in turn retained the living present that preceded it, so we have a whole series of elapsed living presents that are retained through the mediation of prior living presents, through the mediation of prior retentions. In the living present we have a retention of retentions of retentions. We never have an atomic living present all by itself; because of the retentional moment of the living present, the living present always has a comet's tail of elapsed living presents, with their retentions, accompanying it.

We should emphasize the fact that the retention included in the living present is not an ordinary act of remembering; it is much more elementary than memory. Retention functions within the initial establishment of temporal duration. It precedes remembering. What it retains has not yet fallen into the absence of oblivion, and so memory in the familiar sense cannot yet come into play. Likewise, protention, the future-directed counterpart of retention, is not the same as full-scale anticipation or projection, in which we imagine ourselves into a new situation. Protention is more basic and more immediate; it gives us the first and original sense of "something coming" directly upon what we have now. Protention opens the very dimension of the future and thus makes full-fledged anticipation possible.

Protention and retention, along with the primary impression, are the original opening of our experience into the future and the past. The way we break out of the immediate present into the future and past has been called by Heidegger, somewhat dramatically, the *ec-static* character of our experience, and the three forms of opening have been called the *ecstases* of time. The terms are drawn from the Greek preposition *ek*, "out," and the noun *stasis*, which comes from the verb *histēmi*, "to stand," implying that in our most basic temporal experience we are not locked into a solitary presence, but stand out into the future and the past.

This explanation of the structure of the immediate experience of time, with its appeal to primary impression, retention, and protention, has an almost mathematical flavor to it. It is something like an attempt to generate a continuous line by describing points in such a way that any point implies its immediate neighboring points (to the right and left), which in turn imply their next neighbors, and so on. Any point would be related to its more distant neighbors only through the mediation of its closer neighbors. In this understanding, a point would not be a discrete unit, but would point on, so to speak, to the next point, and through it to all the other points on the line. To draw out the analogy a bit farther, it would be as if each point on the line could *be* a point, and could be exposed outward "toward the world," only while also implying its immediate neighbors, and through them its more distant neighbors.

Whether mathematicians would want to redefine a point in this manner is not for us to decide, but in the experience we have of time, the most ultimate unit, the living present (the "point"), must be described in such a way as to include, somehow, a reference to and a containment of the prior and succeeding living presents. If we are dealing with time, we cannot define the momentary point as simply atomic, simply present without any involvement of the special kind of absence that is the rudimentary past and the rudimentary future.

So far we have considered simply the structure of the living present, the presence of temporality. This living present does not just float free; it is intentional, and it intends or manifests temporal objects, such as a melody or a feeling of pain. In our phenomenological analysis, we must also describe the temporal aspects of such objects, which stand over against the living present.

The aspect of the object correlated with an actual living present is its *now phase*. The aspect of the object correlated with an elapsed but retained living present is an earlier now phase. To put this schematically, each retained living present has a now phase of the object correlated with it:

$$\text{Living present}_0 \rightarrow \text{Now phase}_0$$
$$\text{Living present}_{-1} \rightarrow \text{Now phase}_{-1}$$
$$\text{Living present}_{-2} \rightarrow \text{Now phase}_{-2}$$
$$\text{Living present}_{-3} \rightarrow \text{Now phase}_{-3}$$
$$\text{Etc.} \qquad\qquad \text{Etc.}$$

The current living present retains the just elapsed one, which in turn retains the one prior to it, and so on, and on the objective side (the "noematic" side), the temporal phases of the object are held in place in the order in which they succeeded one another. Thus, the phases of a melody (or a feeling) are temporally ordered as soon as they are originally registered. They are stamped with a place in time and internally ordered in their succession. When the melody is remembered, the same ordering returns, because the memory reactivates the temporal flow on both the subjective and the objective sides.

The living present, each segment of the deepest life of consciousness, has a double intentionality. On the one hand, it retains its own preceding living presents and thus builds up a kind of incipient self-identification. On the other hand, through these same retentions, it builds up the continuity of the experienced object as the object unfolds through time. The consciousness of internal time thus exercises what we could call a *vertical* intentionality, building up its own continuous identity, and a *transverse* intentionality, making its objects given over time.

The retentional reach of a living present goes only so far back, however; it does not extend uninterruptedly to the very beginning of our conscious life. At some point the retentions fade off, and the corresponding now phases fall into oblivion. This is the temporal darkness that surrounds all our conscious moments. The light of consciousness goes back a few phases, but then the object and our experience of it cease to be registered. They enter into a more definitive absence. However, we can recover them through memory, in which we relive the earlier temporal flows, both immanent and transcendent, as they were originally endured. We bring them back to life, as represented. We could not remember something that was still going on within the retentional reach of a living presence; the experience and its object have to fall into a forgotten stage before they can be recalled. Remembering is thus a kind of discrete new beginning, going back again to something that had fallen out of consciousness.

In fact, all the displacements of consciousness that we examined in Chapter 5 are a kind of interruption of the present temporal flow of consciousness and the introduction of a new, second flow within it: the flow of ourselves as remembered, imagined, or anticipated. The flow of our current experience can have a parallel flow nested within it. The deliberate exercise of such displacements is analogous to the introduction of categorial activity into perception. The displacements in memory, imagination, and projection allow a heightened sense of self-identity, as well as a heightened sense of the identity of objects, that go beyond the more primitive but more basic identities that occur on the level of the living present.

DETAILS AND PERPLEXITIES IN INTERNAL TIME CONSCIOUSNESS

The domain of internal time consciousness underlies both the subjective flow of internal time and the objective flow of world time, transcendent time. It allows both of these flows to manifest themselves, and it is phenomenologically more basic than they are. However, this domain could not exist by itself. Its whole sense is to manifest the temporal objects in the two streams of time, subjective and objective. We could not isolate internal time consciousness and "have" it by itself alone. To try to do so would be the typical philosophical mistake of making a moment into a piece, an abstract part into a whole. Internal time consciousness adheres to internal time and its objects and, through them, to worldly time and its objects. Although it is more fundamental than they are, it is a moment to them.

Furthermore, the analysis of time consciousness only provides the formal structures of time. Timing is not everything; it is only a form for what is temporal. By providing an analysis of the "origin" of time, we do not explain the origin of trees, cats, bureaucracies, flags, melodies, solar systems, feelings of pain, perceptions, and categorial activities. We have only provided a clarification of the levels of time within which such things exist and manifest themselves. The formal structures of time need to be filled with objects and activities of various kinds, which call for their own specific kind of analysis, since they all have forms of presentation that are distinct from those of temporality. However, because time is so pervasive, temporal structures do apply to all things, both subjective and objective.

The consciousness of internal time is paradoxical when measured by the standards we apply to ordinary objects and processes. As we have seen in Figure 1, the domain of this consciousness is beyond or more immanent than even our subjective temporal processes; it is deeper even than the flow of feelings and intentional acts. Because it is so deep, it calls into question the very use of the terms "internal" or "immanent" to describe it. It moves beyond inside and outside. We come to see that it is not really locatable in space. It evades space as well as time in their ordinary senses, even more radically than does our normal intentional activity.

Internal time consciousness is made up of the living present as it succeeds itself. Is this succession a process? Does it flow along in the way that feelings and intentional acts do? No; its way of changing has to be different from that of feelings and acts, and melodies and races. And yet internal time consciousness has to "change"; it has to have its own kind of flow. One living present does succeed another. Still, the term "succession" when used here cannot mean the same as it does when it is used in regard to a melody or a feeling that waxes and wanes. All we can do is to spell out the peculiarities of such succession, which are expressed by the way retention and protention function in it. Living present$_{-2}$ "preceded" living present$_{-1}$, and both are retained in living present$_0$, which is the only one that counts at the moment, since it is the only one that is actual.

The form of the living present thus chugs along automatically and constantly, neither faster nor slower, always the actuality of temporal experience. It is the little engine at the core of temporality. Because it is the origin of time, it is somehow outside of time (as well as space), and yet it does enjoy differentiation and succession, of a kind proper to itself. It is both standing and flowing, the *stehend-strömende Gegenwart*, as Husserl calls it. It others and gathers, flows and arrests, unfolds and encloses, like the fire and the rose that are one (T.S. Eliot, *Little Gidding*, ad finem). It is the site of the most basic parts and wholes, presences and absences, and identities in manifolds, those that are presupposed by all the more complex forms constituted higher up in experience. This living present is also at the origin of our own self-identity as conscious agents of both truth and action, but because it is at our origin it is prepersonal. It functions anonymously. We could not do anything about it to change it or make it slow down or accelerate. It is not within our power. We do not control our origins. It just keeps on fluttering on its own terms. And yet we are identifiable with it; it is "ours," as our origin and base.

Let us look for a moment at some of the microscopic or "subatomic" identity syntheses that take place within the living present. When an actual living present elapses and becomes retained as living present$_{-1}$, it absents itself, but it does not fall into oblivion; it becomes presented as just gone; its immediate absence is therefore given to us. Here we have something paradoxical, the original givenness of an absence, the original presence of a "past." The modification of the living present introduces an absence (in contrast with the actuality enjoyed before it elapsed), but the absence is presented: the living present$_{-1}$ is given as the same one that just elapsed from centrality, and so it is identifiable as such, but such identifiability depends on the relentless passage into absence. An original absencing takes place within retention, but this absencing is given or presented. In that simple transition of the living present into a retained state, we have absence complementing presence, we have parts coming to be within the whole of the living presence, we have a manifold being generated as the comet's tail of retentions is built up, and in all these things we have identity synthesis of living presences as well as of the temporal phases of their intended "objects" (the phases of the feeling or of the melody).

We have concentrated on the retentional aspect of internal time consciousness, but we should not neglect the protentional side. Protention is the opening to what is coming. It is the original awaiting of something to come. It is formal, awaiting only "something" without any specific content, even though a particular experience always has a content of some sort and hence is specified (more of the feeling of sadness, something from around the corner, more salad, more conversation). Thus, when a phase of a process registers itself in a primary impression, it had already been protentionally "antici-pated," at least as regards its temporal form, and hence it is given as having been awaited. A microscopic or subatomic identity synthe-sis occurs not only in regard to retention, but also in regard to protention.

FINAL REMARKS ON THE APORIAE OF TIME

The things you have been reading about internal time consciousness may seem excessively speculative and almost fantastic. They may seem to go beyond the more accessible descriptions we have been giving of other forms of intentionality. For example, the analyses phenomenology provides for perception and imagination, or for categorial activity and pictures, seem more realistic; they seem to have a foothold in what we actually experience. Distinctions such as those between memory and perception seem to be the kind that the reader could verify or falsify by thinking about his conscious life. But the speculations about internal time consciousness may seem to be utterly foreign to ordinary experience. They seem to drift into the mystical and the hermetic. Are they still part of phenomenology? Are they descriptions, or are they artificial constructions?

One might formulate this objection in the following way: we will grant that temporal experience is not atomic, not a knife edge but a saddleback; we grant that it has something like protention and retention along with its immediate impression. The inclusion of an immediate past and future into the present seems reasonable enough. But why not locate this structure right inside the flow of our feelings and intentional acts, in the second level of temporality? Why not leave it as something psychological? Why posit it as some-thing deeper and more immanent than the subjective stream of consciousness? Why project it into the domain of the living present and its curious mode of elapsing? Why go off into the "precious" language of othering and gathering as a primal event? It is the postulation of the third level of temporality, one deeper and "be-low" the flow of subjective experience, that seems to be philosophi-cally excessive.

In response to the objection, one can say that the analysis of intentionality and presentation cannot rest with just the domain of world time and the domain of subjective time. The back and forth of presence and absence that occurs on these two levels has to be supported by a kind of opening and clearing, a source for distinction, that is not just a worldly process or a psychological event. The fact that things and experiences unfold and persist in time is not just a mechanical or an organic or a psychological fact; it originates from a deeper level. This level is the spring for all formal structures, such as those found in logic, mathematics, syntax, and the various modes of presentation. Furthermore, when we identify and know worldly things, and when we experience our own sensations, perceptions, memories, and intellectual activities, we are always also unreflectively bringing ourselves to light as the identifiable source and receiver of such achievements, without there being any need for another dative that accounts for this manifestation.

Husserl approaches this source in his doctrine on internal time consciousness, while Heidegger focuses on it with his cryptic remarks about *Lichtung* and *Ereignis,* which refer to the "thinning out" of a space where things can be given and we can become their datives. Classical philosophy touches on these matters in its remarks on the emanation of differences from the One (Plotinus), on the interplay of the One and the Indeterminate Dyad (Plato), and even perhaps on the role of the Unmoved Mover (Aristotle). If we are to discuss the presentation and absenting of things, a kind of origin for this push and pull of presence and absence is called for, and it cannot be one of the things that shows up in the world or in our flow of subjective experiences.

A person who feels more comfortable dealing with neurons and computational processes may turn away from such statements in horror and repulsion. He may say that if phenomenology leads to such mystification, he wants no part of it. Instead, he will explain consciousness and knowledge and the experience of time by measuring neuronal activity and locating sites on the cerebral cortex where perceptions and memories and other mental events occur. These are things that we can get our hands on, and such scientific work, he believes, will show what conscious activities really are. But the price of such a person's reserve will be the fact that he will never be able to account for terms like "presentation," "representation," "remembering," and even "computation," terms that he must use but cannot justify. He will be unable to address the sense of pastness, futurity, and identity. He will describe mechanical and organic processes but will not be able to speak legitimately about consciousness in its many forms and will never get to the question of what time is.

The vocabulary and grammar used in speaking about internal time consciousness have their own exactness and rigor. They must use metaphor and other tropes, but this is not surprising, since language could not have originally developed to speak about this domain; we must adjust the terms that are normally used to name things and processes in the world. Worldly terms need to be modified in order to get at what underlies the presentation of things and their very ability to be named. "Being now" and "being here (or there)," being a dative of manifestation and a clearing for things to appear, must be distinguished from physical and psychological facts about ourselves, just as logic and evidence have to be distinguished from physical and psychological processes. The issues of internal time consciousness underlie the issues of truth and disclosure, and they are related to the classical study of being as being, the inquiry into how things manifest themselves.

10

The Life World and
Intersubjectivity

After the extremely formal issues discussed in Chapter 9, we now move on to more concrete topics. In this chapter we will consider the *Lebenswelt*, the life world, the world in which we live, and we will also consider intersubjectivity, the kind of intentionality that functions in our experience of other persons. The familiar character of the lived world and the public character of intersubjectivity will bring a welcome relief from the austere analyses of the preceding chapter.

THE LIFE WORLD AS A PROBLEM

The life world arises as a philosophical issue in contrast with modern science. The highly mathematical form of science that was introduced by Galileo, Descartes, and Newton led people to think that the world in which we live, the world of colors, sounds, trees, rivers, and rocks, the world of what came to be called "secondary qualities," was not the real world; instead, the world described by the exact sciences was said to be the true one, and it was quite different from the world we directly experience. What looks like a table is really a conglomeration of atoms, fields of force, and empty spaces. Atoms and molecules, and the forces, fields, and laws described by science, are said to be the true reality of things. The world we live in and directly perceive is only a construct made by our minds responding to the input from our senses, and the senses react biologically to physical stimuli that are transmitted from objects. The world we live in is ultimately unreal as we experience it, but the world reached by mathematical science, the world that causes this merely apparent world, is real.

Science has great authority in our culture because people think that it tells us the truth of things. Even human things like consciousness, language, and reasoning will, it is said, be ultimately explained in terms of the brain sciences, which in turn will be reducible, in principle if not in fact, to the physical sciences of physics and chemistry. We have two worlds, then, the world in which we live and the world described by the mathematical sciences, and it is generally thought that the life world is a mere phenomenon, totally subjective, while the world of mathematical science is the truly objective world.

The issue of the life world did not arise before the advent of modern science; before then, people simply thought that the world we live in was the only world there was. Premodern science just articulated our familiar world. It did not claim to find a substitute for it. Premodern science tried simply to develop exact terms, definitions, and descriptions of the things we directly encounter, things like living organisms, emotions, rhetorical arguments, and political societies. The problem of how we should interpret the world in which we live – whether we should take it as valid and trustworthy, or purely subjective and unscientific – comes to the fore in response to modern science.

How does phenomenology deal with the problem of the difference between the objective, scientific world and the subjective, lived world? It attempts to show that the exact, mathematical sciences take their origin from the lived world. They are founded on the life world. The exact sciences are a transformation of the experience we directly have of things in the world; they push this experience to a much higher level of identification, and correlatively they transform the objects we experience into idealized, mathematical objects. It may seem that the exact sciences are discovering a new and different world, but what they are really doing, according to phenomenology, is subjecting the ordinary world to a new method. Through this method, the exact sciences merely increase the knowledge we have of the world in which we live; they provide a greater precision in our dealings with things, but they never abandon or discard the world that is their basis. Such sciences are nested within the life world; they do not enter into competition with it.

Moreover, phenomenology does not just assert that the exact sciences are founded on the lived world; it also tries to describe the special kinds of intentionalities that constitute such sciences. It tries to spell out precisely how the life world is transformed into the world of geometric and atomic realities. Then, phenomenology claims that the exact sciences must take their place within the life world. They are one of the established institutions within it, but they never replace the life world by another one. We could not live in the world projected by science; we can only live in the life world, and this basic world has its own forms of truth and verification that are not displaced but only complemented by the truth and verification introduced by modern science.

The move made by phenomenology, then, is to show that the exact sciences are derivative upon the lived world and the things in it. Phenomenology recognizes the value and distinctness of modern mathematical science, but it does not overvalue them; it reminds us that such science is built upon things that are given to us in a prescientific way, and it also reminds us that even science is "owned" or achieved by somebody. Science has to be asserted by scientists, by human beings who carry out the special kind of thinking and intending proper to it. Science involves various kinds of intentionality, various kinds of presence and absence and identity synthesis. It presupposes some forms of intentionality that it has in common with other intellectual endeavors, and it also develops some forms of its own, but it does not float free from the persons, the transcendental egos, who achieve the science.

HOW THE MATHEMATICAL SCIENCES ARE CONSTITUTED

Modern sciences deal with idealized things: with frictionless surfaces, rays of light, ideal gases, incompressible fluids, perfectly flexible strings, ideally efficient engines, ideal voltage sources, and test particles that do not have any effect on the field in which they move. However, such ideal forms are not fabricated out of thin air. Rather, they are projections that have their roots in the things that we directly experience.

For example, consider how we come to the idea of a geometric surface. We begin with an ordinary surface, such as a tabletop. We sand and polish the surface and make it smoother and smoother. At a certain point, however, we can shift from actual sanding and polishing to an imaginative projection. We imagine sanding the surface until it could not be smoothed out any further; we imagine it as having reached the limit of smoothness. In actual fact we cannot polish the surface to this degree, but we can "take off" from the physical steps of refining it and simply imagine it reaching this unsurpassable limit. This limit is the pure geometric surface, and it is reached from a basis in actual experience. It is a transformation of surfaces that we actually experience.

Another example can be found in optics. We start with a beam of light coming from a flashlight. Then we cover part of the light source and cut the beam, say, in half. Then we cover half of the remaining part. We do this a few times, but then we change gears; we shift from actually blocking part of the light to imagining that we block it, and we go on to imagine that we have cut the light down to a very narrow beam, one so narrow that we could not interrupt any part of it without extinguishing the beam entirely. This tiniest of beams, this uncuttable or atomic beam, becomes a "ray" of light, as it was defined by Newton in his *Optics*. We could in actual fact never arrive at such a ray of light, but we can imagine or think about it as a limit.

Both the perfectly smooth surface and the ray of light are *idealized objects*. Such objects could never be experienced in our life world; we establish or constitute them by a special kind of intentionality, one that mixes both perception and imagination. This intentionality starts with something from the life world, but it generates something that seems not to belong to that world any longer. Once we have these idealized objects, however, we may begin to relate them to the concrete objects that we experience. The idealized objects become the perfect versions of what we experience; they seem to be "more real" than the things we perceive because they are more exact. The things we perceive seem to be only imprecise copies of the perfect standard.

Then, if we bring about many such objects, we may think that we have discovered a whole world of things that is far better and more exact than the world of our perception. This is what happens when the kind of science introduced by Galileo, Descartes, and Newton becomes dominant in our culture. People forget that the ideal things referred to in the science have been brought about by a way of thinking; they believe that these things are more real than what we directly experience, and so they credit the sciences that know them with great authority. They take what is the result of a method as being a discovery of a new kind of reality. The scientific experts, the masters in this new domain, are thought to have a much more perfect grasp of the nature of things than the rest of us do, since we deal "merely" with the unscientific world, while they deal with the world as it "truly" is in its perfect exactness. Such idealizations, furthermore, have been projected not only in geometry and physics, but also in the social sciences: in economics, politics, and psychology. Models in game theory, for example, have been used to calculate strategies in warfare and foreign policy.

FURTHER ASPECTS OF SCIENTIFIC OBJECTS

Let us examine in greater detail the procedure by which idealized objects are reached. The object we start with is one in which we can identify a feature in which fluctuations are possible, such as the smoothness of the surface or the size of the beam. There can be variations in these two features: both can be realized in greater or lesser degree, in more or less. The variations are then made smaller and smaller, and the idea arises of a condition in which no further variations are thinkable: they are reduced to zero. The surface becomes perfectly flat, the beam becomes practically a line. We have "geometrized" an object that was once a perceived thing in the world.

It is important to note that when we reach this ideal condition, we retain something of the content or the quality of the thing with which we began. We do not turn everything into pure mathematics. The ideal surface is still a spatial thing, and the ray is still a ray of light. The surface is different from the ray of light, and both are different from, say, the perfectly flexible string or the ideal voltage source, which in their turn are idealizations that began from other worldly objects.

It is the excruciatingly exact identity of the idealized objects that makes them so satisfying intellectually. They are perfect: they are exactly the same wherever they are found, in contrast with the variable surfaces and beams of light that we actually encounter. In earlier chapters of this book, we considered the theme of identity in other contexts; a perceived thing (the cube) was described as an identity in a flow of sides, aspects, and profiles; a mental act was said to be an identity given in the various remembrances we have of it; and even the self was presented as an identity behind our various mental achievements. However, all these identities enclose many variabilities; they are what can be called *morphological* things or essences. In contrast, the ideal things that mathematical science reaches, the *exact* essences, do not tolerate any ambiguity or variation. They positively exclude them.

Not all things can be projected toward a limit and constituted as exact essences; a perception or a memory, for example, always retains some vagueness and variability. It would make no sense to try to project things like them toward an ideal limit; they remain "morphological" and not exact kinds of things. Consequently, such things seem, to some people, to be vague and subjective, and attempts are made to introduce an exact science, a kind of mathematical psychology or cognitive science, that will replace such concepts with more exact ones. The attempt to explain human cognition as a form of neuronal computation is an example.

Phenomenology claims that the exact, mathematical sciences of nature cannot account for their own existence. They do not have the terms and concepts to handle such things as perception, remembering, the experience of other minds, and the like. Phenomenology claims that it can provide the concepts and analyses that will clarify how the exact sciences themselves arise from prescientific origins. Phenomenology presents itself as a science in its own right; it does not behave like the mathematical sciences of nature, but it has its own form of precision, which is unlike the mathematical, idealized precision of natural science. It is, among other things, a science about science itself. It is also a science of the life world, and it tries to show how the life world serves as a foundation and a context for mathematical sciences.

Developments in physics and mathematics in this century have raised questions about the exactness of the natural sciences. Such discoveries as indeterminacy of measurement and observer relatedness in quantum theory, relativity theory, the incompleteness theorem in mathematics, nonlinear systems, chaos theory, and fuzzy logic have cast doubt on the rather tidy understanding of the world that was present in Newtonian physics and the science and mathematics that prevailed during the early years of phenomenology. However, these developments do not affect the problem of the life world and science. All these developments have occurred within the scientific view of the world, which even with them still remains at odds with the world of our spontaneous experience. The newer versions of science may tolerate imprecision, but what they describe is still different from the world in which we live, and the problem of integrating them into that world has not been dissolved. An important contribution to its resolution would lie in the careful analysis of the kinds of intentionalities at work in establishing scientific knowledge.

INTERSUBJECTIVITY: A WORLD HELD IN COMMON

Much of the vocabulary and argument of phenomenology may give the impression that it is a form of philosophy that veers toward solipsism. With its talk about the transcendental ego, the temporal stream of consciousness, and the reduction, phenomenology may seem to neglect the existence and the presence of other persons and communities. Some critics of phenomenology complain that it reduces other persons to mere phenomena and makes the solitary ego the only reality. Such complaints are unfounded. Phenomenology has a lot to say about human community, and it provides an extensive description of our experience of other minds.

There are two approaches to the description of our experience of others. First, we might simply describe how we directly experience other persons, how we recognize other bodies as the embodiment of minds and selves like our own. Secondly, we might take a more indirect route and describe how we experience the world and things in it as being also experienced by other minds and other selves. In this second approach, we do not look at the direct relation between ourselves and others, but at the relation both of us, or all of us, have to the world and the things we possess in common. Let us begin with the second approach.

When I experience a bodily object, such as a cube, I recognize it as an identity in a manifold of sides, aspects, and profiles. The manifold is dynamic; whatever perspective I may have on the cube at any moment, I can move myself or the cube and generate a new flow of sides, aspects, and profiles. What was seen becomes unseen, what was unseen becomes seen, and the cube remains itself throughout. At any moment I anticipate and recall my future and my past views of the thing. These other views are cointended as I enjoy the view that is given to me now. My experience is a mixture of the actual and potential: whenever certain sides or aspects are given, I cointend those that are not but that could be given if I were to change my position, perspective, ability to perceive, and the like.

The mixture of actual and potential is heightened when other perceivers come into play. If others are present, then I realize that when I see the object from this side, the others do actually see it from some other angle, an angle that I would possess if I were to move to where they are. What is potential for me is actual for them. The object therefore takes on a greater transcendence to me: it is not only what I see and could see, but also what they see at this moment. Furthermore, I appreciate the object as so transcending my own viewpoint: I see it precisely as being seen by others and not just by me. That level of its identity is given to me. The object is or can be given intersubjectively, and it is presented to me as such.

The ability of the object to be given perceptually to many viewers, hearers, tasters, smellers, and touchers takes place on a sensory level, but the object can also be categorially articulated by many people and not just by myself. It can be understood and thought about under many guises. I may know Mr. Jones as the post office clerk, but Mrs. Jones knows him as her husband, and I know the post office clerk as also known by others under other forms of description and acquaintance. I am not able to formulate all the ways an object can be known: any acquaintance I have is bound to be limited. Still, I know the object as knowable even in forms I cannot know. I recognize this level of its transcendence to me, this level of the absence that it has to me. Both on the perceptual and the intellectual level, the world and things in it are given to many selves, many datives of manifestation, even though I will always show up for myself as the preeminent one, the one at the center and the one who is an issue for me in a way that no other or others could be, however dear and close they might be. My prominence to myself is a necessity in transcendental logic, not a matter of moral self-centeredness. Some people may be personally closer to me and others may be farther, but the very dimension of proximity does not arise for the way I am given to myself.

INTERSUBJECTIVITY: KNOWING THE OTHER

So far, our discussion of intersubjectivity has focused on objects that we see as being experienced by others as well as ourselves. Let us now make some comments about our direct experience of others as other minds, other embodiments of consciousness. We not only appreciate the world as given to others; we can also turn toward these others and experience them as like ourselves, as datives of disclosure, who can reciprocate our recognition and see us as like themselves.

The experience of another self is based on the experience of another body as like our own. We do not know just the mind of another; we have the body given first, but the body is given as a place in which the consciousness of the other holds sway. Just as I can move and experience my own body, so can the other, whom I recognize as being like me, move and experience his. That body, furthermore, does not just provide a place for the other consciousness and a location for the other point of view. It also expresses the mind of the other. The spoken language, the intentional gestures, and the indeliberate body language all are more than just bodily motions; they signal intentional acts, and they also express a content of thought. They express to me how the world and the things in it seem to be to the one whose body it is. If the other person utters certain sounds or makes certain grimaces, I can be told that "Trouble is coming" or "Don't give up now."

Thus, certain bodies stand out in the world as expressive of meaning (a movement of an arm is not just a mechanical process but a salute, a wave of the hand is a dismissal and not just a motion). These bodies are also capable of conveying to me how the world is: they provide other viewpoints on the way things are. They embody other transcendental egos. I perceive them as the bodies of selves like myself, but in doing so I perceive them precisely as enclosing and expressing a conscious life that will always remain absent to me, a stream of temporality irreducibly different from my own. The distinctive absence of other selves is presented to me. It is a kind of absence different from the absences of the other side of the cube or the meaning of a text that I cannot yet decipher.

One of the more controversial teachings in phenomenology is that it is possible for us to "think away" the intersubjective dimension in principle, and to get down to a level in our own experience that precedes or underlies the intersubjective. This is the so-called *sphere of ownness*. The reduction to this sphere is not the same as imagining a factual solitude; it is not like imagining that I am alone somewhere or even that all other human beings have vanished from the earth and I am the only one left. Such imaginary scenarios would still retain the dimension of other people; they would simply eliminate the others as a matter of fact. The reduction to the sphere of ownness attempts to eliminate the very dimension of other persons. It attempts to reach a level of experiencing in which the very contrast between myself and others does not arise.

Commentators have often criticized Husserl for introducing the concept of the sphere of ownness; they claim that such a domain is unthinkable, because any experience we have must in principle have a rudimentary publicness. However, we should not be too quick to dismiss this doctrine. Certainly, almost all our experiencing involves a dimension of other minds, a meaning that could be shared with others and that is defined by being in contrast with others. But we should not rule out of court the notion that some aspect of our consciousness has a kind of extreme privacy in which the very sense of others does not come into play. There may be a level of experiencing that is, in principle, not capable of being expressed to or shared with others, a domain in which the very sense of others does not intrude. Clearly, such an intense privacy could not be the whole of our experience, nor could it be a major part of it, but there may be a slight touch of the ultimately secret in our awareness. Why should such a dimension be wholly denied? And if there is such a domain, it would deserve exploration to show what sort of identities and differences, presences and absences, and unities in manifold are possible within it.

We should emphasize, however, that this reduction to the sphere of ownness is not the same as the transcendental reduction, the move from the natural attitude to phenomenological reflection. It is a move within the philosophical attitude, uncovering various levels of experience undergone by the transcendental ego.

Reason, Truth, and Evidence

The transcendental ego is the agent of truth. It exercises this agency in many contexts: in speech, picturing, reminiscence, practical conduct, political rhetoric, clever deception, and strategic maneuvers. A special way of exercising the power to be truthful occurs in science, whether the science is empirical or theoretic, and whether it is focused on one region of being or another. In science, we wish simply to find the truth of things; the scientific enterprise is an attempt just to show the way things are, apart from how they can be used or how we might wish them to be. Success in science does not mean victory over other people or the gratification of our various desires; it means purely and simply the triumph of objectivity, the disclosure of how things are.

Philosophy is a scientific effort, but it is different from mathematics and the natural and social sciences; it is concerned not with a particular region of being, but with truthfulness as such: with the human conversation, the human attempt to disclose the way things are, and the human ability to act in accordance with the nature of things; ultimately, it is concerned with being as it manifests itself to us. In science and philosophy we seek truth for its own sake, apart from any other benefit it might bring. In both endeavors we try to reach the highest degree of exactness appropriate to the matter at hand; we are not satisfied by what is just enough to get a particular job done.

We have, in this book, examined many ingredients of truthfulness. We have examined identity in manifolds, categorial articulation, and differences between things like perceiving and remembering. We have explored both the truthfulness of being and the veracity of the agent of disclosure (along with the possible mendacity and confusion that come in their train). In the present chapter, we will consolidate and complete these explorations. We will investigate the phenomenology of reason, the analysis of rational thinking.

When we enter into reasoning, we lift ourselves beyond our biological and psychological life. We live the life of thinking. This means that we, these particular beings, these animals that we are, become able to make claims about the truth of things. We can verify or falsify such claims, we can exchange meanings, and we can praise or blame one another for having been better or worse agents of truth. As we speak with one another and pursue the rational life, we become able to master absences of many kinds and articulate presences in extremely complex ways.

One of the requirements for this kind of life is the sameness of a meaning that we communicate among ourselves and come back to repeatedly in our own mental life. A single proposition returns as identically the same over and over again: we tell it to other people, quote it as having been stated by someone else, use it as a premise, confirm or disconfirm it in our experience, place it within a systematic exposition of a scientific field, or write it down so that it can be read even when we are no longer there to speak it. The sameness of a meaning occurs even across the different interpretations people might give the meaning, and across the differences in vagueness and distinctness the proposition might enjoy in various minds. Unless it were one and the same statement, we could not see such differences as being differences at all; we could not have many *interpretations* if the propositions were themselves different, and we could not speak of a vague possession of a meaning unless a core of sense remained the same between its vague and its distinct states. Sometimes, it is true, a meaning or proposition may fall apart into two or more senses when we think it through more carefully, or it may crumble into incoherence, into no sense at all, but such disintegrations in the realm of meaning are possible only in contrast with meanings that are sustained and confirmed in their identity.

Meanings are presented especially in words. Through language it becomes possible for us to express the way things are and to convey this mode of presentation to other people and to ourselves at other places and other times. The words we exchange capture the way things have appeared to us, and if we are authoritative in our disclosures they capture the way things are. At the same time, the words are flavored by the style with which we have disclosed the things in question, so they indicate to the reader or listener something about ourselves as well.

Physicists and mathematicians do not worry about the fact that a proposition can return over and over again as identically the same, even though physics and mathematics would not be possible if such recurrence did not take place. Philosophers, however, cannot let such identification slip past them; it is the kind of thing they think about as an ingredient in our ability to live the life of reason.

TWO KINDS OF TRUTH

The identity of meaning makes truth possible. There are two kinds of truth that occur in our rational life: the truth of correctness and the truth of disclosure.

1. In the *truth of correctness*, we begin with a statement being made or a proposition being held. We then go on to verify whether the claim is true. We carry out whatever kind of experiencing is needed as a confirmation or a disconfirmation of the statement. If someone says that the porch roof leaks when it rains, we wait until it rains and then see whether or not the roof leaks. If someone makes a proposal dealing with a certain chemical reaction or medical treatment, we carry out the appropriate experiments to confirm or disconfirm the claim. If the results confirm the assertion, we can say that the statement is true because it does express the way things are. It is a correct statement. The sense of falsity that is correlated with the truth of correctness is obvious: it is the falsity of claims that run counter to the way things are, claims that are resisted by the manifestation of things.

2. There is a more elementary form of truth that can occur even apart from the confirmation of a claim. This second sense of truth, the *truth of disclosure*, is simply the display of a state of affairs. It is the simple presencing to us of an intelligible object, the manifestation of what is real or actual. Such a presence could occur immediately during our normal experience and perception: we walk up to the car and are surprised to see that the tire is flat. We need not have been anticipating the tire as flat; our experience of it as such

is not an attempt to confirm or disconfirm a proposition that we have been entertaining. We are dealing not with the truth of correctness, but with the more elementary truth of simple disclosure. An intelligible object, a state of affairs, is presented to us, the object or the situation simply unfolds. We are surprised by a new mathematical relationship, we suddenly realize that John is lying to James, we see why Cézanne arranged the colors and lines the way he did in this particular painting. Such presentations are not confirmations but direct displays. The falsity correlated with this kind of truth is the kind that occurs when appearances mislead, when things seem to be something that they are not: fool's gold, camouflage, the counterfeit, the falsity of the inauthentic, the failure to be genuine as opposed to the failure to tell the truth.

The truth of correctness depends on the truth of disclosure; the latter can serve as the intelligibility that confirms or disconfirms a claim. What the true proposition "matches" or blends with or is measured by is not an inert entity, but a thing being disclosed. The propositional claim is disquoted in favor of a direct display, which is recognized as being identifiable with the claim whose truth was being investigated. As we have seen in Chapter 7, our experience begins with the direct display of states of affairs, of intelligible, categorial objects. This display involves the truth of disclosure. The domain of the propositional comes into play when we become sophisticated enough to take some states of affairs as being merely proposed by someone; they become "states of affairs as proposed," they become propositions, claims, or judgments, they become senses or meanings. It is these propositions, these states of affairs as proposed, that become candidates for the truth of correctness, and they acquire such truth when they are seen to blend with what is given, once again, in the truth of disclosure. The truth of disclosure, therefore, flanks the truth of correctness. It comes before and after.

TWO KINDS OF EVIDENCE

In the two kinds of truth that we have distinguished, the predicate "true" applies either to a proposition or to a displayed entity or state of affairs. We must introduce another term, the word *evidence*, to name the subjective activities that bring truth about. Phenomenology uses the term "evidence" to name the subjective achievement, the subjective having of truth, whether in correspondence or disclosure. Evidence as noesis is correlated with truth as noema.

This usage of the word "evidence" is unusual in English. (It is less strange in German and French.) Normally, "evidence" in English does not mean a subjective achievement; it means, rather, a fact or a datum that serves to prove a claim. Evidence might be a footprint, a bloody glove, a testimony given by a witness, or a document, but in every case it is something objective, a thing of some sort, that is used to prove something else. In normal English usage, a piece of evidence is like a premise that establishes a conclusion, not like an intentionality that discloses an object. When the term is used as an adjective, it is almost always predicated of the object that appears, which then is said to appear vividly and clearly: an evident victory, an evident scheme, an evident deception.

In phenomenology, however, "evidence" takes on the sense of the verbal form, "evidencing." It is the bringing about of truth, the bringing forth of a presence. It is a performance and an achievement. Evidence is the activity of presenting an identity in a manifold, the articulation of a state of affairs, or the verification of a proposition. It is the achieving of truth.

There are some dictionary meanings of "evidence" that come close to the meaning that phenomenology gives to the word. The *Oxford English Dictionary* says that "evidence" can be used as a noun with the sense of a "witness": several persons could be said to be "evidences" in a case, people who can disclose what happened. We can say that someone has "turned state's evidence," that is, he has decided to bear witness to an event. There is even an obsolete English noun "evidencer," which signifies someone who bears witness: "An evidencer of the deed." Also, the word can be used as a transitive verb, and then it means "to make something evident or clear, to show clearly, to manifest something." Thus, we might say, "He evidenced the futility of the plan," or "Her words evidenced the situation they were in." These meanings, though old and rare, are a little more like the sense of "evidence" in phenomenology, but even they do not give us an obvious precedent for the philosophical usage. We will have to make the meaning clear by using the word in ways that will bring out the phenomenon it is supposed to name.

Evidence is the successful presentation of an intelligible object, the successful presentation of something whose truth becomes manifest in the evidencing itself. Such presentation is a notable event in the life of reason. It is the moment when something enters into the space of reasons, the world of intelligibilities. Such an event is not just a perfection of the subject who achieves it; it does not perfect only the person who gets the point or sees what is going on. It is also a perfection in the object; the object is manifested and known, it discloses itself. Its truth is actualized. It is evidenced. When Heidegger uses a rather poetic trope and calls man, or *Dasein*, the "shepherd of being," he means that we are the ones to whom things can be disclosed in their truthfulness, and that we hold a privileged place in the scheme of things because we are datives of manifestation. We evidence things. We let them appear.

The power we have to do so is not the outcome of some plan we contrive, or the result of a government-funded project, or a talent we might try to develop; it comes from what we are even before we begin to make choices or deliberate about what we should do. It comes from our way of being. It allows us to deliberate and choose. Our speech is not just chatter among ourselves; it is also, if we escape the mist of vagueness, the disclosure of things, which come to light in what we say. We provide a light within which things can manifest themselves, a clearing where they can be collected and recollected. Something good and important happens in our life of reason, even though we occupy only a small space and time in the development of things, and even though the exploding sun may, some day in the remote future, consume all the planets including our own. This activity is our achievement as transcendental egos, not simply our behavior as animals or our reaction as bodies embedded in a network of material causes. The light of reason opens up the space of reasons, the kingdom of ends. We are real as datives of manifestation, and what we do as such is to evidence the truth of things.

Why should we strain to adapt the term "evidence" to name this achievement? Why not use some other word? One reason is that the term has a technical sense in phenomenology, in both German and French, where this meaning is more natural. In addition, the word does capture a phenomenon: it expresses the fact that we are active when things present themselves. We *do* something when intelligible objects present themselves to us; we are not mere recipients. We are not only datives, but also nominatives of disclosure (*ego*, and not just *mihi*). Other words like "intuit," "perceive," or "register" seem to make us too passive in accepting what appears. "Evidencing" makes it more clear that we must act as transcendental egos if things are to be given. Such action is most obvious in the case of categorial activity, but it is needed even in perception, with its initial stages of intelligibility, and it is obviously required in picturing, reminiscence, and deliberation. The English term "insight" is a good equivalent, even though it cannot be used as a verb, but it does seem limited to categorial presentation; "evidencing" ranges more widely. Not only speakers and scientists, but also painters and dramatists and their audiences can evidence the way things are. Furthermore, "insight" connotes an action that is accomplished once and for all, while "evidencing" has the sense of continuing and reinforcing itself beyond the initial moment.

We evidence, then, in two ways: in the truth of correctness and in the truth of disclosure. We evidence the correctness of a proposition by seeing how the things are and disquoting the assertion we set out to verify. More fundamentally, however, we evidence an intelligible object by articulating it in its direct presence, when we achieve the truth of disclosure. We see that the squares of even numbers are even, and those of odd numbers are odd; we see that envy is not the same as jealousy; we see that there are only five regular solids in three-dimensional space. These are all facts, intelligible objects, and we register them as true: we display them in their intelligibility. They are understandings. We may want to explain them further and look for the reasons why they are true, but the search for further understanding does not disqualify the initial understanding that is given in the original evidence. Evidence enrolls things into the space of reasons.

TWO WAYS OF TRYING TO ESCAPE EVIDENCE

There are two ways in which we may try, in philosophy and in the common mind, to deny the existence of evidence as the direct display of things. In the first, we reduce evidence to something merely psychological. In the second, we claim that we never really have evidence until we can prove what we know by deriving it from premises or axioms.

1. Because evidencing has to be done by us, we may easily slip

into the belief that it is "just" a subjective event, like a mood or a pain or a feeling of certainty. Evidence may be taken as a mere cognitive state, a temporary condition of our psyche, which in turn may be reduced to a temporary condition of the brain and nervous system. In this view, things are what they are, they are "out there," and cognitive states, evidencing included, are in us, "in here." The cognitive state, say, of belief is a condition we are in, one that we could be aware of in our self-consciousness, but it tells us only about ourselves, not about anything out there in the world.

In German, one of the philosophical meanings of the word *Evidenz* is "consciousness of being convinced of something" (*Überzeugungsbewusstsein*). This meaning too can easily be psychologized. We may take it to mean that we are conscious of firmly believing something, but then the target of our consciousness is just our subjective state, the state of firm conviction. It is like the "belief" that David Hume and John Stuart Mill take to be the target of our inner perception.

Such an interpretation of evidence would be incorrect. What we are subjectively aware of when we are aware of evidencing is not a mental, psychological state, but a display. We are aware of an intellectual achievement, a success in manifestation, not an inner datum. If we are aware of a display, we are also, essentially, aware of what is displayed: the display is not an inner thing over and against the thing displayed. The success in manifestation is reached in our intellectual life, not in our merely psychological life. There may be psychological aspects to our intellectual achievement, but these aspects are not the substance of the action. The act of evidence is an event in the space of reasons, not a mere psychological episode.

An act of evidence is more like a move in logic than like a feeling or a pain. An act of evidence is a move in transcendental logic. It adjusts the network of our propositions and meanings. It may be an episode, but that does not make it psychological; it is an episode of disclosure and truth, a move in the life of reason, an accomplishment of the transcendental ego. In fact, it is the original move in the life of reason. It gets us started in that life: until things have been disclosed by direct evidence and until we enter into the presence of intelligible objects, we do not actively take a position in the game of truth. Until then, we are only rehearsing for the human conversation and have not yet become full-fledged players in it. Any act of evidencing, furthermore, presupposes that the entire game of truth, the human conversation, is already going on; it has to be there for us to enter into it. We are lifted into that life not only by what we are, but also by the rational tradition into which we are rehearsed: both the local tradition into which we are born and the human conversation as a whole. This conversation and intellectual life may be "only" human, but the point is that to be human is to be engaged in truth, to be able to disclose the way things are and to let objectivity triumph in us. We are most ourselves as human beings when we are caught up in that activity.

2. The second way of trying to evade evidence is to claim that the presentation itself is not enough to establish truth. We might think that a presentation gives us only an appearance or an opinion. We would then have to go on to prove the truth of what has been presented, and we would do so by giving reasons for it. We have to explain it; that is, we have to derive it from other, more certain premises, even from axioms, to show why it has to be the way it is. After such proof, we will be sure of the phenomenon. In this view, we do not know anything until we have proved it; we demand a proof for everything. Evidencing alone, therefore, does not present truth. To put it another way, there is no such thing as evidencing. The only source for truth is proof.

This claim reflects the belief that truth is reached by means of methodic procedures. Nothing is directly presented to us, but we can reach truths by reasoning to them. Descartes appealed to such method at the beginning of modernity, and he thought that method could replace insight. Even people of moderate intellectual ability, he said, could follow each simple step of a proof and thus come to a sure possession of the conclusion, with a certainty as great as can be reached by the most intelligent person. Even perception requires proof, he thought, because it involves an inference from the ideas we have to the putative causes "outside" us that must have brought the ideas about. This confidence in method is part of the rationalism of modernity. It lies behind the trust we have in large-scale research projects that promise to discover the truths we need to make life easier and better. The authority of the wise or intelligent person is replaced by the method-driven project sponsored by government, industry, or the academy.

Such trust in method and proof is an attempt to master truth. It is an attempt to get disclosure under control and to subject it to our wills. If we can get the right method in place, and if our methodical procedures can be helped by computers, we will be able to solve many important problems. We will get a hammerlock on the truth of things, coercing consent in ourselves and in others. The philosophical principle behind our confidence in method is the idea that we know things by proving them, not by bringing about evidence.

In contrast with the control over truth that method seems to give us, evidence seems to be unpredictable and unmasterable. It seems to depend too much on people who have the ability to achieve it. It seems to depend on appearances, on how things happen to show up for us. Relying on evidence as opposed to methodical procedures may seem too passive, not energetic enough. The rationalist may find the contingency of evidence unsettling and may regret the fact that we cannot master truth, but such is indeed the case. We do have to wait for the right person and the right moment for the truth to appear, and we must depend on the habituated mind more than on method. Not everyone is equal when it comes to evidence; we must be prepared for it, and even prior to being prepared, we must have the raw native ability to achieve it. We are not equal when it comes to bringing out the truth of things.

HIDDENNESS AND TRUTH

Evidence brings things to light, but every evidence emerges out of absence and vagueness, and the focus on one aspect of an object usually means that other aspects lapse into obscurity. The life of reason is not a matter of one simple evidence, one illumination, following another. Rather, the life of reason is a push and pull between presence and absence, and between clarity and obscurity.

We generally consider presencing to be good, but it does not follow that the absent and the hidden are bad. It may be necessary and good that things go into eclipse. Hiddenness is not just loss; it can also be preservation and protection. Things need their right time to be seen. The fact that Giorgione's painting *The Tempest* was stored unseen for many decades, or that we still are not sure what the figures in it signify, or that no one knew much about Vivaldi for two hundred years, or that we may not really know who Shakespeare was, or that scholasticism suffered a Cartesian overlay in the eighteenth and nineteenth centuries is not necessarily a tragedy. Even when we think we know a lot about something, we may be missing something central: an abundance of historical data about a painting or a text or an event, a mass of information about an illness or a celestial phenomenon, does not guarantee that we can bring out the truth of the things in question. The things may be waiting for the right moment to be understood. As hermeneutics has taught us, *Bergung* is also *Verbergung*, concealment is also preservation.

Concealment can occur in two forms, either as absence or as vagueness, and it is the latter, vagueness, that is the more important. Vagueness occurs first as the hazy presence of an object, the matrix out of which the object can distinctly come to light. Once an object has been evidenced, however, it is possible, and even inevitable, for it to move back again into vagueness. This slippage occurs because we have to take the acquired evidence for granted as we move on to further evidences that are based upon it. The original evidence becomes *sedimented*, as the phenomenological metaphor puts it. It becomes a hidden presupposition that enables something higher to come to light, but when we focus on that higher, newer evidence, the lower, more original one recedes into darkness. It ceases to be authentically articulated. For example, the geometric transformation of nature that took place in Galileo and Newton was an evidencing; it brought a certain categorial structure to presence. As time went on, men simply took it for granted that the world was mathematical in form, and it now requires an effort to reactivate or reconstitute the evidence that is at the heart of modern science.

All our cultural institutions are like this. The sense of what the theater is has also fallen into a sedimented state; it is taken for granted, even though it was originally generated as a specific kind of depiction and categorial articulation. The same could be said of writing or even of human language, with its syntactic structure. The very activity of counting, and the numbers that are constituted in that activity, can lose their original sense and direction. Furthermore, these hidden originals, these sedimented cultural and categorial forms, may be latent and overlooked, but they are effective; they generate a cultural field of force. They are like strong magnets buried in the ground. They determine the scope of what we do and serve as unrecognized premises for much of our human activity. Those who rely on method may wish to pretend that true evidence never lapses into obscurity, that nothing ever goes out of focus when something new comes into focus, because the object is always available through a new application of the procedure. This expectation of sheer presence, however, is doomed to disappointment. The hidden and the lost are as real as the clear and the distinct.

Philosophy attempts to recover the original sense of things by a kind of archaeology, a form of thinking that accepts the cultural and categorial things present in our world and tries to dig through the strata of their categorial sedimentation. It tries to trace back the evidences that were layered one upon the other in our intellectual history; it tries to get back to the point when the primitive differentiations took place that established what we now have given to us. It strives to move backward through the genetic constitutions that lie within the categorial formations we inherit. Getting to the essentials of things also means getting to the archaic and the original.

This philosophical archaeology, moreover, is not a form of empirical history, and it does not find its primary sources in ancient texts, even though it has to make use of history and texts. Its primary sources are the categorial and cultural things that we directly encounter, and what it attempts to do is to dig into them as they stand before us, unpacking them down to their elementary categories and even to their precategorial anticipations. It attempts to "unbuild" them. We take language, for example, and work back to the differentiations through which language emerges from other kinds of signs; we take geometry and work back to the kinds of intentionalities that establish the geometric as such, as it is differentiated from other spatial phenomena. Older texts and primitive forms are indispensable in getting to these beginnings, but such texts and forms do not give us the explanations that we are looking for in our probe into the origins of things, to the primitive differentiations that are more a matter of philosophical than of historical or empirical understanding.

Philosophy depends, then, on the fact that we attain truth but not the whole truth in the natural attitude. There would be no philosophy if we attained no truth at all, if we did not have some right opinion and science. Philosophy reflects on what such a rational attainment means. But there would also be no philosophy, no search for wisdom, if we knew everything, if there were no hiddenness, no vagueness, obscurity, error, and ignorance. The phenomenon of darkness conditions the possibility of light, and it also conditions the possibility of philosophy, which reflects on what light and darkness are. Darkness itself comes to light, as much as it can, in philosophy, but philosophy must have the good sense to let the darkness be. If it were to try to eliminate the darkness, it would become rationalism and would be an attempt to replace the natural attitude instead of contemplating it.

THREE LEVELS OF STRUCTURE IN MEANING

Let us return to the truth of correctness, the kind that occurs when we begin with statements or propositions and attempt to verify whether they are true or false. In dealing with such truth, it is important to distinguish three levels of structure that can be found in propositions. Discussion of these levels will lead us back to themes we examined in Chapter 7 under the heading of vagueness.

Before we work out these three levels, however, we must differentiate between the syntax and the content of a proposition. The *syntax* is the logical grammar of the proposition; it is expressed in terms like "and," "but," "with," and "is." Syntax is the connective tissue of judgments. It serves to join the content terms of statements and, as the "muscle" in judgments, it does the heavy lifting; it pushes, pulls, raises, and lowers the words we use to name things. Sometimes the syntax is expressed in specific terms, such as those words just mentioned, but it can also be expressed by inflections (such as the various cases of nouns) and by the position of words in the sentence: in the sentence, "John hit the car," we can tell which noun is the subject and which the object by seeing where they appear in the sentence; "The car hit John" says something quite different. Syntactic terms are also called the *syncategorematic* parts of judgments (phenomenology borrows the term from medieval logic). These parts are called syncategorematic because they do not appear by themselves as units of meaning; they must be attached to other words, the words that they combine; they need to occur "with" other words.

The *content* of a statement, in contrast, serves not to link other words, but to express the things or aspects that are being talked about. To get at the notion of content, let us imagine the sentence, "John hit the car," as being drained of all syntactic structure. If we were to remove all the syntax, we would be left with a residue of sheer contents: "hit, John, car." We have to project this to an ideal extreme and even imagine that the words "John" and "car" are no longer nouns and the word "hit" is no longer a verb. We would also have to imagine that the relative position of the words does not have any significance. If we could purify the sentence this way, we would have just the contents without any structure. We would have only sheer *categorematic* terms, words that simply name things but without any ordering or articulation. We would have pure semantics without any syntax.

Such a projection into sheer syntax and sheer semantics as totally separated from one another is purely imaginary, of course. In fact, every word that we use has some syntax, and almost all words have some semantics attached to them; the two features are moments to one another, not pieces that can be detached. Still, it is legitimate to distinguish between the syntax and the content as two dimensions of propositions and words. The distinction, furthermore, is very helpful in our phenomenology of reason, and it will allow us to analyze the three levels of structure we set out to examine at the beginning of this section.

1. The first level deals with the kinds of syntactic combinations that yield *meaningful* propositions. If we were to combine a string of terms such as "therefore, is, and, X (the name of any object), with," we would not have a meaningful whole. On the other hand, a combination like "Therefore, X came with Y" is meaningful and could be used in an appropriate situation. The first string is a hodge-podge without a unitary sense, and the deficiency lies in the syntax of the string. This sequence of terms could not be presented as one whole of meaning. Obviously, such a string could not be brought to the truth of correctness, because it is not even a candidate for truth or falsity. It is simply meaningless. Strictly speaking, nothing is being said, even though someone is talking. Furthermore, such a syntactic hodgepodge is not a merely philosophical construct; such garbled strings of words do occur sometimes when people are speaking. They may occur when the speakers are under emotional strain, or when the speakers or writers are extremely confused about what they are trying to discuss. People do fall into babbling. Such speakers do not present a statement that is a candidate for truth, and the reason why they fail lies in the syntactic inadequacy of what they are

saying, not in the falsity of their speech. What they say is not even capable of being false, because it fails to satisfy the preconditions of both truth and falsity.

2. Once we have reached syntactically meaningful propositions, however, a second level of structure arises that is related to the *consistency* of propositions. Two statements can be syntactically meaningful and yet contradict one another: "He came home at five o'clock; he was not home at five o'clock." Even a single statement, if it is complex enough, can be self-contradictory or inconsistent: "He entered the white building that was brown." Such statements are acceptable grammatically, but they "speak against," they contradict themselves. In a contradiction we assert one thing, and then we "unassert" it or say its negation. We do have a meaningful statement, one that is acceptable syntactically, because if we did not, we would not even know that a contradiction has occurred; our speech has satisfied the criteria concerning syntax. However, we still have not said "one thing": we have said two things under the guise of saying one, and the two are irreconcilable. We cannot assert both of them. We are saying something, but we are also unsaying it. There is a meaning, but it flashes on and off, whereas in garbled syntax there is no meaning at all; there, the "meaning" crumbles. An inconsistent statement, although meaningful, cannot be a candidate for the truth of correctness. We know a priori that there is no point in trying to verify or falsify an inconsistency.

Inconsistency is a failure that is different from syntactic garbling, but it is still related more to the syntax than to the content of our statements; it has to do with the combinatorics of propositions, with how they are put together. Syntax deals with the manner in which terms are composed to make up a proposition, and consistency deals with the manner in which propositions can be composed into complex propositions or larger wholes.

3. The third level of structure, however, deals with the content of what we say. It deals with the *coherence* of the statements we make. We may succeed in making statements that are both syntactically correct and consistent but fail because their contents do not have anything to do with one another. For example, a statement like "My uncles are illegible" is unacceptable, not because of syntax or self-contradiction, but because of incoherence: the terms "uncles" and "illegible" do not consort with one another. They belong to differ-

ent categories or different language games, different regions of discourse and being. The statement is "nonsensical," but nonsensical in a way different from statements that are deficient in syntax. There is nothing wrong with the syntax of this proposition, but its contents are wrongly forced together. Other examples of such incoherent statements are "This book is tall"; "My cat is a filibuster"; "That tree is a monoglot"; and "The Tenth Amendment has been broiled."

All such statements, incidentally, could be given a meaning if they were to be taken metaphorically, but we are presuming that they are being stated literally. Indeed, the nature of metaphor is to bring together terms from different regions of discourse in order to articulate new aspects in the things we are talking about. A metaphor flaunts its incoherence in order to make a point.

One might object that no one would make silly mistakes like these; no one would say that his uncles are illegible or that a tree is a monoglot. It is true that the examples just given, which were chosen for the sake of simplicity, are far-fetched, but there are many areas in life in which people do speak incoherently. Incoherence in speech is not a rare phenomenon. Very many statements about political matters, for example, fail in this way, and so do many of the things said about religion, art, education, morality, the human emotions, and philosophy. Any teacher who has graded examinations in political theory or philosophy will know that the major difficulty with weak compositions is not that the statements made in them are false, but that they are incoherent: they blend words that do not belong together. It is very difficult to comment on such essays, because there are no distinct propositions there that can be improved upon or corrected. Nothing specific can be said in response. And more generally, outside the domain of academic examinations, it is very difficult to correct misconceptions that people have in regard to art, politics, or religion, not because what people say is simply erroneous, but because it is incoherent.

The three levels of propositional structure that we have distinguished – syntactic form, consistency, and coherence – help us to make several important points regarding human reasoning. With these distinctions we can, for example, show how formal logic works in the quest for truth. Formal logic provides the rules for the second level, that of consistency. It does not assure us of the truth of propositions, but it spells out conditions for their validity, conditions that the propositions must fulfill if they are even to be candidates for truth. Formal logic shows how propositions can be validly combined into larger wholes, into arguments, without collapsing into contradiction. If a set of propositions is inconsistent, we know we could not confirm them by evidencing the things they express; such evidence is excluded a priori.

Detecting an inconsistency is one way of criticizing an argument, but another is detecting a syntactic flaw, one that shows that the speaker failed formally in assembling a proposition in the first place. An utterance with garbled syntax does not even qualify to be tested for consistency. But incoherence also disqualifies a statement from being tested for consistency. An incoherent statement, such as "My cat is a filibuster," transcends contradiction or noncontradiction. To say the cat both is and is not a filibuster is not to say anything contradictory, because there is no valid propositional meaning there to be contradicted. Incoherence of content, like confusion in syntax, violates the preconditions for consistency.

These three deficiencies in thinking – failed syntax, contradiction, incoherence – can actually occur when our thinking is pervaded by vagueness, and vagueness, as we have seen in Chapter 7, is not rare in human discourse. It is what all of us are in some of the time and some of us are in most of the time when we speak. Indistinct thinking, confusion, is the source for all three muddles, but especially for the third, for incoherence. It is rare that we are syntactically delinquent; if we fell this far, we would be babbling rather than speaking. But incoherence is very common, especially when people begin to speak about things that go beyond simple and obvious facts and get into more reflective issues.

EXPERIENCE OF INDIVIDUALS AS THE BASIC EVIDENCE

Coherence of the contents of propositions, therefore, is a precondition for the consistency and the truth of the propositions. Where does such coherence come from? How do we get the rules that tell us what contents can be blended with others?

It is not the case that we simply devise rules of relevance that tell us that the term "uncles" blends with "male, tall or short, bearded or not, generous or stingy," etc., and that the term does not blend with "illegible, astronomical, feline, molecular," etc. It is not the case that coherence comes just from linguistic rules that govern our vocabulary. Rather, the coherence of the contents of propositions comes from our experience of objects, and specifically from our experience of individual objects. It comes from the fact that in our encounter with particular things we find certain contents or categories belonging together; we articulate the things as having such features. The features emerge as we bring the objects from prepredicative to predicative evidencing. All the propositions we formulate derive ultimately from the experience we ourselves, or other people in our linguistic community, have had of the things in question. For a proposition like "My uncles are bald" to be verifiable, the blend of contents "uncles–bald" must be possible, and its possibility arises because that particular blend can in principle be articulated out of prepredicative experience. We can find those two contents blended together.

In the truth of correctness, we start with the proposition and return it to the evidence of prepredicative experience. The proposition originally arose from prepredicative, individual evidencing, and now it returns to the same source and is melted down into prepredicative experiencing when it is confirmed. If the proposition is falsified, we find that our evidencing resists the intention we try to fulfill in it. We do not find the truth of propositions just by examining the statements themselves; the statements are geared teleologically to confirmation or disconfirmation by the things themselves, by the objects we encounter in our various modes of perception. In the hierarchy of evidences, the intrinsically first and last ones are those of the direct experience of things. All our meanings, with their syntactic and semantic structures, arise from experience and are geared toward experience and the beings disclosed in it.

Human speech, therefore, is directed toward things in their intelligibility, and human reason is ordered toward truth as its end and perfection. Formal structures are not ends in themselves, but instruments in the disclosure of things. Linguistic structures may form wholes of exquisite complexity, and we may at times be so enthralled by them that we think that there is nothing but the play of signifiers and syntax, that they are sufficient unto themselves. Both structuralists and deconstructionists believe this, thinking that there is no "center" beyond the play of significations. But phenomenology sees the formal patterns of language as endowed with an even greater dignity and beauty: they not only interact with one another, but serve to disclose the way things are and the way things can be. The mind that constitutes meaning and its formal structures does so ultimately to evidence the truth of things.

The things we experience, moreover, are not just the material objects perceived through our five senses. It is true that we see that the apple is red and the house is white, but we also see instances of deception, generosity, tools, and sport, and in articulating those instances we flesh out the features that such things have. It is not true that the only individuals we experience are simply material things like stones and trees.

Finally, consistency and coherence are not found only in theoretical matters. Practical thinking is also governed by them. We may criticize a public program or a personal project for being inconsistent or incoherent; its means may contradict one another or the purposes they are meant to serve; several incompatible goals may be sought at the same time (we are acting at cross-purposes); the very sense of the means and the ends may be completely garbled in our planning. Sometimes an inconsistency in action may arise because of unavoidable pressures that are put on the project; we know that the program has problems, but something has to be done, this is the best we can do, and we will try to muddle through. At other times, however, the inconsistencies and incoherences simply reveal the incompetence of the agent.

EVIDENCE AND THE BEAUTIFUL

The things we evidence are not just sources of idle information. We do not just pick up the facts that the tree is tall and the sun is shining. Rather, things, besides being true, are also good and admirable. The things we know are valuable. The reason why we continue to perceive things, the reason why we turn the cube around to see its other aspects or walk into the building to see the parts we cannot see from the outside is that there is something important for us to find out. Things solicit our interest and provoke our articulation: they do so because finding out about them satisfies various needs and interests that we have (the apple is ripe enough to eat, the tree can be climbed), but also because the things themselves are beautiful and reward our curiosity. The things we know are not just dull lists of indifferent information, but sources of marvelous appearances. We are continually astonished to see what a thing is and also what else it can be, what "other sides" it can offer us. No matter how many football games a fan has seen, he is still curious to see how this one will turn out and what face the game will present this time. No matter how often we have heard the *Goldberg Variations*, we are eager to hear this interpretation to see what else the piece can be. No matter how much time two friends have spent together, they will always look forward to another meeting to enjoy the further appearances that will come to light. We do not tire of hearing about human action (heroism or cowardice, generosity or greed) in ever-new situations. Everything – a garden or a tree, a piece of jewelry or a favorite walk – has its *kalon* and is beautiful or admirable after its own fashion.

To say that a thing is an identity in manifolds is not to say that it just rolls out more and more data, like so many copies of one and the same newspaper. Rather, the thing is like a radioactive source that keeps emitting different kinds of energy, even while remaining and being identified as one and the same object. Manifestation does not just give us facts; it reveals the beauty peculiar to the thing in question. And even if we were to be rudely and grossly utilitarian and became blind to the elegance of the thing itself, if our interest in the thing were motivated only by the fact that the thing can serve us in some way, even then, we in our Philistine pragmatism would still be recognizing a kind of good in the thing, a good of utility. Even then, the thing would not be merely a source of information.

Radioactive elements all have a half-life; they become depleted over time, even though they may continue emitting energy for thousands of years. A thing as a source of appearance, as an identity in manifolds, does not have a half-life. It generates new appearances, to a dative that will appreciate them, with greater and greater intensity, not with diminishing strength. It is inexhaustible, an endless reservoir of surprising disclosures. We never know everything that can be said about an object. The thing as an identity has depth; whatever appearances it may have presented to us, there are still others being held in reserve, and all of them belong to one and the same thing: How will the Empire State Building look when we see it at evening from the promenade on Brooklyn Heights? How will

Eisenhower perform as president? How will Hamlet appear through Kenneth Branagh? What will saffron do for this dish? Some of the appearances that have already surfaced, moreover, may go back into hiding and be seen again only at a later time and in other perspectives, to speakers of other languages, to a community that may remember things we have forgotten. All these appearances will belong to the same thing in question. Any truth that we achieve is always surrounded by absence and hiddenness, by mystery, since the thing we know is always more than we can know, the reference is always more than the sense.

The life of reason ranges, then, through the intricate structures of formal logic, the combinatorics of syntax, the cohesion of propositional contents, and the interplay of presence, absence, and vagueness. It covers both direct disclosure and correctness. It moves between sedimentation and revival. It is a life led by the transcendental ego and is ordered toward evidencing the way things are.

12

Eidetic Intuition

In our experience, we deal with more than individuals and groups. We also have insight into the essence of things. For example, we can see not only that all the human beings we have encountered are capable of speech, but that the ability to use language is necessarily and universally a part of being human. It is part of the essence of man; we could not be human without it. We can see not only that material objects interact causally with their surroundings, but that they must do so; without the possibility of such interaction, a material object would not be what it is. Likewise, a perceived object's being an identity in a manifold of sides, aspects, and profiles is universal and necessary, and we can see that it is so. Essences are evidenced to us.

Insight into an essence is called *eidetic intuition*, because it is the grasp of an eidos or a form. We can intuit, or make present to ourselves, not only individuals with their features, but also the essences that things have. Eidetic intuition is a special kind of intentionality with a structure of its own. Phenomenology offers an analysis of this intentionality; it describes how we can intuit an essence.

ANALYSIS OF EIDETIC INTUITION

Like all intentionalities, eidetic intuition is an identity synthesis. Through it we recognize an identity within manifolds of appearance, but the identity and the manifolds are different from the kind that occur when we intuit individual things. To show how eidetic intuition makes essences present to us, we must trace it through three levels of intentional development.

1. On the first level, we experience a number of things and find similarities among them. We might find, for example, that this piece

of wood floats, and that this other piece of wood floats, and that this third one does so as well. At this stage we discover the rather weak kind of identity that is called *typicality*. This level could be symbolized by the following series: A is p_1, B is p_2, C is p_3. The predicates in this series are not, strictly speaking, the same; they are only similar to one another. We have achieved an identity synthesis based simply on association, as the presence of one feature makes us rather passively expect other features associated with it to follow in its train. Floating has, for us, been associated with wood, or biting has been associated with dogs, so we expect the next piece of wood to float or the next dog to bite us, but we have not made an explicit judgment about wood floating or dogs biting. Our experience is stylized or typified, but it has not been elevated into distinct thinking.

2. On the second level, we come to see that the three individual pieces of wood can be said to have not just similar predicates, but the very same predicate. This level could be symbolized by the following series: A is p, B is p, C is p. A kind of identity synthesis now occurs in which we recognize not just similars, but the very same, a "one in many." It follows that the mere use of the word for the predicate, such as the word "floats," does not by itself indicate whether the word is being used to name similars or the very same. The use of one word masks two different kinds of intentionality, two different identifications. When we do take the word to mean the very same feature, we reach an *empirical universal*, because all the instances in which we have found the predicate are things we have actually experienced. So far, all the cases of wood we have encountered do float, and empirically we express this finding in a universal manner, as "Wood floats," but our evidence only goes so far as our experience has gone. Our claim is falsifiable by further experience; it is conceivable that we might encounter pieces of wood that do not float. The discovery of black swans was able to falsify the universal claim, "All swans are white," because the claim was based on an empirical universal.

3. In our third and final stage, we strive to reach a feature that it would be inconceivable for the thing to be without. We try to move beyond empirical to eidetic universals, to necessities and not just regularities. In order to do so, we move from perception into the realm of imagination. We go from actual experience to armchair

philosophizing. If we are successful, we will have achieved an eidetic intuition.

We proceed in the following manner. We focus on a universal that we have reached. We posit an instance of that universal kind. We then attempt to imagine changes in the object, in a process called *imaginative variation*. We let our imagination run free, and we see what elements we could remove from the thing before it "shatters" or "explodes" as the kind of thing that it is. We try to push the boundaries, to expand the envelope of the thing in question. If we can discard some features and still preserve the object, we know that those features do not belong to the eidos of the thing. However, if we run into features that we cannot remove without destroying the thing, we realize that these features are eidetically necessary to it. If, for example, we tried to imagine a perceived object that did not get larger as we came closer and smaller as we went farther from it, we would say we are no longer perceiving a material, spatial object: spatial expansion and contraction as a function of approach and withdrawal are essential features in the perception of spatial things. If I tried to imagine someone else's experiences arising within my memories, I would see that such a thing is not possible: only my own experiences can be remembered by me. If we tried to imagine time without succession, or speech without a rhetorical aspect, we would see that such things could not be. When we bump up against such impossibilities, we have succeeded in reaching an eidetic intuition. We evidence an essence. We achieve an identification that is "more necessary" than the kind achieved in empirical universals. We know that such things "must be" in a stronger way than things like the facts that wood floats and swans are white. When we reach an eidetic intuition, we see that it would be inconceivable for the thing in question to be otherwise. The move into imagination gives us a deeper insight than does empirical induction.

Eidetic intuition is not easy. It calls for great strength of imagination. To be able to try to imagine the impossible, and to see that it is impossible and therefore cannot be thought, demands that we be able to go beyond the things we are accustomed to, the things we have regularly experienced. Most of us live in empirical universals; we take it for granted that things will be the way we have always experienced them to be, but we have not tested their necessity by trying to imagine their being otherwise. To be able to ferret out the eidetic within the customary and the empirical requires creative imagination. For example, the transformation of space and time that occurred when Newton introduced absolute space and time as a kind of eternal container for the universe, and the further transformation of space and time that occurred in the theory of relativity, were attempts at eidetic intuitions, based on imaginative variations that Newton and Einstein were able to perform. Those men had the imagination to project this new possibility. They pushed space and time beyond the customary and the received. Obviously, not everyone can do this sort of thing.

Imaginative variations occur in fiction, where circumstances are imagined that depart from the ordinary but serve to bring out a necessity. They show how things have to be. It is not the case that one just imagines bizarre settings. The purely fantastic projection is easy enough, but what must happen if there is to be insight is that within the imaginative circumstance a necessity has to be brought to light. For this to occur, the imaginative variation has to be cleverly contrived; we must have the talent to know what imaginative presentation will do the trick. Imagination gives us a glimpse of necessity. That insight, which the Greeks called *nous*, is the reward we get for our imaginative effort.

Two things must be done, therefore: the imaginative projection beyond what is possible, and the insight that what we have projected cannot be. A necessity comes to light in the impossibility of what we tried to imagine. These requirements are found even in science fiction. The most outlandish circumstances are imagined, but within them the basic human exchanges all seem to recur: honesty and deceit, prudence and foolishness, courage and cowardice. Such actions seem to be inevitable so long as rational agents are being depicted, and their necessity comes to light when they are found to persist even in the exotic settings of the remote future or cosmic space. We can imagine human beings living in spaceships instead of on earth, but we could not imagine them without the possibility of communicating with one another or without the ability to be courageous, rash, or cowardly. What is noteworthy about science fiction is not how different its locale and technology are from ours, but how much like us the protagonists are.

Imaginative variation and eidetic insight are used everywhere in philosophy. Because they involve fantasy, they give the impression that philosophy deals with unreal situations. The point of philosophical imagination, however, is not to concoct fantastic scenarios, but to use these projections to bring out the inexorable necessity of certain things: to show that, say, human beings find their moral perfection in civic life, or that material things involve networks of causation, or that space and time involve parts that are outside one another, or that there is a difference between human action and human making, between *praxis* and *poiēsis*. These eidetic necessities are deeper and stronger than empirical truths. In fact, they are so deep and strong that people generally take them for granted and see no reason to assert them. When such truths become formulated by philosophers, they may provoke another common complaint against philosophy, that it deals with the most patent trivialities. Why do such obvious things need to be stated? Who on earth would ever question them?

They need to be stated for two reasons. First, despite their obviousness, some people do deny them. There are people who say, for example, that human fulfillment is achieved in the economic life rather than the moral and political, or that there are no perceptions, or that time is illusory, or that there are no such things as truth and evidence. The Sophists made some of these claims when philosophy was just beginning, and they or their equivalent are always around in human life. Philosophy always has to recall things that are obvious because people do in fact overlook or even deny them. Philosophy has to defend the true opinions of the natural attitude.

But besides this protective task, philosophy states its "trivialities" for a second, more positive reason. It is humanly gratifying to become aware of eidetic necessities. It gives us pleasure to contemplate them. They are good to know. If some writers can use their imaginations to generate insight into what has to be, they help us see the eternal things. Not everyone wants to see these things, but many of us do, and insight into eidetic necessities is its own justification for those who are able to enjoy it.

Philosophy is falsely accused, then, of dealing either with the fantastic or with the trivial. These reproaches are made because philosophy makes use of eidetic intuition, which employs imagination to bring out the way things have to be.

FURTHER COMMENTS ON EIDETIC INTUITION

This discussion has given a general idea of what eidetic intuition is. There are many further details that can be brought out concerning such intuition and the three stages that lead to it. Let us spend a few moments browsing through this form of intentionality.

We distinguished a first stage, in which we experience merely similar things, and a second, in which we experience empirical universals. Only on the second level does the full sense of an individual arise for us. Only when we reach the sense of a true universal, such as "red" or "floats" or "square," as identically the same in many instances, do we attain the contrasting sense of an individual or a particular under that universal. On the first level we experience individuals, but we do not yet see them as individuals. Their sense of being individual has not yet been constituted for us, because we need the foil of the universal for this to happen.

On the first level, where we experience only similars, we may use the same word for many instances, but the word is being used analogously. A child may call all men "daddy" or "uncle," or use the word "go" for all sorts of situations, but in doing so he does not use the term to express anything univocal or specific. At this stage, the mind is awash in similarities, and the distinction between universal and singular has not yet arisen. This level of intentionality is submerged in association and does not reach exact identifications. The associative level, furthermore, remains with us as a kind of foundation for our higher intentionalities. Even in our mature thinking, we sometimes fall back into these primitive stages, when we lapse into vagueness or when we search for the right word or the right metaphor for a new situation. Eidetic intuition moves us into the domain of the Platonic forms; it takes us into the highest section of the Divided Line described in book 5 of the *Republic*, but the associative level, the domain of mere similarities, places us in the lowest section of that line, where we live among insubstantial images. But no matter how much we may enjoy living among the forms, we never abandon the appearances on the lower levels, and only through them can we come to the higher intelligibilities.

We do not always succeed in our eidetic intuitions. We may think we have one when we do not. Our attempt may misfire. We may overshoot. We may imagine something new and think we have revealed something necessary about the thing in question, but we may be mistaken: we may have slipped into sheer fantasy without essentials. Socrates imagines a city in which women, children, and property will be held in common. He thinks he has discovered a truth about human families and possessions, but Aristotle criticizes him for mistaking pure fantasy for what could be real (*Politics* 2.6). Newton's postulation of absolute time and space may be criticized as an excess, as an overstatement of what could possibly be. Hobbes imagines man into a state of pure nature and then imagines a contract that establishes a sovereign who rules over perfectly equal subjects; he thinks he is discovering the true nature of man and society, but he may well have drifted off into fantasy without insight. Socrates' city, the Hobbesian sovereign, Marxist utopias, Cartesian consciousness, and mathematically ideal nature all suffer from an excess of imagination. They are misplaced intuitions, projects of fantasy and not expressions of the world in which we truly live.

When we err in regard to eidetics, when we take as necessarily true what is only a fantastic projection, we have made a mistake precisely in regard to an eidetic necessity. We have not erred in regard to simple facts or empirical universals. We have made a "philosophical" mistake, not an error in factual judgment, a misperception, or a failure in memory. Not all imaginative variations are successful, and when they fail they do not turn into another kind of intentionality. They remain an attempt at an eidetic intuition, but a failed one. Because eidetic intuition works with imagination, it plays with fire: it is easy to let our imagination run out of control.

How do we correct mistakes in eidetic intuition? By talking with others about them, by imagining counterexamples, and most of all by seeing how our eidetic proposals conform to the empirical universals we had identified before we reached the eidetic. Empirical universals are constituted on the second of the three levels we have distinguished, and they serve as a foundation for eidetic universals. Eidetic universals go beyond the empirical, but they rest on them and should not destroy them. What we find in an eidetic intuition should confirm the empirical truth and not subvert it. The empirical universals serve as a control on our imaginations. When we say our philosophy should conform to "common sense," what we are appealing to are the empirical universals that are the fruit of our standard experience. Empirical universals give us a foothold in the real world, and our eidetics would fly off into unreality if it disregarded them.

Another point to be made concerning eidetic intuition concerns the role of impossibility, of negative necessity. We do not see positively the necessary link between the thing and the feature we are testing it for. Instead, we see the necessity by a rebound from the negative insight: we see the impossibility of the thing's being without the feature, so we know the feature is essential; we could not imagine the thing being deprived of it. The negative impossibility brings the eidetic necessity to light. The fact that we must make a foray into the impossible is what forces us to appeal to the imagination in eidetic intuition; the imagination could attempt to portray the impossible and thus bring out the necessary, but how could perception ever do so?

Imaginative variation and eidetic insight can be carried out within the natural attitude. This *eidetic reduction* focuses on the essential form of things. The eidetic reduction, however, is different from the transcendental, which turns us from the natural attitude to the phenomenological. Phenomenology itself makes use of both reductions, the transcendental and the eidetic. By virtue of the transcendental reduction, it contemplates intentionality and its objective correlates, but it also brings out the eidetic structures of such noeses and noemas, and hence engages the eidetic reduction. It is concerned not with the experiences and objects that I happen to have, but with the eidetically necessary structures of such experiences and objects, as they would hold for any consciousness whatever. Phenomenology aims at discovering how things and the mind have to be for disclosure to take place.

13

Phenomenology Defined

Our exmination of evidence in Chapter 11 interpreted reason as being ordered toward the truth of things. Reason is the disclosure and the confirmation of what things are. Even in the natural attitude, the mind finds its completion in truth. Phenomenology, working from the transcendental viewpoint, is also an exercise of reason and shares in the teleology of thinking. It too is ordered toward manifestation, but in a way different from the science and experience that occur in the natural attitude. The language we have called "mundanese" serves to disclose truth; "transcendentalese" does so as well, but in a different way.

In our natural achievements of evidence, in our ordinary experience and in science, we let things appear to ourselves and to the community within which we converse. We let plants and animals, stars and atoms, heroes and villains manifest themselves. In phenomenological reflection, however, we turn our focus toward these disclosures themselves, toward the evidences that we have accomplished, and we think about what it is to be datives of manifestation and what it is for beings to be manifest. Phenomenology is the science that studies truth. It stands back from our rational involvement with things and marvels at the fact that there is disclosure, that things do appear, that the world can be understood, and that we in our life of thinking serve as datives for the manifestation of things. Philosophy is the art and science of evidencing evidence.

Phenomenology also examines the limitations of truth: the inescapable "other sides" that keep things from ever being fully disclosed, the errors and vagueness that accompany evidence, and the sedimentation that makes it necessary for us always to remember again the things we already know. Phenomenology acknowledges these disturbances of truth, but it does not let them drive it to despair. It sees them just as disturbances and not as the substance of our being. It insists that along with these shadows, truth and evidence are achieved, and that reason finds its perfection in letting things come to light. Reason does not perfect itself in error, confusion, and forgetfulness.

Philosophy begins when we take up a new stance toward our natural attitude and all its involvements. When we engage in philosophy, we stand back and contemplate what it is to be truthful and to achieve evidence. We contemplate the natural attitude, and hence we take up a viewpoint outside it. This move of standing back is done through the transcendental reduction. Instead of being simply concerned with objects and their features, we think about the correlation between the things being disclosed and the dative to whom they are manifested. Within the transcendental reduction, we also carry out an eidetic reduction and express structures that hold not just for ourselves, but for every subjectivity that is engaged in evidencing and truth.

We examined philosophical thinking in Chapter 4, where we explored the transcendental reduction at length. We can now examine the nature of philosophy from a slightly different angle: we will make use of some thoughts developed in Chapter 7, where we saw that propositions and concepts need not be posited as mental things or mediating conceptual entities. We noted in that chapter that a proposition arises in response to a special kind of reflection, one that we called "propositional" or "apophantic" reflection. A state of affairs is turned into a proposition or a sense when we take that state of affairs as being proposed by someone. We change its status; it becomes not just the way things are, but the way someone has articulated and presented them. Such propositions, constituted by propositional reflection, then become candidates for the truth of correctness. They are said to be true judgments when they can be disquoted and blended with the direct evidence of things themselves.

What we will do in the present chapter is to discover more precisely what philosophical reflection is by contrasting it with propositional reflection. The two forms of reflection, the propositional and the philosophical, are often confused with one another. Because of this confusion, the special character of philosophical thinking is frequently misunderstood. We will bring out the differences between philosophical and propositional reflection, and these distinc-

tions will help us pin down more clearly the nature of phenomenological inquiry.

We live in the world and articulate things, whether in theoretic or
in practical contexts. Suppose you and I are conversing about a
house. Among many other statements, you say that the house is fifty
years old. I have been listening to you and unreflectively going along
with everything you said, and I have been articulating the world
under your guidance, but now this assertion makes me pause. It
does not seem quite right. I interrupt my naive acceptance of everything you say; I switch into the propositional mode: I take the house
as being fifty years old not simply as the way things are, but only as
you are presenting them. I shift gears; I move into a propositional
reflection. I put quotation marks around the house's being fifty
years old. I treat that state of affairs not as an evident fact but as
your proposition, your meaning, the sense of your words. I treat the
state of affairs as merely being proposed, as being presented by you.
The original state of affairs has become a proposition.

Suppose that my further experiencing leads me to agree that the
house is fifty years old. Then I disquote what I had put into quotation marks. I abandon the propositional reflection. I realize that the
proposition is correct, that it identifies with what is the case, with
what can be given in straightforward evidence. The proposition (the
state of affairs taken as proposed) blends with the fact and is seen
to be true. On the other hand, suppose that my further experiencing and inquiry lead me to conclude that the house is not fifty years
old but only twenty. Then I would rivet the quotation marks to the
house's being fifty years old; I would see that the proposition, your
proposition, is false, that it cannot be disquoted and made into a
simple fact again, that it cannot enjoy the truth of correctness. It is
discarded as a candidate for truth. It is only a proposition, only a
state of affairs as proposed, only your opinion, and it could not be
anything else. I can no longer relax my propositional reflection in
this instance and take what you say as simply the way things are.

This movement back and forth between the state of affairs and
the proposition, between the state of affairs as simply taken and as
taken as merely proposed, is a highly sophisticated human achieve-

ment. It is an essential part of human reason. We could not imagine a rational animal that failed to have this power; an entity bereft of this ability would not possess reason. Nonhuman animals cannot propositionalize a state of affairs except perhaps in the most rudimentary way; they cannot reflect propositionally and see a situation as merely being presented by someone or as confirming what someone has said. This zig-zag motion between what is, what seems, what is said, and what confirms is inscribed in the grammar of human languages, in phrases such as "I claim that *p*," "You say that *q*," "What you said is true [or false]," and in many other dimensions of syntax.

Our ability to shift into propositional reflection allows us to take a distance toward any issue we are involved in. When we are caught up in a conversation about something, and even when we are thinking about an issue by ourselves, we can shift into the propositional mode and take what is being presented as *merely* presented, as just a proposition or a sense and not the way things simply are. The ability to shift into the propositional mode, and then to confirm or disconfirm what has been said, establishes us as responsible speakers who can say "I" and identify ourselves as the agents of this or that claim to truth.

However, this ability to shift into propositional reflection and to exercise the kind of truth that it makes possible, glorious as it may be as an emblem of our rational nature, is not the same as the ability to move into philosophical reflection. We must distinguish propositional from philosophical reflection. If we succeed in doing so, we will gain a much better understanding of both the propositional and the philosophical domain.

When I engage in a propositional reflection, when I take the house's being fifty years old as merely your proposition, I reflect *only* on this one state of affairs: on the house's being fifty years old. Everything else is left in place and not reflected upon: your being there as my interlocutor, my being here as yours, the sounds we make, the trees, the lawn, the sky, the weather, the house itself as white, wooden, and colonial in style. I also leave in place, undisturbed and without reflection, the world belief that underlies all my more particular convictions. When I propositionalize, I take a distance to a particular salient state of affairs, or even to a group of them, but my reflective critique leaves an unlimited array of states of affairs, things, and contexts totally untouched. Their doxic quality stays intact. They all remain in place as a kind of floor on which I find the leverage I need to reflect on the simple state of affairs I turn into a proposition.

On the other hand, when I engage in philosophical reflection, when I exercise the phenomenological reduction, I take a distance toward absolutely everything in the natural attitude: not just the house's being fifty years old, but the whole house, the trees, the lawn, you and me as conversationalists, the weather, the earth, the sky, the stars, the sun and moon, and even the world that underlies all these things and the world belief that is its correlate. This is reflection with a vengeance; it is wholesale reflection. Nothing is left out. We take a distance toward everything, even to the world as such and ourselves as having a world. We do not hold on to several beliefs as a base to give us leverage; we do not retain a floor to stand on. We do not leave any convictions untouched. All of them, even the most basic, are suspended and reflected upon. This all-encompassing reflection is philosophical; the more restricted reflection is propositional.

The initial difference between philosophical and propositional reflection, then, is one of scope: philosophical reflection is universal, propositional reflection is limited and targeted just toward this or that state of affairs.

"All right then," you might ask, "is the difference between propositional and philosophical reflection just the fact that the former is limited and the latter is comprehensive? Does propositional reflection deal only with this or that state of affairs, while philosophical reflection deals with absolutely everything? Is philosophy just the propositional reflection enlarged to cover any and all convictions that we have? Are they both the same kind of reflection, and do they differ only in their range?"

The answer to this question is negative. Propositional and philosophical reflection do not differ only in their extension. They are different kinds of reflection, and they differ in the following way.

A propositional reflection is carried out in order to test the truth of the proposition that emerges from it. It is carried out so that we can verify a proposal that has become questionable. There is something pragmatic about propositional reflection. We execute it in order to find out more accurately what is the case. If we find out that the proposition is true, we accept it again, with the new, stronger evidence that the confirmation brings, but if we find out that it is false, we reject it. It becomes a discarded, erroneous judgment. Propositional reflection is carried on in the interest of truth, in the interest of verification. Our overall truth interest is never neutralized when we shift into the propositional mode.

Philosophical reflection, on the other hand, is not carried out for such pragmatic reasons. It is not done in order to verify or falsify a claim. It is more purely contemplative, more purely detached. When we take a distance philosophically toward all our convictions, including our world belief, and toward everything given to our intentionality, including the world, we are not putting all these convictions and things into quotation marks until we can verify whether or not they are true. They are not being suspended in the way we suspend propositions. They are neutralized, but only to be contemplated, not to be verified.

When we propositionalize a state of affairs, when we enter into *propositional* reflection, we question the state of affairs. We do not assert it any longer. We change its modality: it was a conviction, but now we make it doubtful or at least questionable. When we enter into *philosophical* reflection, we do not change the modality of the convictions we have in the natural attitude. We take a distance to them, and hence we contemplate and do not, at the moment, share in them, but we do not make them doubtful or questionable. We do not try to verify or falsify them. We merely think about them and try to tease out their intentional structure and teleology. We leave everything as it was when we enter into philosophy. We do not try to transform our prephilosophical opinions or verifications or evidences. We must leave everything as it was, for otherwise we would change the very thing we wish to examine.

In a manner that should not be taken amiss, philosophy is indifferent to the truth or falsity found in the natural attitude. Philosophy contemplates the truthful, but it also recognizes the falsity, vagueness, empty intentions, and error that are part of the natural attitude, and it does not try to erase these shadows that accompany truth. It acknowledges their inevitability in the quest for truth. It does not take over and try to get rid of them. It does not try to substitute its own perspective, with its calm detachment and greater lucidity, for the perspectives of the natural attitude. It does not become imperialistic and does not claim that its mode of truth is the only one there is.

If philosophical reflection were to be taken as the same as propositional reflection, then philosophy would indeed become imperial. It would try to elbow its way into our prephilosophical inquiries and actions. It would try to take over. It would try to correct everything. It would try to clean up the mess in the natural attitude, with all the partial perspectives, vagueness, and deceptions, and would try to make us live in pure light. It would intrude on the human conversation, and its voice would drown out all the other voices in the human condition. If philosophy is to be faithful to its own destiny, it has to be more modest than this. It is the crown of human rationality, but it has to restrict itself to its own kind of truth, to its own purely contemplative teleology; it must refrain from trying to substitute for the skills and expertise of the natural attitude. The philosopher would look silly if he were to try to replace statesmen, lawyers, scientists, and craftsmen. It is also true, of course, that the experts and the statesmen look silly in turn if they think that what they do is the summit of human reason.

So far, we have seen that philosophical reflection differs from propositional reflection in two ways: in scope (the former is universal while the latter is limited) and in kind (the former is merely contemplative and not an attempt to verify; the latter is geared to determining the correctness of statements). There remain two further differences that must be considered.

DIFFERENCES BETWEEN NOEMA AND SENSE, BRACKETING AND QUOTING

In both kinds of reflection, the philosophical and the propositional, we modify the way the objective correlates of our intentions are given to us.

When we shift into philosophical reflection, when we execute the transcendental reduction, we do not concern ourselves only with our intentionality; we also consider the targets of that intentionality, the things that are given to our various modes of intending (perception, memory, imagination, anticipation, judgment, and the rest). From our philosophical vantage point, however, we do not directly and naively focus on these objects; rather, we focus on them precisely as being intended by, or presented to, our intentionalities in the natural attitude. We consider them not simply as things, but as "things being intended." That is, we consider them as noemas. We consider them noematically. For example, the perceived object looked at from the philosophical viewpoint and considered precisely as perceived, as the objective correlate of perception, is the noema of perception. The asserted state of affairs, looked at from the philosophical viewpoint and considered precisely as asserted, as the objective correlate of assertion, is the noema of assertion. The task of phenomenology is to explore the correlations between noemas and their corresponding noeses, the intentional activities that constitute the noemas and allow the things disclosed to be presented to us.

The phenomenological reduction turns objects into noemas. Propositional reflection, in contrast, turns objects into senses. When I begin to question a state of affairs and take it as merely being proposed by you, I turn the state of affairs into a sense or a proposition. I see it just as your meaning. I can then test it for correctness. Being a sense, however, is not the same as being a noema. A sense or a proposition is a candidate for verification, for the truth of correctness, but a noema is merely the target of philosophical analysis. The world, along with everything in it, is turned into a noema when we enter into phenomenological reflection, but it would be impossible to turn the world and everything in it into a sense or a proposition, into something that needs to be verified.

As we have seen in Chapter 7, when we carry out a propositional reflection, we can be said to have put quotation marks around the state of affairs we are questioning. You tell me that the house is fifty years old, and I, in my hesitation to agree with you, transform the house's being fifty years old into your opinion, "The house is fifty years old." Something analogous to this kind of citation also happens in phenomenological reflection; there is a kind of citation in phenomenology that resembles the quotations done in the natural attitude, but it must be distinguished from them.

In the phenomenological attitude, we do not merely focus on objects; we focus on them precisely as the targets of the natural attitude, precisely as given to our intentionalities in the natural attitude. Therefore, we in a way "quote" the natural attitude when we speak philosophically. We "quote" ourselves as we intend things in the natural attitude. But let us avoid the word "quotation" here, lest it lead us into confusion. Let us follow the accepted phenomenological terminology and say that we *bracket* the world and everything in it when we carry out philosophical reflection. We put the world and everything in it into brackets or into parentheses. Brackets are the quotation marks for philosophy. They express the kind of distance we take to things when we are engaged in philosophy (we see them as they are presented to prephilosophical evidences), just as quotation marks express the kind of distance we take to a state of affairs when we are engaged in propositional reflection. Brackets mean we are taking what is bracketed as a noema, while quotation marks mean we are taking what is quoted as a sense.

DIFFERENCES IN PERSPECTIVE

There is one more difference between philosophical and propositional reflection that we must examine. We recall that propositional reflection is carried out in the natural attitude. Propositional reflection suspends belief in one intentionality and its object, but it does not suspend our world belief, as phenomenological reflection does. If you tell me that the house is fifty years old, and if I exercise a propositional reflection toward that state of affairs, I still remain in the natural attitude. The state of affairs (the house's being fifty years old) has been turned into a proposition or a sense, but as such it too is still encased within the natural attitude.

A sense or a proposition is itself, as such, the objective correlate of a special kind of intentionality. It is the correlate of a propositional reflection, just as the perceived object is the correlate of a perception and an articulated object is the correlate of an assertive articulation.

Now, when we shift into the phenomenological attitude, we contemplate the proposition or sense as the objective correlate of a propositional reflection. We focus noematically upon the proposition or sense. The proposition or sense is a noema, just like any other objective correlate of any other intentionality. In fact, the entire description we have been developing of the establishment of the propositional domain, the domain of sense, was done from within philosophical reflection. It was as phenomenologists that we pointed out that a proposition or a sense arises in response to a propositional reflection.

Thus, the phenomenological reflection is not just more radical than the propositional, in the sense that it cuts all the way down to world belief; it is also more encompassing, in the special sense that it focuses on propositional reflection and describes what it accomplishes. Phenomenological reflection comes on top of propositional reflection and explains what it does: it explains how propositional reflection constitutes propositions. Propositional reflection, however, does not explain the turn into phenomenology. The turn into phenomenology is off the radar screen of propositional reflection.

We noted in Chapter 4 that the noema should not be equated with sense. Now we can say why the two should not be identified. To equate sense and noema would be to equate propositional and phenomenological reflection. It would be to take philosophy simply as the critical reflection on our meanings or senses; it would equate philosophy with linguistic analysis. The special stance from which we think philosophically, the distinctive nature of philosophical analysis, would not come to light. Philosophy would be assimilated to one of the activities within the natural attitude. Sense or meaning differs from the noema because propositional reflection is different from philosophical reflection.

A GRAPHIC ILLUSTRATION OF THE TWO REFLECTIONS

I would like to try to clarify the interplay between philosophical and propositional reflection by drawing an analogy. I wish to use comic strips to bring out the difference between the perspective we take on when we are engaged in philosophy and the perspective we have when we simply propositionalize and test a statement for the truth of correctness.

Suppose we have a comic strip in which one speaker, Alpha, is talking to another, Beta. Alpha says something to Beta about trees. What Alpha says is enclosed in the balloons that are used in comic strips to designate speech. Suppose the balloon attached to Alpha contains the words, "These trees will fall over the next time there is a strong wind." Beta, within the comic strip, would normally be taking Alpha's words at face value and would be thinking about the trees as he hears what Alpha says. But suppose Beta gets suspicious. He wonders if Alpha is right. He propositionalizes the state of affairs that Alpha has articulated. When Beta does so, it is as though he turned his focus from the trees to the "conceptual content" of the balloon attached to Alpha, and the "conceptual content" of that balloon is the trees' being ready to topple (taken as proposed).

When Beta carries out this propositional maneuver, however, he remains entirely within the frame of the comic strip. He remains within the natural attitude.

How would philosophical reflection be illustrated in this setting? The philosopher could not be depicted inside the comic strip. The philosopher is something like the person who is reading the comic strip, not like one of the personalities within it. He stands "outside" the frame of the natural attitude, outside the comic-strip cartoons. The philosopher (perched or suspended in the phenomenological attitude) contemplates the goings-on in the comic strip (the exchanges in the natural attitude). The comic-strip characters, Alpha and Beta, carry out all sorts of intentional acts (perceptions, imaginations, recollections), they constitute categorial objects, and they converse with one another. They also engage in propositional reflection, as they turn a state of affairs into a proposition or a sense and test it for truth.

The one thing the comic-strip characters cannot do is to crawl out of the cartoon frames and read the comic strip. That performance is logically and metaphysically impossible. They cannot escape being in the funny papers. To draw out the analogy, the one thing they cannot do is to take on a phenomenological perspective. Likewise, the one thing the reader of the comic strip cannot do is to crawl into the comic strip and replace the intentions and evidences of the characters therein. The philosopher, to draw out the analogy, cannot intervene in the natural attitude. In effect, however, such intervention by philosophy in the natural attitude is what Descartes tries to do in regard to our perceptual experience and what Hobbes tries to do in regard to our political life. They try to use philosophy as a replacement for our natural lives. Rather than save human life, however, the rationalism that they introduce threatens to ruin it, as we will presently see in the final chapter.

But before leaving this analogy with the comic strip, we must qualify it and make it more complex. Like all analogies, it limps a little. It is true that the philosopher cannot be simply depicted inside the comic strip, and that he cannot intervene in the comic-strip story as one of its normal characters. However, it is also true that he is not totally detached from that story and its characters. He is the same person who also lives in the natural attitude; when he enters into the phenomenological attitude he does not step out of the world, as the image of the reader of the comic strip might suggest. In this respect, the spatial difference between the reader and the papers being read might mislead us when it is translated into the relationship between philosophy and the natural attitude. The philosopher as such does transcend the world, but he does so while remaining a part of it. Phenomenology gives us an immanent way to be transcendent. Philosophy does not show up as one of the standard "careers" within the natural world, but it does have a public presence of some sort, one that often perplexes those who are not philosophical.

IMPORTANCE OF THE TWO REFLECTIONS

The distinction between phenomenology and propositional reflection, which we have explored in this chapter, is particularly important in bringing out the nature of philosophical thinking. If we had omitted the treatment of this distinction, and had spoken only about the contrast between the natural and the phenomenological attitude, our exploration would not have faced up to one of the most common confusions regarding the nature of phenomenology. Philosophy is often not understood radically enough; it is taken to be a mere reflection on and clarification of meaning; that is, it is taken to be what is done from the perspective of propositional reflection.

Philosophy can arise only after propositional reflection has taken place. It is a rational step beyond such reflection. In the natural attitude, we go through three levels in the movement toward truth: first, we simply perceive and intend things; second, we articulate things categorially, introducing syntax into our experience; and third, we reflect propositionally on the things we have articulated and thus take up a critical attitude toward them. All three levels belong to the natural attitude. Only after we have passed through these three stages, and specifically only after we have achieved propositional reflection, can we enter into philosophical thinking. The critical thinking involved in propositional reflection, the effort to determine the correctness of propositions, must have already occurred if we are to move on to the more detached thinking we call philosophy. The "I" expressed in philosophy presupposes the "I" expressed in phrases like "I think this is the case," or "I know that this is true."

Philosophical reflection is more than just reflection on propositional reflection – it ranges over all intentionalities and their objective correlates – but it can be triggered only after propositional reflection, with the kind of truth that it permits, has taken place. Critical, propositional reasoning is a condition of possibility for philosophical reasoning.

Because propositional reflection has to precede the phenomenological, it is not surprising that we find it difficult to distinguish the one from the other. We find it hard to stretch far enough into the new dimension that philosophy brings. We tend to think that reflection on meaning is the highest form of reflective analysis. For this reason, it is essential for us explicitly to draw the distinction between propositional and phenomenological reflection, and to distinguish between sense and noema, if we are to sharpen our understanding of what philosophy, as the science of truth, is.

14

Phenomenology in the Present
Historical Context

We will now gain a final perspective on phenomenology by looking at how it fits into the present philosophical scene. Toward the end of Chapter 13, we noted that both Descartes and Hobbes try to replace the natural attitude by the philosophical. They think that philosophy can not only clarify but also replace the knowledge proper to prephilosophical thinking. This belief in the power of philosophical reason, along with this suspicion about other forms of experience, is typical of modernity. Phenomenology understands philosophy very differently. It believes that prephilosophical intelligence ought to be left intact, that it has its own excellence and truth, and that philosophy contemplates the prephilosophical without replacing it. Thus, while phenomenology originates within modern philosophy, it also takes a distance from it. To show how it does so, let us begin with an interpretation of modernity.

MODERNITY AND POSTMODERNITY

Modern philosophy has two major components: political philosophy and epistemology. In both these components, modern philosophy defined itself, in its origins, as a revolution against ancient and medieval thought. Machiavelli, at the beginning of the sixteenth century, prided himself on initiating new modes and orders in political life, and Francis Bacon and Descartes, in the early seventeenth century, declared that they were introducing new ways of thinking about nature and the human mind, ways which require that we abandon our inherited and commonsense convictions and take up a new method of directing our minds in the search for knowledge.

The new politics begun by Machiavelli and systematized by Hobbes was not just a theoretic innovation. It had a practical outcome, the establishment of the modern state. The modern state is different from previous forms of political rule. In all premodern forms, one part of the society – whether one man, the wealthy few, the many poor, the middle group, or the better people – rules over the whole. The rulers might exercise their rule for the common good or for their own benefit, but in any case the political community involves some human beings ruling over others. Even in a republic, in which the laws are said to rule, men still form the establishment, because there have to be enough citizens endowed with the political virtue and intelligence to allow the laws to rule.

The modern state is very different from this. In the modern state, a new entity is created, the sovereign. The sovereign is not one group of people in the body politic. The sovereign is a construct, not a spontaneous human development or a natural form of human association. It is an invention of philosophers. It is proposed as a permanent solution to the human political problem. The introduction of the sovereign is to put an end to the interminable human struggle, carried on by individuals and by groups, to rule. The concept of sovereignty is meant to rationalize human political life. It puts in place a structure that is impersonal, in contrast with the personalized forms of rule found in the ancient and medieval city. The introduction of the sovereign, it is promised, will bring about civic peace. The only requirement the sovereign makes is that all the subjects (for they are subjects now, not citizens) renounce any claim to public action and speech. They will be protected by the sovereign from one another's aggression and will be allowed to pursue their own private comforts and preferences, but all public decisions and speech must be left to the sovereign alone.

The modern state, shaped by the idea of sovereignty, worked its way through the political and intellectual history of the past five hundred years. It was first embodied in the absolute monarchs of the seventeenth and eighteenth centuries. It then discarded these monarchs and showed its face more clearly in the French Revolution. After germinating in nineteenth-century France in the aftermath of the Revolution, in Germany in the work of Bismarck, and in the United States in the Civil War and its consequences, the modern state appeared again vividly in the Russian Revolution and the Soviet state that followed. The idea of sovereignty remains in our contemporary political societies, in the tendencies that still exist to centralize all authority in a single impersonal source of power, an omnicompetent government that dissolves all other forms of social authority.

Besides being embodied in these diverse ways, the modern state went through theoretical refinements after Machiavelli and Hobbes. It found its final statement in Hegel, whose formulation was adapted by Karl Marx. Since Hegel, what we have had is an intellectual standoff between proponents of sovereignty and the modern state and political thinkers who recall the alternative to sovereignty, the political forms described by ancient and medieval theory. There are writers like Alexis de Toqueville, who reminds us of earlier political forms; Leo Strauss, who plays the ancients and the moderns off against each other; and Michael Oakeshott, who tries to work out adjustments between ancient and modern political concepts, with the goal of garnering the advantages while excluding the disadvantages of each. It can be said, however, that modern political philosophy has finished its work. It has reached its conclusion in the concept and the political establishment of the modern state, which is now generally considered to be the only legitimate form of government: the modern state does not need to be justified, and everyone agrees that the form of a modern state ought to be installed everywhere.

Phenomenology has nothing directly to say about the political dimension of modernity. Some of the writings of Sartre and Merleau-Ponty are related to politics, but they are little more than minor contributions to socialist theory. The work of Alfred Schutz is concerned more with social than with political philosophy. It is striking how completely devoid phenomenology is of anything in political philosophy. It has much to say, however, about the other component of modernity, epistemology and method.

Modernity involved not only a new conception of political life, but also a new conception of the mind. In the classical writings of modern philosophy, we are told that human reason must take possession of itself. Reason cannot accept what it inherits from the past or from others. The opinions that are given to it by others, and even the apparent truths that the senses present to it, are misleading. Reason must learn to conduct itself according to new procedures, new methods that will guarantee certainty and truth. All the sciences must be built up again on new and better foundations. Reason must even develop a method that will allow it to test our sense perceptions and make it possible for us to distinguish between the true and the false impressions made on our sensibility.

Like the political, the epistemological component of modernity has also had its history: it moved through the rationalism of Descartes, Spinoza, and Leibniz, through the empiricism of Locke, Berkeley, and Hume, through the critical philosophy of Kant and his followers, through the idealism of Fichte, Schelling, and Hegel, and through the positivism and pragmatism of nineteenth- and twentieth-century thought. There is a difference, however, in that epistemology has not come to closure as political philosophy has. Despite the great success of the modern sciences, and despite the strenuous efforts of movements like artificial intelligence and cognitive science, there is no epistemological equivalent of the modern state in uncontested possession of the field. As a theory of knowledge and method, modernity is still unfinished, and it is to this branch of modern thought that phenomenology makes its contribution.

Before we consider phenomenology, however, we must examine one more point about both components of modernity, the political and the epistemological. What is common to modern political philosophy and modern epistemology is that they both insist that the mind is to be understood as the power to rule. In political philosophy, the mind, in the persons of Machiavelli and Hobbes, generates a new entity, the sovereign state, which is not present among the more spontaneous forms of human association that have arisen in history. From now on the uncertainties and tensions of human competition for rule are to be replaced by a construct brought about by philosophical insight. Something new, something transhuman, the Leviathan, replaces the old conflicting authorities, and this new thing is reason expressing itself as ruling over men.

Also, in regard to human knowledge, reason takes possession of itself and rules over its own experiences by generating methods of inquiry and carrying out a critique of its own powers. The mind establishes itself as reason. The mind rules over itself and its power to know. The mind is not conceived as ordered toward the truth of things, but as governing its own activities and generating the truth through its own efforts. The mind is not receptive, but creative. It does not accept itself as teleologically ordered toward truth, but invents itself and constructs its truths by means of critical methodologies. In both cases, therefore, in both politics and science, reason or the mind is understood as ruling and as autonomous. This is the major difference between the philosophy of modernity and ancient and medieval philosophy, in which reason is understood as finding its perfection in the manifestation of things, in the triumph of objectivity and the attainment of truth. In premodern philosophy, even political excellence is subordinated to the truth of being that is presented to the theoretic life. Rule is subordinated to truth.

During the first centuries of its influence, modernity expressed itself as rationalism. The name given to this period of its history and this style of thinking was the Enlightenment. Modernity promised a purely rational political society and a secure, scientific development of human knowledge. But more recently, after the initial proclamations made by Nietzsche, it has become more and more clear that the heart of the modern project is not the exercise of reason in the service of knowledge, but the exercise of a will, the will to rule, the will to power. As this insight becomes more and more evident, modernity fades away and postmodernity takes over. Postmodernity is not a rejection of modernity, but the flowering of the deepest impulse in it. At this moment in our academic and cultural life, the natural sciences are still serving the project of classical modernity, but the humanities have been given over quite entirely to postmodernity.

THE RESPONSE OF PHENOMENOLOGY

How does phenomenology fit into this development of modern philosophy? Is it a continuation of the rationalist strain in modernity? Some of the hopes and arguments found in Husserl would seem to say so. Or is it a contribution to postmodernity, as some passages in Heidegger, and everything in Derrida, would seem to indicate?

I would claim that phenomenology breaks out of modernity and permits a restoration of the convictions that animated ancient and medieval philosophy. Like premodern philosophy, phenomenology understands reason as ordered toward truth. It sees the human mind as geared toward evidence, toward manifesting the way things are. Furthermore, it validates this vision of reason and the mind by describing, in convincing detail, the activities by which the mind achieves truth, along with the limitations and obscurities that accompany such achievement. Because of its understanding of reason and truth, phenomenology allows us to reappropriate the philosophy of antiquity and the Middle Ages.

Does this mean that phenomenology simply restores the ancient understanding of philosophy and abandons the modern project? Or that it merely plays off the ancients and the moderns as two basic alternatives for thinking? No; it does more. It responds positively to issues that have arisen in modernity. By drawing on modern philosophy and also restoring the ancient understanding of reason, phenomenology goes beyond ancients and moderns. For example, it deals with the modern epistemological problem and the place of mathematical science in human life. It shows how perception should not be understood as a barrier between ourselves and things, and how things can be given in various perspectives and still maintain their identity; it examines the interplay of presence and absence in all our experiences; and it unravels the intentionalities by which the sciences are constituted out of the lived world.

But while addressing the epistemological concerns of modernity, phenomenology also improves on the ancient understanding of science. It brings out the role of the ego, showing that human knowledge is not the work of an agent intellect separate from human beings, but the achievement and possession of someone who can say "I" and who can take responsibility for what he says. Because it recognizes the transcendental ego as a dimension in human beings, phenomenology is able to introduce a historical and hermeneutical dimension to human knowledge. It does so, however, without submerging truth into subjectivity and historical circumstances. Having had to deal with modern skepticism, phenomenology gives a more thorough analysis of experience and of intentionality than ancient philosophy did, as well as a more explicit treatment of the difference between philosophy and the prephilosophical. Phenomenology is neither a rebellion against antiquity and the Middle Ages nor a rejection of modernity, but a recovery of the true philosophical life, in a manner appropriate to our philosophical situation.

Phenomenology has not developed a political philosophy, but because it sees human reason as ordered toward truth, it can make an important contribution to political philosophy. If the human mind finds its end in the evidence of things, then political rule cannot be the highest good for man. Politics has to be subordinated to the truth of things, that is, political rule has to be exercised in accord with human nature. Sheer ruling does not provide the utmost satisfaction. Rule must be exercised according to human excellence, and it must also recognize that there is a life higher than its own. These truths have been lost from view in the political thinking inaugurated by Machiavelli.

If human beings are recognized as agents of truth, their political association must reflect this dimension of their being. An impersonal system of sovereignty cannot replace responsible human rulers and citizens. The civic and intellectual virtues of those who hold public office cannot be disregarded; ruling is not simply a matter of automatic procedures and electoral processes. The urgent problems of civic education, family stability, and social order that have arisen in recent years show that the teachings of ancient political philosophy are not out of date in our times. A better understanding of human responsibility, based on an understanding of reason as ordered toward truth, is sorely needed in the education of citizens and statesmen, if men are not to become slaves of a despotic state.

The modern state is not the same as a republic, the political society in which the laws rule. The sovereign is a construct deliberately fabricated by reason, whereas the laws are the inherited customs of a community, some of which become codified into explicit statutes; they are the common laws, the way of life of a people. More basic than statutes, of course, is the constitution of the political society, which determines the offices and the people who will be eligible to hold them; that is, it determines who shall be citizens. The republic assumes that men have been born and educated into prepolitical societies, into families and tribes, and that they have associations (friendships) that are prepolitical. Sovereignty is much less restrained. It claims to supersede all other authorities and associations, which it regulates. It claims to be able to make men human. It is essentially totalitarian.

Another difference between the republic and the sovereign is that the republic draws on elements from many other forms of government: it is made up of democratic, oligarchic, aristocratic, and royal components, and this variety gives it great tensile strength. The sovereign, in contrast, is univocal. There is just the single rule of the one or the group who are said to represent all the subjects. Because it is univocal, sovereignty is not adaptable to circumstances. It is what has been called the universal and homogeneous state, the one form of rule that is expected to be found everywhere. It is purely "rational," but rational in the sense modernity gives to the term: an expression of calculative, methodic reason, not the reason that evidences the way things are. The moral and social ruin left behind by the collapse of soviet states shows how effectively the sovereign can destroy the social authorities that try to rival its power.

The best political societies in the modern world, such as that formed by the original American Constitution, have been republics. They are a rule of laws and are composed of elements from many different forms of government: democratic, oligarchic, aristocratic, and royal. They run counter to the centralizing forces that have also developed in the modern world. To the extent that they remain republics, they treat their people as citizens, not as subjects, and consider it essential to educate their people as citizens, not as subjects. To be educated as a citizen is to be capable of entering into the human conversation as a responsible agent of truth. Phenomenology can strengthen or restore this civic self-understanding; such is the donation it can make to contemporary political philosophy and practice.

For the study of human consciousness and thinking has a value that goes beyond epistemology. When we describe human reason philosophically, we provide a human self-understanding, and such an understanding is not unrelated to political philosophy. The most systematic picture of the sovereign state is given by Thomas Hobbes in *Leviathan*, a work that begins with a mechanistic theory of knowledge. The conjunction between politics and epistemology is not accidental. If human beings are to be made abject subjects of a sovereign, they have to understand themselves in a certain way. Since they will not be permitted to act in the public domain (only the sovereign can carry out public actions), they must take themselves as neither moral agents nor agents of truth. They have to understand their intellect as a mechanical, impersonal process, not a power of disclosure. They cannot understand themselves as datives of manifestation. The sovereign state and modern subjectivism go hand in hand. The "egocentric predicament" and the reduction of mind to brain, the cancellation of public truth in favor of private relativism, are not just epistemological theories, but also political predispositions. If we become persuaded that we do not enter into the game of truth, we will see ourselves as solitary players who can act only within our internal life. There is no public game but only private fantasy, no football or baseball but only a mental tic-tac-toe. The understanding of human reason as boxed into the brain, the understanding that serves the sovereign state, is widespread in our culture, but it is not yet universal. It has the weakness of being counterintuitive and logically self-dissolving, as postmodernism has shown. In Platonic terms, what is needed is a new "musical trope" that makes us more clearly aware of what we are, and the political role of philosophy is to help make such music possible.

PHENOMENOLOGY AND THOMISTIC PHILOSOPHY

Since we are trying to define phenomenology by showing how it fits in the modern philosophical situation, it would be helpful to compare it with scholastic philosophy, and more specifically with the most prominent representation of scholasticism, Thomism. Thomism is like phenomenology in providing an alternative to modernity and postmodernity, but the two alternatives differ. Thomism is a premodern or nonmodern form of thinking. Its roots lie in antiquity and in the Middle Ages. Historically, it ran parallel to the early development of modern thinking, when it was represented by such sixteenth- and seventeenth-century writers as Cajetan (1468–1534), Suarez (1548–1617), and John of St. Thomas (1589–1644). Thomism receded somewhat during the next two centuries, but after the revival prompted by Pope Leo XIII, with his encyclical *Aeterni Patris* (1879), it became a conspicuous presence in nineteenth- and twentieth-century thought, primarily but not exclusively in Roman Catholic educational and intellectual circles. It was represented by many scholars and commentators, but also by such independent thinkers as Jacques Maritain (1882–1973), Etienne Gilson (1884–1978), and Yves R. Simon (1903–1961). Its presence was much diminished in the aftermath of the Second Vatican Council. Furthermore, the neoscholastic philosophy of Franz Brentano exercised a significant influence on Husserl, so there was some continuity between Thomistic thought and the early stages of phenomenology.

Thomism shares with phenomenology the conviction that human reason is ordered toward truth, but there is an important difference between the two traditions. Thomism develops its philosophy within the context of Christian faith and revelation. It works within the intellectual dimensions opened by Saint Anselm, who provides a kind of "theological deduction" of the possibility of philosophy, analogous to Kant's "transcendental deduction" of our cognitive powers. The first step that had to be made in medieval philosophy was to show that reason has its own domain, its own sphere of operation, and that it is not absorbed by faith. Saint Anselm and the scholastics "made room" for reason within faith. They knew about philosophy because they found it among the ancients, but their own appropriation of it had to begin within revelation. Among the great achievements of scholasticism were the distinctions between faith and reason and between grace and nature. Medieval thinkers, and Saint Thomas Aquinas in particular, taught that natural evidences have their own integrity, and that reason can achieve truth through its own powers. This teaching, however, has to be justified from within biblical faith.

In ancient philosophy, no such theological justification was needed, because philosophy did not have to find its place within divine revelation. It defined itself within the inherited opinions of the Greek cities. There, philosophy understood itself as the natural culmination of human thinking. Men had opinions about the way things are, they were able to acquire some scientific knowledge, they had viewpoints on the right and the just thing to do, they made statements about the gods; beyond such exercises of the mind, they began to think about the whole and about themselves as displaying the whole and the parts in it. Whether in the Presocratic study of nature or in the Socratic investigation of man and the political order, they began to exercise philosophical thought.

Phenomenology offers us just this kind of understanding of philosophy as a natural human achievement. Phenomenology does not try to derive philosophy from within religious faith. Rather, it takes philosophy simply as a natural human excellence, one that completes the prephilosophical exercises of reason. Phenomenology thus begins philosophy in a manner different from the way Thomism begins it, but in a way that complements and does not contradict the Thomistic approach. Thomism offers a legitimate way of entering into philosophy, but it is not the only way. Taking possession of philosophy from within faith does not deform philosophy, but it does give it a distinctive look and feel, a distinctive presentation. Another way of entering philosophy, the older way, is to begin within the natural attitude and to distinguish the philosophical from it. Indeed, taking the route offered by phenomenology can be of benefit to Thomism: it becomes possible to show how the context assumed by Thomism is itself distinguished from the natural whole we call the world. Phenomenology can help Thomistic philosophy and theology understand their own origins.

Phenomenology escapes the voluntarism of postmodernity because it avoids the apparent rationalism of modernity. It is more moderate than such rationalism. It recognizes the validity of prephilosophical experience and thinking and does not try to substitute for it. Still, it may seem excessive to say, as I have stated earlier, that phenomenology is indifferent to the truth or falsity found in the natural attitude. Does phenomenology do nothing for the experience that comes before it? Does it just stand back and reflect for its own benefit?

Phenomenology can clarify the intentionalities at work in the natural attitude. It can show, for example, how logic differs from mathematics, and how both differ from natural science; it can show what each of these forms of intentionality is after, what evidences it aims at. Phenomenology assists prephilosophical experience by clarifying what such experience discloses and how it fits in with other forms of evidence. In doing so, however, phenomenology or philosophy does not substitute a new method for what was already there. All it does is to distinguish more sharply the intentions that have already established their own integrity. It removes confusions in these intentions and resolves ambiguities in the speech that expresses them.

Phenomenology also helps prephilosophical thinking because such thinking inevitably goes beyond itself and tries to formulate an opinion about the whole. Every partial science, as well as human common sense, expresses an opinion about the whole. It formulates this opinion, however, in terms of its own partial view. Physicists think of the whole as a physical whole, politicians think of it as political, psychologists think of it as psychological. Each partial view stretches out its own philosophical pseudopod. In contrast, phenomenology, like every true philosophy, sees the difference between a partial view of the whole and a view that is appropriate to the whole. It avoids the positivity of partial sciences. Instead of plunging ahead with blinders on, it knows that thinking about the whole requires subtlety, reserve, nuance, analogy, and metaphor. It makes more basic distinctions than the partial sciences do. It is sensitive to the transformations of language that must occur when we speak about the widest context.

Phenomenology thus helps the partial sciences and the natural attitude by clarifying their partiality, by bringing out what is absent to them, and by showing that what they identify can be seen from perspectives they do not enjoy. It does not doubt or reject, but clarifies and restores. In clarifying the partiality of other ways of thinking, it formulates its own sense of the whole. In speaking about the whole it also calls the self to mind, and thus counters both the self-forgetfulness of modern forms of science and the self-denial of postmodernity. Phenomenology helps us to think about the first and final issues and helps us to know ourselves.

Appendix
Phenomenology in the Last One Hundred Years

The phenomenological movement fits very neatly, almost exactly, into the twentieth century. The work that is generally considered to be the first true phenomenological work, Edmund Husserl's *Logical Investigations*, appeared in two parts in the years 1900 and 1901, so the new movement began precisely with the dawning of the century. Moreover, this date was literally a new beginning, because Husserl was so truly an original philosopher. He cannot be considered as continuing a tradition that had taken shape before him; even Martin Heidegger, as strong a philosopher as he was, can be understood only in the tradition opened up by Husserl, but Husserl did not have any such overshadowing predecessors. He drew on the work of Franz Brentano and the psychologist Carl Stumpf, but he greatly exceeded them. His theory of intentionality, for example, is far superior to that of Brentano. Husserl's written work before 1900 (his *Philosophy of Arithmetic*, which appeared in 1891, and the few essays that followed the book), although it foreshadows some of his later thought, is justly considered to be prephenomenological, in the way that Kant's writings before the *Inaugural Dissertation* of 1770 are taken to be precritical. So now, as we stand at the end of the twentieth century, we can look back at the philosophical movement that began in the year 1900 and attempt to survey it.

Husserl had been a Privatdozent at the University of Halle for fourteen years when, because of the success of *Logical Investigations*, he was invited to become professor at Göttingen. He was at Göttingen from 1901 to 1916, when he moved to Freiburg, where he taught from 1916 to his retirement in 1928. He remained at Freiburg another ten years until his death in 1938 at the age of seventy-nine. Husserl published only six books during his lifetime: *Philosophy of Arithmetic* (1891), *Logical Investigations* (1900–1), *Ideas I* (1913), *Lectures on Internal Time-Consciousness* (1928), *Formal and Transcendental Logic* (1929), and *Cartesian Meditations* (1931), which appeared in French. However, he composed thousands of pages of manuscripts: course lectures, philosophical sketches and meditations, commentaries, drafts for possible publication; he philosophized by writing. All these materials were collected in the Husserl Archives, and many volumes were published posthumously in the series *Husserliana*, which now numbers twenty-nine titles and is still counting. A total of about forty volumes is planned.

Elisabeth Ströker (personal communication) has observed that Husserl always remained something of a natural scientist even when he turned to philosophy; he had begun his studies and written his doctoral thesis in mathematics, and also studied astronomy and psychology before entering philosophy. As a natural scientist, he was, Ströker says, more inclined to the experiment than to the monograph, and his many philosophical compositions were like so many empirical studies or experiments. Even his larger books were more like collections of small studies rather than architectonically structured compositions.

Through his teaching and writings, Husserl stimulated the growth of several branches of phenomenology during his lifetime. Another important way in which he exercised influence was through his editorial work on the *Jahrbuch für Philosophie und phänomenologische Forschung*, which he founded in 1913. Many important German monographs appeared in that yearbook, including Heidegger's *Being and Time*, Husserl's own *Ideas I* and *Formal and Transcendental Logic*, Max Scheler's *Formalism in Ethics*, and works by Adolf Reinach, Alexander Pfänder, Oskar Becker, and Moritz Geiger. A total of eleven volumes, some of which contained more than one work, were published in this series between 1913 and 1930. The last was a study by Eugen Fink entitled *Vergegenwärtigung und Bild* (Representation and image).

Two philosophical groups were influenced by Husserl during his teaching period, one at Göttingen and one at Munich. The one at Munich arose spontaneously through the reading of *Logical Investigations*. At the University of Munich, students of Theodor Lipps had organized a philosophical group around the turn of the century; the group, including such figures as Alexander Pfänder and Johannes

Daubert at the beginning, and later Adolf Reinach, Theodor Conrad, Hedwig Conrad-Martius, Moritz Geiger, Dietrich von Hildebrand, and Max Scheler, was influenced by Husserl's written work and gradually became an independent center of phenomenology. Members met frequently with Husserl at Göttingen, they invited him to lecture at Munich, and some transferred to Göttingen to study with him. What interested the Munich philosophers was Husserl's overcoming of psychologism and his restoration of realism in philosophy. They disliked his later development of a transcendental philosophy, however, thinking it to be a relapse into idealism, and they thought of their own work as phenomenology without the reduction. At Göttingen, subsequently, another group was formed. Some of its members came from Munich, such as Reinach, Daubert, Conrad, Conrad-Martius, and von Hildebrand, and they were joined by such figures as Alexandre Koyré and Jean Héring. Roman Ingarden and Edith Stein became members of this group and later went with Husserl to Freiburg.

When Husserl moved to the University of Freiburg in 1916, no formal circle of phenomenology was established there, but many prominent figures worked with him: Stein, Ingarden, Fink, Ludwig Landgrebe, and especially Martin Heidegger. Others who were influenced by him while studying elsewhere in the 1920s were Jacob Klein and Hans-Georg Gadamer, who were at Marburg and were more directly influenced by Heidegger.

THE SECOND STAGE: HUSSERL, HEIDEGGER, AND SCHELER

During the 1920s Husserl's philosophical movement, as a cultural phenomenon, was somewhat derailed by the appearance of Martin Heidegger on the academic and intellectual scene. Heidegger made a tremendous impression on the philosophical world in Germany and stole Husserl's thunder. Husserl and Heidegger form one of the great pairs of thinkers in the history of philosophy, and to understand their relationship let us move back a few years to 1907, when Heidegger read Brentano's book on the many senses of being in Aristotle. Two years later as a student at Freiburg he read Husserl's *Logical Investigations.* He completed his doctoral dissertation under the Neokantian Heinrich Rickert in 1913, wrote his habilitation in 1915, and then began teaching at Freiburg, just as Husserl was coming there. As a young teacher, Heidegger lectured on Greek philosophers and on phenomenology, and also on the philosophy of religion. He was invited to teach at Marburg and left Freiburg in 1923. In the winter of 1923–24 he composed the first draft of *Being and Time*, and he began teaching at Marburg in 1924. *Being and Time* was published in 1927. Heidegger was invited to succeed Husserl in Freiburg on the latter's retirement in 1928. Heidegger had remained at Marburg for four years, 1924 to 1928, but his lectures, both there and earlier at Freiburg, had already made him famous and had revealed his own independent philosophical position.

Heidegger read about Aristotle when he was seventeen years old, and he read Husserl's *Logical Investigations* when he was nineteen. It was the combination of these two sources that deeply shaped him philosophically. In *Being and Time* §7 he asserts that the method of his analysis will be phenomenological, and he provides a lucid explanation of what phenomenology means, but despite the influence Husserl exercised on him, there are a number of obvious differences between the two philosophers.

First, Heidegger formulates his task in classical terms and shows a great knowledge of the history of philosophy. Husserl was a mathematician who came to philosophy, while Heidegger was educated as a philosopher from the beginning. *Being and Time* quotes such sources as Aristotle, Augustine, Saint Thomas, Suarez, Descartes, Kant, and other philosophers and theologians, as well as the Book of Genesis, Calvin, Zwingli, and Aesop, and it sets as its goal the rejuvenation of the issue of being. Heidegger was able to make use of what Husserl accomplished by applying it to more classical philosophical issues. He was also better able than Husserl to use a classical philosophical vocabulary.

Second, Husserl is very much a rationalist in the style and content of his work, while the style and content of Heidegger's writing and teaching engage the reader and put existential questions to him. This is both good and bad. It is good in that it brings out explicitly the fact that philosophy is not merely unconcerned or carefree speculation, but a way of life and a great benefit for those who practice it. However, it is bad in that when pursuing his philosophical project, Heidegger did not distinguish adequately between the theoretical and the practical life, between philosophy and prudence; he also did not distinguish clearly between the theoretic life and religion. He wanted to be a prophet and moral leader as much as a thinker, and the oscillation between these forms of life confused his own work and affected the thought of those who were influenced by him. The main purpose of Heidegger's analysis of being-toward-death, or of anxiety, or of authenticity, is not primarily to give us grounds for worry or make us earnest about life or get us out to vote; rather, he is using these phenomena as approaches to the question of being. They have an analytic function, not an exhortative one. They are to show that the question of being is disclosed not only in speculative metaphysics, but in all the varieties of human existence. However, even in Heidegger's own writings, the analytic purpose does blend with a religious and moral exhortation. There is something prophetic about them. One can be a prophet, awaiting the new coming of the gods, and one can be a philosopher, but it is misleading to try to be both at the same time.

Another way of expressing this difference between Husserl and Heidegger is to say that Husserl began with the impulse of a scientist and a mathematician and transformed it into philosophy, while Heidegger began with the religious impulse and blended it into the philosophical one. Husserl, the rationalist, thought of himself as a free, nondoctrinal, and nondogmatic Christian, but he used religious categories very sparingly in his work. He was intent on philosophy as a rigorous science. He respected religion, but was somewhat distanced from it. Heidegger, in contrast, seemed to present his philosophy as a resolution of the religious problem. It has been observed that several followers of Husserl converted to Catholicism or Protestantism; this occurred not because Husserl encouraged such a move (indeed, he seemed somewhat embarrassed by it), but because his work restored respectability to various domains of experience and thus allowed people to cultivate their own religious development without hindrance. Such conversions were not common among Heidegger's followers, however, and I would suggest that in the human context that Heidegger formed the opposite of a conversion would be more likely to take place. People would be inclined to turn from religious faith to philosophy as a way of dealing with the religious impulse. Questions of mortality, authenticity, decisiveness, the hermeneutics of human existence, and temporality and eternity would be treated by philosophical analysis and exhortation rather than by religious dedication in its traditional form. The philosophical response would even be taken as the more authentic of the two. No one tried to interpret the New Testament in Husserlian categories, but Rudolf Bultmann tried to do so with the categories of Heidegger, and one might claim that others did something similar in regard to Catholic belief.

What was it in Husserl that most influenced Heidegger? I would suggest that it was the fact that in Husserl the Cartesian or the modern epistemological problem had been dissolved and overcome. The notion of a solitary, self-enclosed consciousness, aware only of itself and its own sensations and thoughts, was disposed of by Husserl's concept of intentionality. Indeed, the epistemological problem is ridiculed in *Being and Time* §13. We experience and perceive things, not just the appearances or impacts or impressions that things make on us. Things appear to us through a manifold of presentations. Husserl presented this realism not only by pointing out the self-contradictions of the Cartesian and Lockean position, of the way of ideas, but also by working out detailed descriptive analyses of various forms of intentionality, analyses that proved themselves by virtue of their precision and convincingness. One does not prove realism; how could one do so? One displays it.

More particularly, this breakthrough in the doctrine of intentionality expressed itself in two more particular doctrines of Husserl: first, his analysis of categorial articulation, and second his insistence that we truly do intend things in their absence. Both of these teachings are vividly present in the early Heidegger. In his doctrine of categoriality, Husserl shows that when we articulate things, when we judge or relate or compose or structure things, we do not merely arrange our own internal concepts or ideas or impressions; rather, we articulate things in the world. We bring out parts within wholes. Our judgments, for example, are not internal compositions that we try to match against some sort of "external" world; they are, in their most elementary form, the assertive articulation of the things we experience; we articulate the presence of things, the manner in which they are given to us. Thus, Husserl's doctrine of intentionality should not be taken only in regard to perception, in which we are told that the things we perceive do immediately present themselves to us. It should be taken especially in regard to the categorial articulation that is built upon perception. The doctrine of categorial presentation in Husserl, as given in the sixth of the *Logical Investiga-*

tions, was crucial for Heidegger's formulation of the question of being.

Also, through the doctrine of intentionality Husserl is able to say that we actually intend things that are absent. It is not the case that we always deal only with immediate presences; it is not the case that when we refer to something absent, we are really talking about an image or a concept we have of the thing. Human thinking is such that it transcends the present and intends the absent; the absent, what is not there, is given to us as such. There are, furthermore, different kinds of absence, corresponding to the different kinds of empty intendings our intentionality can take on: the absence of the other side of things we perceive, the absence of things meant only through words, the absence of things being remembered, the absence of things only depicted, the absence of those who are far away as opposed to the absence of those who have died, the absence of the past and that of the future, the absence of the divine. Another important kind of absence that Husserl described is that of vagueness, in which things are given to us, but given only indistinctly, in need of further articulation and possession. This theme of absence was, I believe, a stimulus to Heidegger's notion of unconcealedness as involved in truth.

Heidegger saw the philosophical possibilities in Husserl's discovery of intentionality and exploited them with a vengeance. Other philosophers had been impressed by what Husserl opened up. The members of the Munich and Göttingen schools, for example, rejoiced in the "realism" that was made possible by Husserl's discoveries. None of them, however, had the depth and originality and philosophical energy of Heidegger or the seductive charm of his religious tonality.

I would like to mention one more difference between Heidegger and Husserl. Husserl is very skimpy in his use of the history of philosophy. He does provide occasional surveys of that history, and he uses Descartes, Galileo, Locke, Hume, and Kant, but he does so with an obviously limited knowledge of these writers. He makes some incisive comments about them and usually gets to the heart of issues in their philosophy, but he has a rather simplified, textbook knowledge of their work. On the other hand, the content of what Husserl proposes for philosophical analysis is rich and wide-ranging. He opens up issues in the structure of language, perception, time in its various forms, memory, anticipation, living things, mathematics, numbers, causality, and so on. He proposes many regions of being as subjects for analysis. Husserl, then, is oversimplified in his treatment of authors but rich in his treatment of speculative topics.

Heidegger is the opposite of this. He seems concerned with only one issue, the question of being and its implications. It is true that in *Being and Time* he introduces a number of what could be taken as "regional" issues, such as instrumentality and speech and death, but all of them are subordinated to the one question of being. He does not spread out various regional tasks before us, various domains to be analyzed; he is philosophically a monomaniac, always on the way to the first principles, while Husserl both moves toward the first principles and then spends much time moving away from them and embodying them in the various things we experience. As regards content, Husserl seems variegated while Heidegger seems oversimplified.

As regards authors, however, Heidegger is positively exuberant in his variety. He discusses in great detail and in sophisticated interpretations the Presocratics, Plato, Aristotle, medieval thinkers, Leibniz, Kant, Hegel, Kierkegaard, and Nietzsche, as well as poets such as Hölderin and Rilke and religious writers such as Angelus Silesius and Luther. All these writers, however, are examined in regard to how the question of being is raised in them. I would also like to mention the importance Heidegger had for a new approach to Greek philosophy, for the interpretation of the Presocratics, Plato, and Aristotle, especially in Germany and France during the rich period of the last one hundred years.

Before closing this survey of the German phase of phenomenology, I should say a word about Max Scheler. Scheler cannot be placed as clearly within the phenomenological movement as Husserl and Heidegger can; he was an independent thinker who at some times developed and commented on phenomenological themes, at other times criticized and distanced himself from that form of philosophy. What makes him seem to be a phenomenologist is that he pays attention to concrete, specific issues, especially human issues such as religion, sympathy, love, hate, emotions, and moral values, and he analyzes them in detail. His marginal affiliation with phenomenology helped popularize the movement, but he also moved freely outside it. After a dramatic and turbulent life, Scheler died in 1928 at the age of fifty-four.

It would be an understatement to say that political and historical events intruded on the phenomenological movement in the 1930s. With the rise to power of the National Socialists, Heidegger became involved with the party and acted and spoke accordingly as rector of the University of Freiburg in 1933. Husserl, in contrast, suffered many indignities and dangers before his death in 1938. Events among European nations led to a deep separation between German and continental philosophy and the British and American world.

Just before the outbreak of war, the Franciscan Herman Leo Van Breda of Louvain came to Freiburg to study phenomenology and, seeing the situation there, acted to save Husserl's written materials and library, having them shipped to Louvain in the fall of 1938, some six months after Husserl's death. He also rescued and protected Husserl's widow, Malvine, who was sheltered in a convent at Louvain for the duration of the war. Van Breda's actions led to the establishment of the Husserl Archives at the University of Louvain after the war. The archives became an important international center for the editing and publication of Husserl's writings and for research into his thought. Affiliated archives were later established at Cologne, Freiburg, Paris, and New York.

PHENOMENOLOGY IN FRANCE

After the German, it was certainly the French branch that was of greatest significance for the phenomenological movement. Emmanuuel Levinas studied with Husserl and Heidegger in the 1920s, wrote a thesis on the concept of intuition in Husserl's thought, which was published in 1930, and cotranslated *Cartesian Meditations*, which appeared in 1931.

Jean-Paul Sartre (1905–1980) spent two years in Germany (1933– 35), in Berlin and Freiburg. His early works show the strong influence of Husserl, but transformed into an existentialist humanism. In fact, many of Sartre's early works are excellent phenomenological analyses that develop important themes in Husserl. I would mention especially *The Imagination* (1936), "The Transcendence of the Ego" (1936), *Sketch of a Theory of the Emotions* (1939), *The Imaginary* (1940), and *Being and Nothingness* (1943). What strikes one in reading these works is how well Sartre grasped the concept of intentionality and saw its philosophical potential, and how effectively he used the element of absence as a philosophical theme, both in his descriptions of various kinds of human experience and in his analyses of the ego. Sartre's respect for Husserl certainly helped greatly in making Husserl's thought accessible and interesting to a wider public after the war.

In particular, Sartre has excellent descriptions of how we actually perceive or experience nonbeing, the absence of things; negation is not merely a feature of our judgments, but is given in the intuitive experience that precedes judgment. The transforming power of the various emotions, as well as the lively movement and projection of imagination, are described in ways that complement Husserl's own descriptions. Sartre speaks of imagination, for example, as "*perception renaissante*" and describes prereflexive consciousness in great detail. He also stresses the acting self, showing the distinction between abstract possibilities and possibilities that are there for an agent as his own, those that would not come about without his own presence in a situation. He describes the difference between facticity and transcendence and provides a remarkable analysis of determinism as a form of avoiding the anxieties that freedom brings. His style is fluid and engaging.

However, Sartre consciously incorporated phenomenological themes into his own philosophical project of existential humanism, which involved elements from many other sources, especially Descartes, Hegel, and Marx. He even criticizes Husserl, in *Being and Nothingness*, for a kind of philosophical timidity; he says Husserl restricted himself to neutral analysis and avoided existential and ontological commitments ("he remained fearfully [*craintivement*] on the level of functional description"). I believe, incidentally, that Sartre misinterprets Husserl on the concept of noema and the nature of appearance when he claims that the noema is like the Stoic lekton and when he claims that Husserl remained a phenomenalist rather than a phenomenologist, always tottering on the brink of Kantian idealism.

Sartre's radical contrast between the "in itself" and the "for itself" overlooks intermediate distinctions that should be respected, such as those that occur in animal awareness. In particular, when speaking of the phenomenon of nothingness, *le néant*, as being founded in human consciousness, he so stresses difference and otherness as to overlook elements of identity that always come along with these negatives. His description of *le rien* as permitting the ego to become alien to itself in consciousness anticipates Derrida's introduction of *différance* and "traces," but both French thinkers seem to neglect the corresponding sameness and identity that Husserl would recognize in such phenomena. Sartre made use of phenomenology within a philosophy that was not only analytic but also exhortative, a kind of dramatic humanism, and in such rhetorical writing one always emphasizes some aspects of things to the neglect of others.

Maurice Merleau-Ponty's (1908–1961) development followed a few years after that of Sartre. Merleau-Ponty never studied in Germany, but among other influences in his studies he was helped in his understanding of both phenomenology and Gestalt psychology in the early 1930s by Aron Gurwitsch, who had fled Germany and taught in Paris before coming to the United States, where he became an important figure representing phenomenology at the New School for Social Research in the 1960s and 1970s. Merleau-Ponty's first major writings, and perhaps his most enduring, were *The Structure of Behavior* (1942) and *Phenomenology of Perception* (1945). Both were criticisms of positivist psychology. Merleau-Ponty stresses the prereflexive, the prepredicative, the perceptual, the temporal, the lived body, and the life world. The richness and complexity of his descriptions match the quality of Sartre's work and remain as important phenomenological achievements. Merleau-Ponty appealed mostly to Husserl's later work and made use of unedited materials in the Husserl Archives. Perhaps because of his criticism of positivist science, but also because of the excellence of his work, Merleau-Ponty exercised a great influence in the United States during the 1950s and 1960s. Many found his work more accessible than the rigorous, almost mathematical writing of Husserl himself.

I should also mention Paul Ricoeur (b. 1913) as a member of the French branch of the phenomenological movement. He translated Husserl's *Ideas I*, commented extensively on him, and carried out independent philosophical analyses of human freedom, religion, symbolism, myth, and psychoanalysis. It is interesting that his study of human freedom, *The Voluntary and the Involuntary*, was very much influenced by Alexander Pfänder, one of the Munich phenomenologists.

The German root and French branch of phenomenology were certainly the main parts of this movement, but other significant parts arose in other countries. In the United States, William Ernest Hocking had studied with Husserl for a semester in 1902, and so did Dorion Cairns in the late 1920s and early 1930s. Cairns wrote a Harvard thesis on Husserl in 1933 and became a superb translator of Husserl's works. Marvin Farber wrote a dissertation on Husserl at Buffalo in 1928 and later wrote about his thought and founded the review, *Philosophy and Phenomenological Research*, but he remained more of a naturalist philosopher than a phenomenologist. The main impact of phenomenology in the United States occurred in the 1950s and 1960s, when it became established as one of the major schools of philosophy in this country, even though it was overshadowed by other more native and more anglican forms. In the North American philosophical world, phenomenology has enjoyed a durable but relatively small presence, compared with that of analytic philosophy in its various styles. Significant centers of phenomenology have been present in many universities, and several associations and journals dedicated to it have been established. The earliest center, dating from the 1950s, was at the Graduate Faculty of the New School for Social Research, where Dorion Cairns, Aron Gurwitsch, and Alfred Schutz taught.

Phenomenology was never very prominent in England, although through the efforts of Wolfe Mays at Manchester and his students Barry Smith, Kevin Mulligan, and Peter Simons a vigorous group of scholars was founded about twenty years ago with the intent of exploring the early period of phenomenology and showing its relation to the origins of analytic philosophy in Gottlob Frege and other thinkers in Austria in the early part of this century.

This development in England, incidentally, has a counterpart in the United States, an interpretation of Husserl that is inspired by Frege and analytic philosophy. It is centered in California and is represented by such writers as Dagfinn Føllesdal, Hubert Dreyfus,

Ronald McIntyre, and David Woodruff Smith. It draws especially on Husserl's earlier writings. This "West Coast" reading of Husserl has as its antithesis an "East Coast" interpretation, situated largely in the Boston-to-Washington corridor, that takes its bearings especially from Husserl's later philosophical and logical works and does not use Frege and analytic philosophy as its starting point. It reads Frege in the light of Husserl and not vice versa. It is expressed in the writings of John Brough, Richard Cobb-Stevens, John Drummond, James Hart, Robert Sokolowski, and others. The present book is written in its spirit. The two "schools" differ especially in their understanding of noema, sense, and the phenomenological reduction. The basic theoretic difference between them is that the West Coast group identifies sense and noema and posits them as mediators between the mind and world, whereas the East Coast group distinguishes sense and noema as the outcomes of two different kinds of reflection upon the intended object; it does not posit them as mediating the intentional relation of mind to world. J. N. Mohanty has developed an independent interpretation of both Husserl and Frege and has also related phenomenology to ancient Indian philosophy.

José Ortega y Gasset was an independent philosopher who both represented and criticized Husserl and Heidegger in Spain; Xavier Zubiri could also be mentioned as involved in phenomenology. In Italy, phenomenology and existentialism were developed in Milan by Antonio Banfi in the period between the two world wars and by Enzo Paci after the Second World War. Also, Sofia Vanni Rovighi related Husserl's thought to themes from Aristotle and Aquinas. The existentialism of Nicola Abbagnano should also be mentioned. In Poland, Roman Ingarden, who studied with Husserl in 1912–18 and remained in close contact with him later, initiated a branch of the phenomenological movement and wrote several important phenomenological works on aesthetics, ethics, and metaphysics. He taught at Lwów in the 1930s and at Cracow after the war. This tradition was later continued as a partial influence on the work of Karol Wojtyła and the work of the Lublin school of Thomism. In Czechoslovakia, Jan Patočka, a student and friend of Husserl's, was a strong representative of phenomenology in Prague and a courageous defender of civic freedom. He died in 1977 after having been interrogated by the police. Phenomenology was influential in prerevolutionary Russia. *Logical Investigations* was translated into Russian in 1909 and exercised an indirect influence on structuralism and formalism in literary theory through the work of Roman Jakobson, who always referred to Husserl's theory of parts and wholes as an important philosophical doctrine. Gustav Shpet is mentioned as a representative of phenomenology in Russia at that time, but the First World War and the Communist Revolution prevented any development of these beginnings. Efforts are now being made to translate Husserl into Russian.

HERMENEUTICS AND DECONSTRUCTION

After this geographic survey of what came after the main period of phenomenology, I could mention two further metamorphic forms that have followed and are somewhat on the margins of phenomenology – hermeneutics and deconstruction.

Hermeneutics began as a specifically German movement, with Friedrich Schleiermacher (1768–1834) and especially Wilhelm Dilthey (1833–1911), who was a senior contemporary of Husserl. Hermeneutics originally stressed the structures of reading and interpreting texts from the past and presented its work as a philosophy of biblical and literary interpretation and of historical research. Heidegger expanded the notion of hermeneutics from the study of texts and records to the self-interpretation of human existence as such. The person primarily associated with hermeneutics is, of course, Hans-Georg Gadamer, who was not only a student of Heidegger but also a learned interpreter of Plato, Aristotle, and poetic texts. He has also been a living Boswell of the phenomenological movement, able to represent it to other countries and to younger generations; he does so as an independent witness of its major figures and events, and as a person whose congeniality and vivacious lecturing have helped him establish contacts all over the world. Gadamer was influenced by Heidegger, under whom he studied at Marburg, but less influenced by Husserl, with whom he also studied for a while at Freiburg. Some of Husserl's concepts are helpful in hermeneutics – the concepts of ideal meanings, sedimentation, and language, for example – but they play a relatively small role in Gadamer's thought. It is regrettable that hermeneutics is often taken as a license for relativism, a use that Gadamer would certainly dispute. The fact that there can be multiple interpretations of a text does not destroy the identity of a text, nor does it exclude erroneous or totally inappropriate readings, those that destroy the text.

Deconstruction should also be mentioned in a survey of the phenomenological movement, albeit with some embarrassment, the way a family might be forced to speak about an eccentric uncle whose antics are known to everyone but whom one tries to avoid mentioning in polite society. Jacques Derrida's first writings were translations and interpretations (highly questionable interpretations, to be sure) of short works by Husserl, but he soon abandoned Husserl and moved into wider philosophical fields. Deconstruction is more strongly influenced by figures like Hegel, Heidegger, Sartre, and Jacques Lacan, and in a deeper sense by Nietzsche and Freud. I would also claim that Husserl has a much more subtle treatment of absence and difference than Derrida gives him credit for, one that recognizes these phenomena but does not fall into the extremes of deconstruction. One of the most appropriate comments I have heard about deconstruction was made in a lecture by the Scottish literary theorist Alasdair Fowler; he observed that deconstruction in moderate sips provides a welcome correction to traditional literary theory, which might have become a bit too tidy and rationalist, but that in the United States it became absorbed into a political ideology and hence developed beyond all proportion.

FINAL REMARKS

Phenomenology still continues in a somewhat less spectacular way as one of the major traditions in philosophy. Its leading works will continue to be read as classics, and time will tell how high the stars will rise. The thinkers in the first part of this century will certainly stand among the significant figures in the history of thought, and they will inspire philosophical thinking as the best writings of the past have done. Phenomenology's strength as a movement is evidenced by the fact that it presents to us not only obvious major figures, but also a wide range of minor writers, those who fill out the possibilities in the niches and corners of the phenomenological style of philosophy.

Furthermore, a great deal of scholarly work continues to be accomplished in this tradition, such as the edition of texts (with Louvain and Cologne as especially important centers), commentaries on major works and major thinkers, and controversies about the meaning of various terms and concepts. Although the edition of Husserl's work is arriving at the point at which one might well say "enough," some important materials, such as his later manuscripts on the consciousness of internal time, still await publication. The edition of Heidegger's lectures has shed much light on the development of his thought and provided us with texts that are of great philosophical value.

One of the great deficiencies of the phenomenological movement is its total lack of any political philosophy. This is clearly an area in which a supplement is needed. Indeed, one might say that the lack of political acumen was not only a speculative, but also a practical catastrophe in the case of Heidegger. Alfred Schütz (1899–1959), who taught at the New School and commented in part on Husserl's thought, had been most influenced by Weber and Scheler and did important work in social philosophy and a humanistic sociology, but he too did not really develop a political philosophy.

I would also say that its established terminology is a handicap for the phenomenological movement. Words like "noesis" and "noema," "reduction," "life world," and "transcendental ego" tend to become fossilized and provoke artificial problems. They substantialize what should be an aspect of being and of the activity of philosophy. The very name "phenomenology" is misleading and clumsy. The terminology translates badly into English and seems pompous; English writers in phenomenology ought to learn from authors like John Findlay, Michael Oakeshott, and Gilbert Ryle.

There are important theoretical resources in phenomenology that are still unexploited, mineral deposits, so to speak, that still remain to be mined. Husserl made a decisive breakthrough in modern thought; he showed the possibility of avoiding the Cartesian, Lockean concept of consciousness as an enclosed sphere; he restored the understanding of mind as public and as present to things. He opens the way to a philosophical realism and ontology that can replace the primacy of epistemology. Many of these positive possibilities in Husserl's thought have not been appreciated because the Cartesian grip – "la main morte de Descartes" – is so strong on so many philosophers and scholars. All too frequently, everything in Husserl is reinterpreted according to the very positions he rejected.

The way of ideas, the idea of the isolated consciousness, still holds many of us captive, and it is very difficult, if not impossible, to dislodge people from this way of thinking once it has taken root, once they have become used to a certain set of problems and a certain way of reasoning. But much remains in phenomenology for those who want it. The phenomenological movement, with its origins in Husserl at the beginning of this century and its rich history in the past one hundred years, furnishes many resources for an authentic philosophical life.

Select Bibliography

Bernet, Rudolf, Iso Kern, and Eduard Marbach. *An Introduction to Husserlian Phenomenology*. Evanston, IL: Northwestern University Press, 1993. The authors are prominent Swiss scholars who studied at the University of Louvain during the 1960s. They have each edited texts of Husserl and have written many works in phenomenology. Rudolf Bernet is currently director of the Husserl Archives at Leuven.

Brough, John Barnett. "Translator's Introduction." In Edmund Husserl, *On the Phenomenology of the Consciousness of Internal Time (1893–1917)*, trans. John Barnett Brough. Dordrecht: Kluwer, 1991, pp. xi–lvii. In this introduction and in other essays, Brough provides the clearest English treatment of the phenomenological doctrine of temporality.

Cobb-Stevens, Richard. *Husserl and Analytic Philosophy*. Dordrecht: Kluwer, 1984. There are a number of books, by various authors, that compare phenomenology and analytic thought, and this is one of the most successful. It studies primarily the differences between Husserl and Frege but also shows how Husserl resolves problems that have dominated philosophy since Descartes. The role of categorial intuition is emphasized.

Dillon, Martin C. *Merleau-Ponty's Ontology*. Bloomington: Indiana University Press, 1988.

Dreyfus, Hubert L., ed. *Husserl, Intentionality, and Cognitive Science*. Cambridge, MA: MIT, 1982. This collection contains several important essays by Dagfinn Føllesdal as well as papers by authors such as Dreyfus, J. N. Mohanty, John Searle, and David Woodruff Smith, dealing with intentionality and cognitive science.

Drummond, John J. *Husserlian Intentionality and Non-Foundational Realism: Noema and Object*. Dordrecht: Kluwer, 1990. This volume is a thorough and systematic evaluation of the Fregean interpretation of Husserl. It presents the "East Coast" critique of the "West Coast" form of phenomenology, dealing especially with the themes of noema, sense, and reduction.

Elveton, R.O., ed. and trans. *The Phenomenology of Husserl: Selected Critical Readings*. Chicago: Quadrangle, 1970. Six classical essays, written between 1930 and 1962. Of special importance are the essays by Eugen Fink, "The Phenomenological Philosophy of Edmund Husserl and Contemporary Criticism," pp. 73–147, and by Walter Biemel, "The Decisive Phases in the Development of Husserl's Philosophy," pp. 148–73.

Embree, Lester et al., eds. *Encyclopedia of Phenomenology.* Boston: Kluwer, 1997. Articles in this encyclopedia treat the major concepts in phenomenology, developments in various countries, major authors, and important new areas of controversy, such as language, artificial intelligence, cognitive science, and ecology. It is very well organized, and the articles are written by recognized scholars. This work will probably remain the most authoritative reference work on phenomenology for many years.

Gadamer, Hans-Georg. "The Phenomenological Movement." In his *Philosophical Hermeneutics*, ed. and trans. David E. Linge. Berkeley: University of California Press, 1976, pp. 130–81. A personal review of the main themes in the history of phenomenology.

Guignon, Charles, ed. *The Cambridge Companion to Heidegger.* Cambridge: Cambridge University Press, 1993. Books in the "Cambridge Companion" series are collections of about ten newly written essays on a given philosopher. Each volume has an introductory essay by the editor that gives an overview of the philosopher's thought, and an extensive bibliography is provided.

Hammond, Michael, Jane Howorth, and Russell Keat. *Understanding Phenomenology.* Oxford: Blackwell Publisher, 1991.

Howells, Christina, ed. *The Cambridge Companion to Sartre.* Cambridge: Cambridge University Press, 1992.

Kisiel, Theodore. *The Genesis of Heidegger's "Being and Time."* Berkeley: University of California Press, 1993. Spells out in detail the historical circumstances, personal interests, and intellectual developments that helped shape Heidegger's first major publication as well as his entire philosophy.

Kockelmans, Joseph J. *Edmund Husserl's Phenomenology.* West Lafayette, IN: Purdue University Press, 1994.

Langiulli, Nino, ed. *European Existentialism.* New Brunswick, NJ: Transaction, 1997. This is the third edition of a book that appeared in 1971 under the title, *The Existentialist Tradition.* It contains selections from authors ranging from Kierkegaard to Camus. Besides the major authors in this tradition, the book contains writings from Ortega y Gasset, Abbagnano, Buber, and Marcel. The selections are valuable and unusual, and the introductions, written by various scholars, are very helpful.

MacQuarrie, John. *Existentialism.* Baltimore: Penguin, 1962.

Madison, Gary Brent. *The Phenomenology of Merleau-Ponty.* Athens: Ohio University Press, 1973.

Manser, Anthony. *Sartre: A Philosophical Study.* Oxford: Oxford University Press, 1966.

McIntyre, Ronald, and David Woodruff Smith. *Husserl and Intentionality: A Study of Mind, Meaning, and Language.* Boston: Reidel, 1982. This is the most comprehensive study of Husserl's philosophy from the Fregean and analytic point of view.

McKenna, William R., and J. Claude Evans, eds. *Derrida and Phenomenology.* Dordrecht: Kluwer, 1995. A review of the relationship between phenomenology and deconstruction.

Mohanty, J. N. *Transcendental Phenomenology: An Analytic Account.* New York: Blackwell Publisher, 1989. Mohanty is the author of many works in phenomenology, philosophy of language, and Indian thought. This book describes the nature of transcendental phenomenology, using categories and issues familiar to analytic philosophers.

Mohanty, J. N., and Richard McKenna, eds. *Husserl's Phenomenology: A Textbook.* Lanham, MD: University Press of America, 1989. Essays that introduce various aspects of Husserl's thought.

Natanson, Maurice. *Edmund Husserl: Philosopher of Infinite Tasks.* Evanston, IL: Northwestern University Press, 1974. This volume won an American Book Award in 1974. It is a clear and colorful exposition of Husserl's thought.

Ott, Hugo. *Martin Heidegger: A Political Life,* trans. Allan Blunden. New York: Basic Books, 1993. The author of this biography is professor of history at the University of Freiburg. The book is an accurate and dispassionate biography of Heidegger. It addresses the political controversies in which Heidegger was involved.

Pöggeler, Otto. *Martin Heidegger's Path of Thinking,* trans. Daniel Magurshak and Sigmund Barner. Atlantic Highlands, NJ: Humanities, 1987. An introduction to Heidegger by one of his most authoritative interpreters.

Sepp, Hans Reiner, ed. *Edmund Husserl und die phänomenologische Bewegung. Zeugnisse in Text und Bild.* Freiburg: Karl Alber, 1988. This work was composed as a catalogue to accompany an exhibit that commemorated the fiftieth anniversary of the Husserl Archives. The book contains many pictures of people and places, as well as images of documents related not only to Husserl and his life but to other people and developments in phenomenology. It includes reminiscences by Hans-Georg Gadamer, Emmanuel Levinas, Herbert Spiegelberg, and others, five essays about the phenomenological movement, biographical sketches for almost ninety persons associated with the movement, a historical time line for the period 1858–1928 (giving events parallel to events in phenomenology), bibliographies of major works in phenomenology and their translations, and a bibliography of selected secondary sources.

Smith, Barry, and David Woodruff Smith, eds. *The Cambridge Companion to Husserl.* Cambridge: Cambridge University Press, 1995. This "Cambridge Companion" volume contains essays by important British and American commentators on Husserl. The introduction surveys Husserl's philosophy and sketches various interpretations of his thought. Essays cover the development of Husserl's philosophy, the phenomenological perspective, language, knowledge, perception, idealism, mind and body, common sense, mathematics, and part–whole logic.

Sokolowski, Robert. *Husserlian Meditations: How Words Present Things.* Evanston, IL: Northwestern University Press, 1974. A study of major concepts in Husserl's thought, with reference to authors like Strawson and Austin.

Sokolowski, Robert. *Pictures, Quotations, and Distinctions: Fourteen Essays in Phenomenology.* Notre Dame, IN: University of Notre Dame Press, 1992. A collection of essays describing phenomena such as picturing, quoting, making distinctions, measurement, reference, temporality, and moral action. The essays attempt to clarify philosophically things that are part and parcel of the human condition.

Spiegelberg, Herbert. *The Phenomenological Movement.* Third, revised and enlarged, edition, with Karl Schuhman. The Hague: Nijhoff, 1982. This is the classical history of phenomenology. The first two editions (which comprised two volumes) were written by Herbert Spiegelberg; the third (in one volume) was written with the assistance of Karl Schuhman. The book goes into great detail in treating developments in various countries, with ample coverage of even the minor figures.

Ströker, Elisabeth. *Husserl's Transcendental Phenomenology,* trans. Lee Hardy. Stanford: Stanford University Press, 1993. The author was director of the Husserl Archives at Cologne for many years. She specializes not only in phenomenology, but also in the philosophy of science.

Warnke, Georgia. *Gadamer: Hermeneutics, Tradition, and Reason.* Stanford: Stanford University Press, 1987.

Willard, Dallas. *Logic and the Objectivity of Knowledge.* Athens: University of Ohio Press, 1984. A clear and exact exposition of Husserl's early work, with a thorough study of major themes in *Logical Investigations.*

Index

absence: in perception, 17; and other selves, 34, 154; as contrasted with presence, 35; importance of in phenomenology, 36; as truly presented, 36–7; varieties of, 37; in memory, 68, 76; in signitive intentions, 78–9, 81–2; of categorial objects, 96–7; in internal time consciousness, 139,142; and intersubjectivity, 152–3; in Husserl and Heidegger, 217; *see also* presence and absence

abstract parts, 2–4

adequacy in phenomenological analysis, 58

advertising and imagination, 73

aesthetic objects, identity of, 29–30

analytic philosophy and phenomenology, 3, 222–3

animals and transcendental ego, 119

apodicticity of statements in the phenomenological attitude, 57

apophantic reflection, *see* propositional reflection

appearances: in modern life, 3; and phenomenology, 3–4; reality of, 15; as studied from phenomenological viewpoint, 50

archeology: involves special intentionality, 13; philosophical, 167

Aristotle: and parts and wholes, 22; and rational soul, 44; and science of being as such, 53; and prephilosophical truth, 64; and Unmoved Mover, 144; and idealized societies, 183

aspects as different from sides, 19

association as lowest form of identity, 182

beauty and manifestation, 174–6

Beckett, Samuel, 10–11

belief: in natural attitude, 45–6; *see also* world belief

biologism, 113–16

bracketing: in phenomenology, 49–50; as different from quotation, 192–3

brain: and egocentric predicament, 9–10; and intentionality, 25; and memory, 68–9; and ego, 113; and internal time consciousness, 144–5; and political life, 205

Brentano, Franz, 206, 211, 213

bricolage, 4

Cairns, Dorion, 222

categorial intuition: described, 90, 96; as confirming a claim, 97

categorial objects: as discrete identities, 91–2, 110; as communicable, 92, 102–3; as in the world, 95–6; as usually absent, 96–7; and falsehood and contradiction, 103

categoriality: and intelligible objects, 5; etymology of the term, 88; arising in three stages, 89–90; and language, 91, 103; as discrete, 91–2, 110; as humanizing perception, 94, 111; and logic, 103–4; articulates the whole, 110; as sedimented, 166–7; *see also* syntax

chessman, as analogy for transcendental ego, 118–19

coherence: of propositional contents, 170–1; founded on experience of individuals, 172–3; in practical matters, 174

comics, as illustrating phenomenological reflection, 194–6

concepts: problem of, 5–6; as substitute presences, 36, 79; as mental or semantic entities, 97–102; *see also* meaning; propositions

Index

concretum, 24

consistency: as second level of propositional structure, 170; in practical matters, 174

constitution, as presentation of intelligible objects, 92–3

corporeality: and the ego, 124; and sense of touch, 124–5; and mobility, 125–6; and location, 126; and memory, 126–7; and intersubjectivity, 154

correspondence theory of truth: and meanings, 98; defined as disquotational, 101, 187; and correctness, 158–9

dative: for appearances, 4, 32, 65, 153, 161, 175; and temporality, 132, 144–5

deconstruction: and modern predicament, 3–4; and speech about being, 173–4; outcome of modernity, 202; and phenomenology, 225

deliberation: and imagination, 72–4; and vagueness, 108; and ego, 128; and consistency and coherence, 174

Derrida, Jacques, 202, 221, 225

Descartes, René: and radical doubt, 54–6; rationalism of, 63, 201; and concepts, 98; on mastering evidence by method, 164–5; and pure consciousness, 183; as supplanting prephilosophical truth, 195, 198; influence on current thinking, 226

detachment in philosophy, 190

disclosure, truth of, 158–9

displacement: in memory and imagination, 74–5; and internal time consciousness, 140

disquotation, 101

distinctness, as achievement of judgment, 106–7

doubt: attempt to, 54–6; whether subject to free choice, 54–5; needs reasons, 55

drama and identity, 29

dreams, 75

East Coast interpretation of Husserl, 222–3

education and modern political life, 204

ego: identity of, 5–6; empirical and transcendental, 112–13; and world, 113; and phenomenological attitude, 122; and corporeality, 124–7; as nonpunctual, 127–9; and deliberation, 128; as always preeminent, 153; see also self; transcendental ego

egocentric predicament: described, 9; and brain sciences, 9–10; and relativism, 10; overcome in phenomenology, 11–12, 216; cannot be original condition, 46; and categoriality, 89; and political life, 205

eidetic intuition: described, 178–84; and errors, 182–3; and negative necessity, 184; and eidetic reduction, 184

Einstein, Albert, and eidetic intuition, 180

Eliot, T. S., 142

empirical ego and temporality, 132

empirical universals: defined, 178; as controlling eidetic intuitions, 183–4

empty intentions: defined, 33; varieties of, 34–5; see also signitive intentions

epistemology: in modernity, 7, 61, 200–2; countered by phenomenology, 203, 216, 226

epochē: neutralization, 49; term from Greek skepticism, 49; importance of, 64

error and world belief, 46

essences, insight into, 177

evidence: defined, 159–62; dictionary meaning of, 160–1; two senses of, 162; not a mere subjective experience, 162–4; unmasterable, 164–5; more basic than proof, 164–5; and beauty, 174–6

exprimend and meaning, 27–8

extramental world, so-called, 10, 12, 25, 62, 64, 67, 216

Farber, Marvin, 222

fiction and eidetic intuition, 150

filled intentions, 17, 33

formal apophantics and ontology, 104

founding, relation of, in parts and wholes, 24

Frege, Gottlob, 222–3

fulfillment: introduced, 33; as graded, 39; as additive, 39–40; see also intuition

Gadamer, Hans-Georg, 213, 224–5

genetic constitution, 93

Index

Göttingen school of phenomenology, 212–13

Gurwitsch, Aron, 221–2

hallucinations, 14–15

Hegel, G. W. F.: and modern state, 200; and theory of knowledge, 201

Heidegger, Martin: and phenomenology, 3; and ontological difference, 50; and ecstases of time, 138; on *Lichtung*, 144; on *Dasein*, 161; and postmodernity, 202; and Husserl, 213–18; prophetic tone, 214–15; and religion, 215–16; and history of philosophy, 218; and question of being, 218; political involvements of, 219

hermeneutics: and hiddenness, 166; prepared by phenomenology, 203; as a movement, 224–5

hiddenness: present in all experience, 31; as essential to presence, 165–8; as vagueness, 166; as sedimentation, 166–7; and philosophy, 167–8; and mystery in things, 176

historical event, as an identity, 28–9

Hobbes, Thomas: and parts and wholes, 27; and mechanistic theory of man, 205; as supplanting prephilosophical truth, 195, 198; and the modern state, 198, 200–1

Hocking, William Ernest, 222

Husserl, Edmund: his introductions to phenomenology, 2; founder of phenomenology, 2–3; original treatment of presence and absence, 22, 37, 225; on ways to reduction, 52; and internal time consciousness, 141, 144; and sphere of ownness, 155; and modernity, 202; and Thomism, 206; life and work, 211–13; originality of, 211; and Heidegger, 213–18; and history of philosophy, 217–18

Husserl Archives, 219, 225–6

idealization: in exact sciences, 148–50; as retaining some content, 150; identity in, 150–1

identity: introduced as issue, 3–5; as beyond sides, aspects, profiles, 20; and intentionality, 20–1; in manifolds, 27–33; of historical events, 28–9; of artistic objects, 29–30; of religious events, 30; as not part of manifold, 30–1; of self, 32–3; across presence and absence, 37–8; in memory, 66–7; in imagination, 72; in memory, imagination, and anticipation, 85–6; in words, pictures, and symbols, 86; in categorial intentions, 91–5; as what is named through words, 95; and verification, 102; of transcendental ego, 122–4; of self as nonpunctual, 127–8; in internal time consciousness, 132, 139, 142; in exact sciences, 150–1; of objects and intersubjectivity, 152–4; of meaning, 157–8; and beauty, 175–6; and eidos, 177–8; and mere similarity, 178, 182; *see also* self

illusions: as not requiring mental entities, 14–15; as modifying belief, 45

image: as substitute presence, 36; as putative meaning, 78

imagination: contrasted with memory, 71; changes modality, 71–2; and identity of object, 72; and deliberation, 72–4; and anticipation, 73–4; and idealization, 148–9; and eidetic intuition, 178–81

imaginative variation: described, 178–80; and philosophy, 181

incoherence: and vagueness, 107; as prior to consistency, 172

inconsistency and vagueness, 106–7

indeterminacy in science, 151–2

indexicals: and transcendental ego, 118, 121–2; in phenomenological attitude, 122–3; and quotation, 128–9; and ego strength, 128–9; and propositional attitude, 188; in philosophy, 197; and responsible speaker, 203

indications: described, 84–5; as not engaging syntax, 85

individuals: experience of, 172–3; and empirical universals, 182

Ingarden, Roman, 223

intentionality: as consciousness of something, 8, 12; distinguished from practical intentions, 8; and egocentric predicament, 9; publicness of, 10–12; varieties of, 12; and physics, 13; and identity, 20–1; not equivalent to empty intentions, 40; enrichment of, 40; and exact science, 147–8; in Husserl and Heidegger, 216–17

Index

intermediate fulfillments, 38

internal time, 130–1

internal time consciousness: described, 131; as most basic level of time, 131–4; as hard to express, 132, 134, 141, 143, 145; diagrammed, 133; as different from memory, 135; compared with linear extension, 138; as formal, 140–1; and succession, 141; and original presence of the past, 142; why located in a third level of temporality, 143–4; *see also* living present

intersubjectivity: and identity in manifolds, 31–2; and categorial domain, 102; and common world, 152–3; as knowing other person, 153–5; and corporeality, 154; and absence of other self, 154

intuition: and filled intentions, 34–5; not mysterious, 35, 39; contrasted with signitive intentions, 81

James, William, on consciousness of time, 136

Kant, Immanuel, on kingdom of ends, 117

language: and categoriality, 91; and syntax, 108–9; and identity of meaning, 157–8

Levinas, Emmanuel, 3, 219

life world: and modern science, 6, 146–7; and premodern science, 147

living present: not episodic, 135; involving special kind of succession, 135–6; includes protention and retention, 136; diagrammed, 137; compared to point on line, 138; enjoys a double intentionality, 139; *see also* internal time consciousness

logic: and categoriality, 103–4; and evidencing, 163; related to consistency, 171–2

Machiavelli: and rationalism in politics, 63; and modern state, 198, 200–1; and reason understood as rule, 204

manifolds: and identity, 27–33; visible to phenomenological reflection, 50; new and higher levels in complex intentions, 85–7

Marx, Karl: on parts and wholes, 27; and idealized societies, 183; and modern state, 200

mathematics: contrasted with philosophy, 1, 7, 156; and life world, 147–8, 150–1

Mays, Wolfe, 222

meaning: as not mediating entity, 5, 79, 97–102; identity of, 27–8; established by signitive intentions, 81–2; and correspondence theory of truth, 98; as objects as proposed, 99–100; and words, 157–8; as requiring correct syntax, 169–70

medieval philosophy and phenomenology, 207

memory: and identity of object remembered, 66–7; and mental images, 66–7; as different from picturing, 67; as reviving earlier experience, 68–9; neural basis for, 68–9; and errors, 69; and self, 69–70; and regrets, 70–1; and imagination, 71; and body, 126–7; and internal time consciousness, 139–40

Merleau-Ponty, Maurice, 3, 200, 221

metaphor and incoherence, 171

method, as attempt to master truth, 164–5

mobility and corporeality, 125–6

modern state: and sovereignty, 199; and republics, 199, 204–5

modernity: and rationalism, 164; politics of, 198–200; epistemology of, 200–2; understands reason as rule, 201–2

Mohanty, J. N., 223

moments: as nonindependent parts, 23; mistaken for pieces, 24–7

morphological essences, 151

mundanese, as language in natural attitude, 58–9, 185

Munich school of phenomenology, 212–13

natural attitude: introduced, 5; described, 42–3; and absence, 43; and world, 43; incapable of handling appearances, 50–1; validated by phenomenology, 56, 64; and imagination and memory, 75–6; achieves many intentionalities, 87; and transcendental ego, 122–3

neutralization: described, 48; preserves intentionalities in natural attitude, 63; and philosophy, 190–1

235

Newton, Isaac: and life world, 146; and idealization, 149; and indeterminacy, 151; and hiddenness, 166; and eidetic intuition, 180, 183
Nicklaus, Jack, 38–9
Nietzsche, Friedrich, and postmodernity, 202
noema: differs from sense and meaning, 59–60, 191–4; term used in phenomenological attitude, 59–61, 192; not a mediating entity, 60–1; etymology of, 60–1; and mental representation, 104
noesis: term used in phenomenological attitude, 59–61; not substantialized, 60

Oakeshott, Michael, 200, 226
Ortega y Gasset, José, 223
ownness, sphere of, 154–5

parts and wholes: introduced, 3–5; treatment of, 22–7; and philosophical analysis, 24–7; necessity in sequences of, 27; and categorial genesis, 89–90; and categoriality, 92; and syntax, 109; and rationality, 118; in internal time consciousness, 132, 142
Patočka, Jan, 223
perception: internal and external transformation of, 5; and sides, aspects, profiles, 17–20; as dynamic, 18; as revived in memory, 68; modified by memory and imagination, 75; modified by signitive intentions, 78; modified by words, 81; and picturing, 82–4; humanized by categoriality, 94, 111
phases in temporality, 139
phenomenological attitude: introduced, 5, 6; differs from natural attitude, 47; not shift within natural attitude, 47; detached and theoretic, 48, 190; anticipated in natural attitude, 48–9; focuses on objects as well as intentions, 50; capable of treating imagination and memory, 75–6; examines intentionalities of all kinds, 87, 102; and ego, 122–4; contrasted with propositional attitude, 186–94; scope of, 189; not imperial, 191; illustrated by comics, 195
phenomenology: defined, 2, 4; and classical philosophy, 2, 7; sees reason as or-

dered toward truth, 6–7, 173–4, 202–3; etymology of, 13; as restoring theoretic philosophy, 15–16, 48; as realist, 21, 216; as describing identities in manifolds, 31; anticipated in natural attitude, 51–2; as the more concrete science, 53–4; as validating the natural attitude and prephilosophical reason, 56, 62, 198, 208–9; and epistemology, 62, 216; as not rationalistic, 62–3; as not introspective, 80; and psychologism, 114–15; as study of truth, 185–6; as seeing limits in truth, 185–6; defined in contrast with propositional reflection, 186–7; response to modernity and postmodernity, 202–6; and ancients and moderns, 203; and political philosophy, 203–5, 226; and Thomism, 206–8; and religious belief, 207–8; stilted vocabulary of, 226
philosophy: compared with mathematics, 1–2; and moments and pieces, 24–7; and theoretic life, 64; as dealing with truth, 156, 197; follows upon evidences and hiddenness, 167–8; and trivial truths, 181; and imaginative variation, 181; not merely analysis of meaning, 196–7
physics: intentionality of, 13; and moments, 23; as claiming to be science of the whole, 63, 208; and life world, 146–7; and indeterminacy, 151–2; and philosophy, 156
picturing: as founded on perception, 13; as public, 14; different from remembering, 67–8; different from signitive intentions, 82–3; and perception, 83–4; not mere similarity, 84
pieces: as kind of part, 22–3; in philosophical analysis, 24–6
Plato: and phenomenology, 2; and appearances, 3; and identity, 22; and internal time consciousness, 144; his *Republic*, 182; new "musical trope," 206
Plotinus and internal time consciousness, 144
political philosophy: in modernity, 7, 198–200; politics as not highest good, 7, 203–4; and phenomenology, 203–4, 226; political events related to phenomenology, 219

Made in the USA
Monee, IL
28 March 2021